# EXPORTERS' CHECKLIST

## A step-by-step guide
## to successful exporting

by

## Harry Twells, ACIB, MIEx

**FOREWORD BY SIR DEREK HORNBY**
*Chairman, British Overseas Trade Board*

**Recommended by The Institute of Export**

## 2nd Edition

**Lloyd's of London Press Ltd**
**1995**

Lloyd's of London Press Ltd.
Legal Publishing Division
27 Swinton Street,
London WC1X 9NW

USA AND CANADA
Lloyd's of London Press Inc.
Suite 308, 611 Broadway
New York, NY 10012 USA

GERMANY
Lloyd's of London Press GmbH
59 Ehrenbergstrasse
22767 Hamburg
Germany

SOUTH EAST ASIA
Lloyd's of London Press (Far East) Ltd.
Room 1101, Hollywood Centre
233 Hollywood Road
Hong Kong

First published in Great Britain, 1992
Second edition published 1995

British Library Cataloguing in Publication Data
A catalogue record for this book is available from the British Library
ISBN 1-85044-864-7

Text set in 10 on 12pt Helvetica by
Cotswold Typesetting Ltd, Gloucester
Printed in Great Britain by
Bookcraft Ltd, Midsomer Norton

UK Exporters are becoming increasingly successful in winning business opportunities abroad. Nevertheless there is still even more potential for UK businesses to win in world markets.

There is no doubt that exports are vital to the country's economic growth and we are in an exciting period of redefining the way UK business is helped to export. I believe we all have an important part to play in ensuring that UK firms are best placed to achieve rapid and sustained success when they trade overseas.

The Government's Overseas Trade Services aim to reinforce and back up this success by providing a wide range of advice, information and assistance. This partnership between business and government will build on our reputation for industrial and commercial excellence and competitiveness, and this year OTS will be able to provide an even better service to its customers through local Business Links.

I believe "Exporters' Checklist" is an invaluable guide to the many practical questions which an exporter needs to know. It is set out in a clear, logical and well constructed manner and answers many of the simple questions that are very often overlooked. This book draws together many of the threads in an accurate guide which reflects the experience and knowledge that Harry Twells has gained over the years.

I think this booklet is useful to all traders; but perhaps particularly to the small and medium-sized company exporters who may not have a large export department to back them up. This book will, I am sure, prove an invaluable source of reference.

May 1995                                    SIR DEREK HORNBY
                            Chairman, British Overseas Trade Board

# PREFACE

The United Kingdom is a major exporter to all parts of the world, and in 1993 and 1994 real increases in the total value of UK exports have been achieved. Annual increases in export values, well ahead of the rate of inflation, mean that UK businesses are winning new business in overseas markets, and yet there is still much greater potential. Overseas sales underpin profitability for businesses and security of employment for our communities in the United Kingdom, and we must continue to encourage and support exporting businesses and those wishing to become exporters.

Information and support services to help UK exporters abound – there is no shortage. In the past few years the services provided by the Government Offices, principally the Department of Trade and Industry, have been more precisey focused on providing accurate and directed information to businesses to help them ACTIVELY seek new opportunities, rather than wait to respond to opportunities which come to hand. And there are many other organisations which provide important information and support through seminars, workshops, trade missions etc, and a guiding hand at local level – all aimed at increasing the confidence of British businesses to trade professionally, and successfully win new business around the world.

The First Edition of EXPORTERS' CHECKLIST, published in 1992, was designed to help businesses become more aware of the intricacies of exporting practice, so necessary to win new business, and to help with establishing a RIGHT FIRST TIME culture within businesses. I have been very encouraged by the letters and comments received, and I am therefore pleased that EXPORTERS' CHECKLIST has been read and used by so many.

This Second Edition has been up-dated and hopefully improved. I trust it will continue to be a very useful reference guide for everyone engaged in the art, the industry, the profession of exporting successfully and profitably.

However, it is **not** the definitive textbook on all matters 'exporting' – rather it is a CHECKLIST of points, an easy HANDS-ON REFERENCE MANUAL, with information on a wide range of topics, and contact references to enable more detailed information to be obtained.

This checklist is based on 18 years' first-hand experience of being closely involved with and meeting the needs of exporting businesses, and involvement with many export-support organisations. During this period I have managed two International Banking Centres for National Westminster Bank Plc – Sheffield and Nottingham – and for the past two and a half years have been the Bank's International Trade Consultant.

I trust this Second Edition of EXPORTERS' CHECKLIST will be of continuing benefit to business people exporting, or wishing to become exporters.

June 1995                                    HAROLD NELSON TWELLS,
                                                              OBE, ACIB, MIEx

---

Publisher's note: Harry Twells is currently Chairman of the Export Clubs' Advisory Committee of the British Overseas Trade Board. He was awarded the OBE for services to export in the 1995 Queen's Birthday Honours List.

## ACKNOWLEDGEMENTS

I would like to express my very sincere thanks to a number of friends and colleagues for their continuing encouragement for the Exporters' Checklist. It is three years since the first edition was published, and in that time I have been delighted that so many people have expressed their appreciation for the book, both verbally and to me in writing, and the reception the book has had has spurred this second edition.

The "International trade scene" is an ever-changing one. It is a fascinating arena and there are many equally fascinating segments to successful exporting practice. EXPORTERS' CHECKLIST was, and is, intended to help exporters to export more professionally, to have a ready reference manual to sources of information and help, and to assist in a Right First Time approach to export documentation. I trust it has helped to fulfil these objectives, and that this Second Edition will continue to serve this purpose. This Second Edition has been updated to reflect changes generally to the end of March 1995, although certain contact addresses and numbers have been amended to early May.

I would like to express my sincere thanks to Sir Derek Hornby, Chairman of the British Overseas Trade Board, for the Foreword he has kindly written for this Second Edition.

I am very pleased too that Ian Campbell, Director General, The Institute of Export, has provided the introduction, and my sincere thanks go to Ian for his and the Institute's support. Robin Bussell, Director of Exports, British Chambers of Commerce, has been very helpful in checking sections which carry reference to Chambers of Commerce, both in the UK and those overseas, and I extend my sincere thanks to Robin for his support.

The changes caused by the issue of the new Uniform Customs & Practice UCP 500 have been included, and I am most grateful to my friend and colleague, Ruth Walker, Manager, Documentary Credits Section (NatWest International Banking Centre, Nottingham), for checking the detail in Sections 14 to 17, to reflect the changes as a result of UCP 500, and for her support for Exporters' Checklist's publication.

Paul Lewis, awarded the MBE for services to export in the 1995 New Year Honours, has given much encouragement for Exporters' Checklist and I appreciate his raising various points over the last three years, which I trust I have added correctly to the text for this new edition. My sincere thanks too to Sarah Barrow, Bernie Harris and Stephen France for their support and encouragement.

There is always a danger that someone is inadvertently omitted from these acknowledgements – if perchance I have omitted anyone who should have been named, then may I offer my very sincere apologies for such omission.

Finally, may I extend a very warm thank-you to everyone who purchased a copy of the First Edition, particularly those who have written or expressed their appreciation to me when we have met – it is very encouraging to know that Exporters' Checklist has been found useful by so many.

H. N. TWELLS

I am delighted to welcome the second edition of Harry Twells's "Exporters' Checklist". Several thousand copies of the first edition have helped exporters – especially new ones – to locate help and guidance, and to avoid making costly mistakes.

Exporting is vital to the United Kingdom, and it is our exporters who have led us out of the recession which beleaguered us in the early 1990s.

As with many other facets of life, the biggest obstacle to exporting is fear – fear of the unknown. Exporting may be different, but it need not be difficult – providing you know where to obtain assistance.

The second edition of Harry's book lists many new sources of help and updates those areas where changes have occurred since 1992.

It also gives both the new exporter, and the more seasoned overseas trader, helpful guides to "getting it right – and right first time".

The Institute of Export's principal role is to educate and train those engaged in international trade, enabling them to become more professional in their approach.

But even the most well-trained professional needs to update his/her knowledge, and to be able to check that s/he is working to current best practice.

Here, in a convenient, well-researched and well-written handbook, are the practical guidelines you need.

IAN CAMPBELL, BA, MBIM, MIEx, FRSA                May 1995
DIRECTOR GENERAL
THE INSTITUTE OF EXPORT

# CONTENTS

* denotes Sectional Index provided

# Winning Business in Overseas Markets

---

# Sources of Help and Information

## SECTIONAL INDEX

# 1. WHAT PRODUCTS AND SERVICES WILL SELL ABROAD?

THE FIRST QUESTIONS ARE

– Will my products and/or services sell abroad?
– If so, what will sell and where?
– How do I assess the potential?

---

A CAREFUL SYSTEMATIC APPROACH IS NECESSARY

The opportunities will seldom fall into your lap

They have to be sought, fought for and won, often against stiff competition from other suppliers

BUT

British products and services are amongst the best in the world

There are opportunities in overseas markets which can lead to good new business for British businesses

British businesses can win more business abroad, through COMMITMENT, DETERMINATION, the QUALITY of what is offered, prompt DELIVERY, and by offering competitive credit and payment terms

---

**IF YOU TRADE IN SECOND-HAND GOODS you should be aware that Consumer Protection Law and Product Safety Regulations now apply to second-hand goods sold in the UK and within the EU**

Second-hand goods are now required to perform as new

Businesses which import goods into the EU in an already reconditioned state, are now regarded as the manufacturer under EU law

**IF YOU TRADE IN SECOND-HAND GOODS YOU SHOULD DISCUSS YOUR TRADING TERMS AND CONDITIONS WITH YOUR COMMERCIAL LAWYER**

---

*Section 1 sets out a number of sources of information for those seeking to sell their products and/or services into overseas markets*

---

THERE IS NO CAST-IRON ANSWER, but:

- if you currently manufacture either wholly, or part-manufactured/finished products, there is every likelihood there will be opportunities for your products in one or more overseas markets
- if you provide professional services there could be opportunities for you to sell these into overseas markets
- if you are an Agent for a UK or Overseas Manufacturer or Supplier, there could be opportunities for you to Export or re-Export goods, or provide services into overseas markets
- THERE IS NO EASY SOLUTION, NO SHORT-CUT WAY INTO SELLING ABROAD – A STRUCTURED APPROACH WILL ENSURE COSTS AND VALUABLE TIME ARE CONTROLLED

THERE ARE OPPORTUNITIES FOR BRITISH BUSINESSES IN OVERSEAS MARKETS

- NOT ONLY IN EUROPE
- BUT IN MOST OTHER COUNTRIES AROUND THE WORLD
- But Britain's market share in many countries outside Europe is often as little as 3 or 4%
- and Britain's export trade could be increased substantially
  - if more businesses became exporters
  - if those who 'respond' to enquiries took a more active role to seek out suitable opportunities

---

THERE IS NO SHORTAGE OF INFORMATION AND ADVICE TO ASSIST BUSINESSES

---

Who buys your products or services in the UK?

- if you supply to industrial users
- if you supply components to manufacturers
- if you sell finished products to
  - stockists
  - distributors

5

- direct to retailers*
- direct to the end user*

THERE IS A GOOD CHANCE THAT THE SAME SUPPLIER-TO-BUYER ROUTE WILL APPLY IN A GOOD MANY OVERSEAS MARKETS

* Sales to individual retailers, or to retailer chains, or to the end user customer may well be handled more effectively through appointed distributors and stockists, or agents

---

### 1.1.1 EXPORT CONTROL REQUIREMENTS

EXPORTERS SHOULD BE AWARE THAT CERTAIN GOODS ARE SUBJECT TO SECURITY EXPORT CONTROL

**APPROVAL PRIOR TO THE EXPORT OF CERTAIN TYPES OF GOODS WHICH ARE SUBJECT TO CONTROLS, IS VITALLY IMPORTANT**

Export controls are imposed for a variety of reasons, including:

- the collective security of the UK and its allies in NATO
- national security
- foreign policy requirements
- international treaty obligations and commitments
- the UK's non-proliferation policy
- concerns about terrorism or internal repression

---

To determine whether there are restrictions on the type of goods you wish to export, you should contact:

> **EXPORT CONTROL ORGANISATION,**
> **DEPARTMENT OF TRADE & INDUSTRY,**
> **Kingsgate House, 66-74 Victoria Street,**
> **London, SW1E 6SW**
> **Enquiries – Tel:  0171 215 8070**
> **Fax: 0171 215 8564**

**IF YOUR GOODS AND/OR SERVICES ARE SUBJECT TO EXPORT CONTROL COMPLIANCE, YOU SHOULD ENSURE THAT CLEARLY**

**DEFINED AREAS OF RESPONSIBILITY FOR COMPLIANCE ARE SET DOWN IN WRITING, THAT THERE IS A RESPONSIBLE OFFICER OF THE COMPANY NOMINATED TO ENSURE COMPLIANCE, AND RECORDS DETAILING APPROVALS ARE KEPT UP-TO-DATE**

**THERE ARE SEVERE PENALTIES FOR THOSE WHO DO NOT COMPLY FULLY WITH EXPORT CONTROL PROCEDURES**

---

The DTI Export Control Organisation will advise on the availability of training courses covering Export Control subjects

---

## 2. SOURCES OF INFORMATION

If you think your product may be affected by the standards/
technical requirements of your target market, you should
consult:

**THE TECHNICAL HELP FOR EXPORTERS BUREAU**
**389 Chiswick High Rd**
**Chiswick**
**London W4 4AL**
**Tel: 0181 996 7111, Fax: 0181 996 7048**

They will advise on:

– which markets accept the same technical standards and
  specifications as the United Kingdom
– what modifications would be necessary for a product to be
  acceptable and gain certification and entry into specific
  overseas markets
– British Standards specifications and the corresponding
  European and International Standards
– labelling to meet standards requirements
– foreign standards and regulations and provide up-to-date
  information on requirements
– which countries require 'Manufacturer's Declaration of
  Conformity with Relevant Standards', and assist exporters with
  preparation of the necessary paperwork
– electrical and other types of standards for individual countries

They will translate into English relevant sovereign standards,
codes, laws, etc.

They will supply all handbooks published by The International
Standards Organisation

# BRITISH PATENT OFFICE

### Information on Overseas Products

For manufactured products the **BRITISH PATENT OFFICE** can assist in identifying whether Patent protection is registered against like and similar products, and details of patents pending

- they have access to Patent data-bases worldwide
- can advise on patented designs
- can advise on patent protection procedures
- can advise on patent infringement positions
- assist with the evaluation of new inventions
- have details of Trade Marks registered worldwide

The PATENT OFFICE can provide invaluable information on virtually all Patented work around the world

This is available to British businesses to assist in assessing product potential for selling into overseas markets

Dates when patents have been recorded give an indication of the development and sophistication of particular overseas target markets

Can assist with identification of potential competitors and competing products

In addition to the protection of patents and trade marks, there are other sections which deal with protection of designs and copyright.

---

**MANUFACTURERS, DESIGNERS ETC MAY WISH TO SEEK PROTECTION IN ONE OR MORE OF THE FOLLOWING CATEGORIES:**

**PATENT PROTECTION**

- up to 20 years' protection for a new product, a material, or a technical process, which includes an inventive step and is capable of industrial application

**REGISTERED DESIGN**

- protection for up to 25 years for registered designs which must have æsthetic appeal

9

## COPYRIGHT

- copyright protection lasts for at least 50 years and can be claimed for any original written work, by authors of books, by publishers, by authors of computer software programs

## UNREGISTERED DESIGN RIGHTS

- ownership of a defined but unregistered design right enables the owner to prevent copying of the design by others for a period of five years, and for the ensuing five years the owner is entitled to a royalty in respect of any copies made, used or sold in the UK

---

## TRADE MARKS

Trade Marks and Brand Names which are distinctive in the market place, can be protected under the Trade Mark Act 1994

Trade Marks should be registered at the earliest opportunity to gain maximum protection and to avoid mis-use and mis-representation

**Trade Mark Registry Contact Address:**

see Appendix C5.2

For Patent Office addresses see pages 321/322.

---

## THE SINGLE EUROPEAN MARKET

The need to meet European Standards is important, and will be increasingly important in the years ahead

New European Union rules mean that many products have to:

Carry the C E mark

- to show they meet the common rules

Carry the C E mark

- to show they have passed the required tests and checks

Carry the C E mark

- to be sold legally in the United Kingdom or elsewhere in the EU

So, no C E mark . . . NO SALE

For further information contact:
**BUSINESS IN EUROPE HOTLINE**
– see below

---

**BUSINESS IN EUROPE HOTLINE**
The following free publications relating to Standards and the
European single market are available from the:
BUSINESS IN EUROPE HOTLINE
      Tel: 01179 444888
  Keeping your product on the market – new common rules
  Toy safety
  Simple pressure vessels
  Construction products
  Electromagnetic compatibility
  Machinery safety
  Personal protective equipment
  Gas appliances
  Active implantable medical devices
  Preventing new technical barriers
  Conformity assessment
  Non-automatic weighing instruments
  Telecommunications terminal equipment
  Equipment for use in potentially explosive atmospheres

# WORLD AID SECTION, DTI, LONDON

## Organisations available to assist

**WORLD AID SECTION** is part of the Department of Trade & Industry and maintains a comprehensive database of information on Aid Funded projects worldwide. There are opportunities for UK suppliers of services and equipment, contractors and consultants.

---

WORLD AID SECTION collects and monitors information on projects being financed by the following agencies and funds:

| | |
|---|---|
| ADB | Asian Development Bank |
| ADFAED | Abu Dhabi Fund for Arab Economic Development |
| AFDBG | African Development Bank Group |
| AFESD | Arab Fund for Economic & Social Development |
| ABEDA | Arab Bank for Economic Development in Africa |
| CDB | Caribbean Development Bank |
| CID | Centre for Industrial Development |
| EBRD | European Bank for Reconstruction and Development |
| EEC | European Economic Community |
| EIB | European Investment Bank |
| IDB | Inter-American Development Bank |
| IFAD | International Fund for Agricultural Development |
| IFED | Iraqi Fund for External Development |
| ISDB | Islamic Development Bank |
| KFAED | Kuwait Fund for Arab Economic Development |
| OECF | Overseas Economic Cooperation Fund |
| OPECF | OPEC Fund for International Development |
| SFD | Saudi Fund for Development |
| UN | UN (UN Agencies not otherwise specified) |
| UNIDO | UN Industrial Development Organisation |
| UNDP | United Nations Development Programme |

---

The database Project Listing will include:
- date information entered
- WAS reference and country listing
- project value and currency
- the funding authority
- industry sector of project
- current stage of development of a project
  - project identification
  - information available on the project
  - whether tenders have been awarded and to whom

---

There are good opportunities for British businesses to gain business from Aid Funded projects, either directly or on a sub-contract basis to the major contractor

There is a very wide range of goods and services required under many of the projects

---

The Section holds files of more than 5000 current projects in various stages of development.

They also have available:
- economic reports
- sector analyses
- tender notices
- procedural guidelines
- details of contracts awarded
- the various agencies organisational listings

Details of relevant business opportunities are published through the DTI's Export Intelligence Service

---

British exporters are welcome to visit WAS to examine documents and seek opportunities

Visit World Aid Section:         2nd Floor, Ashdown House,
                                 123 Victoria Street, London,
                                 SW1E 6RB
                                 Telephone: see page 324
Give 24 hours notice of intended visit if possible

---

## WORLD BANK PUBLIC INFORMATION CENTRE

Located at:    The World Bank,
               New Zealand House,
               15th Floor,
               Haymarket,
               London, SW1Y 4TE

               Tel: 0171 930 8511
               Fax: 0171 930 8515

---

- Complete set of World Bank Project Information Documents available
- Each P I D consists of two pages of information on the designated project
- Information is available to interested parties during the project preparation and discussion stages
- P I Ds allow for progressive monitoring of individual projects, including:
    - country and location of the project
    - objectives
    - expected or probable components
    - costs and financing
    - environmental and other issues as appropriate
    - procurement arrangements
    - studies to be undertaken
    - prospective implementing agency
    - relevant points of contact
- Once a project has been approved by the World Bank Executive

14

Board, information on any approved changes to the project are
made available
- Environmental Data Sheets, prepared and updated quarterly
  for each project in the World Bank lending program are
  available from the P I C
- A booklet, '*The World Bank Policy on Disclosure of Information*',
  is available from above address

---

**EXPORT INTELLIGENCE – Prelink Ltd.**
**Prelink classifies and distributes export sales leads to UK
businesses on behalf of the DTI. This information, sent from global
sources such as diplomatic posts, ranges from specific
opportunities to notification of major infrastructure projects.**
- information gathered daily from Diplomatic Posts, the Official
  Journal of the EU, the World Bank, providing opportunities for
  UK firms to win new business
- data converted into Prelink notices, with precise information on
  the requirement/opportunity, and details of the potential buyer
- database of UK companies registered with Prelink, with details
  of a member company's Products and Services, the markets of
  interest, and specific information requirements, are matched
  to opportunities and advised daily
- **historical search to assist with market analyses and research**
- tender documents service

---

The **EXPORT INTELLIGENCE SERVICE** is available from:

    Prelink Ltd.,
    Export House,
    87A Wembley Hill Road,
    Wembley, Middx HA9 8BU
    Tel: 0181 900 1313
    Fax: 0181 900 1268

---

**AN EXPORT OPPORTUNITIES SERVICE IS ALSO AVAILABLE FROM:**

> FT Profile,
> PO Box 12,
> Sunbury-on-Thames,
> TW16 7UD
> Tel: 01932 761444
> Fax: 01932 781425

## EXPORT PROMOTERS

**AVAILABLE TO HELP INCREASE EXPORTS FROM THE UK**

Export Promoters are seconded to DTI for a period of two years initially, and it is anticipated new EPs will join the programme as individual two-year secondments are completed

Each has responsibility for one or more overseas countries and/ or industry sectors

They are experienced exporting businessmen, with many years of practical experience

They are available to assist UK businesses with information and guidance

Export Promoters accompany UK Trade Missions to their respective markets, and assist with cultural and market briefings

They are available to visit UK businesses for discussions

---

**To contact the EXPORT PROMOTER for the market you sell into, or are targeting, telephone the appropriate DTI COUNTRY DESK**
**– See Appendix C3**

---

**Government Regional Offices, Business Links and Chambers of Commerce can also assist with contact numbers**

## EXPORT DEVELOPMENT ADVISERS

**EDAs** are experienced export managers from industry operating through Chambers of Commerce and/or Business Link offices
– they are available for consultation on an appointment basis
– they identify and assist businesses with potential to export successfully, and offer expert advice on developing a planned and successful approach to exporting
– their objective is to increase UK exports
– a key service for new and the less-experienced exporting businesses

CONTACT YOUR LOCAL BUSINESS LINK
(see Appendix J for contacts)
or CHAMBER OF COMMERCE
(see Appendix D for contacts)

## MARKET INFORMATION ENQUIRY SERVICE

Provides:
– information about a particular market relevant to your product, process or service, to meet your specific needs
– an assessment of your market prospects
– general background to the market, political and economic information
– recommendations for future activity
– list of individually checked contacts
– details of relevant legislation
– 4–8 weeks' response time

To use the service, contact your local BUSINESS LINK office – see Appendix J
or
G.O. – DTI REGIONAL OFFICE – see Appendix C1

## TRADE FAIR PAMPHLETING SERVICE

**For UK products and services only**

- your company literature displayed on a UK stand at an overseas trade fair
- provides initial exposure in overseas markets
- feed back with list of potential contacts who have expressed an interest in receiving further information on your company's products and/or services
- one use of this service per market
- not available if your company has exhibited at a particular event
- **hot leads identified passed on by fax or telephone direct to you**

To enquire about this service, contact:

your local BUSINESS LINK – Appendix I

or

G.O. – DTI REGIONAL OFFICE – see Appendix C1

## THE INSTITUTE OF EXPORT HELPLINE

**See Appendix B1 for details of qualifications, professional export training courses by Accredited Training staff, College courses for the Institute's qualifications, and local centre information**

THE INSTITUTE'S **HELPLINE**

    **Tel: 0171 247 9812**

- available to members free of charge
- experienced and qualified exporters available to assist with your queries, solving problems and guidance on all matters related to exporting practice
- professional support

18

# INSTITUTE OF EXPORT RESEARCH ASSISTANCE

EXPORT MARKET INFORMATION RESEARCH SERVICE

The Institute of Export and their joint venture partners, Business & Trade Statistics Ltd, have a Research manager located in the DTI Export Market Information Centre Library in Victoria SW1 to assist UK businesses to gain access to the unique collection of business and trade statistics/information held there

- the Research Manager will discuss your requirement and identify the scope of the information available
- you will be provided with a quote identifying the scope and fee
- the fee is nominal and is cost effective when compared with other costs

FOR INFORMATION CONTACT EXPORT MARKET INFORMATION RESEARCH SERVICE – Tel: 0171 215 5707, Fax: 0171 233 1853

# EUROPEAN CONSTRUCTION CENTRE

The Centre is adjacent to the BUILDING CENTRE in London

A ONE-STOP-SHOP to assist UK suppliers to the Building and Civil Engineering industries TO SEEK OUT AND SECURE OPPORTUNITIES IN EUROPE

**THERE ARE MANY OPPORTUNITIES IN CONSTRUCTION AND RELATED INDUSTRIES IN EUROPEAN COUNTRIES, AND THE ECC CAN HELP UK COMPANIES WIN BUSINESS**

The Centre has direct links with a network of specialist European centres, consultancies and business service organisations, and with the European Commission

Close links are maintained with the Department of Trade & Industry, and the Department of the Environment

Database information on opportunities in European Union countries, in both the public and private sectors

Pan-European contacts service for businesses looking for contacts, partners and agents in the local construction markets of Europe

19

Information services staff, and business development specialists are available for discussions

Membership scheme available to all UK businesses supplying into the Building Construction and Civil Engineering industries

For further information contact:

**THE EUROPEAN CONSTRUCTION CENTRE**
26 Store Street, London, WC1E 7BT

Tel: 0171 637 1581, Fax: 0171 637 1582

## JOINT ENVIRONMENTAL MARKETS UNIT – JEMU

A joint co-operation unit between the Department of Trade & Industry and the Department of the Environment

A unit to promote UK exports into the world-wide 'environmental' sector

The 'environmental' sector has a multi-billion spend-resource through past the millenium

Several Export Promoters are closely involved with the JEMU

If you have services, processes, or manufacture or provide equipment suitable for the UK environmental sector, there could be opportunities in overseas markets for you

**You can contact JEMU** on 0171 215 1079

## KNOW-HOW FUNDING FOR TRAINING & INVESTMENT

Funding is available for approved Training schemes in former Eastern Bloc countries

Provision of planned training resource in a wide range of subjects can be submitted for approval and, if the application is successful, an allocation from the Know-How Fund

For investment in former Eastern European countries a Pre-Investment Feasibility Grants Scheme is available

The Know-How Fund is administered by the Foreign & Commonwealth Office

**Tel: 0171 270 3469**

## BRITISH CONSULTANTS BUREAU

The Association of British Consultants operating worldwide

The Bureau exists to:

– promote British consultancy of all disciplines internationally
– provide a forum in which consultants of all disciplines can meet
– provide information to assist member firms win projects in all corners of the world
    – to find the very latest leads to projects
    – explore opportunities by country, sector, field of interest
    – analyse funding
    – identify the buyers
    – access data not available elsewhere
– act as a focal point for governments as far as British consultancy overseas is concerned
– publish a Journal which is distributed to a controlled list of readers mostly overseas
– raise the profile of members to a key audience
– organise regular Seminars targeted at 'Creating the marketing culture to win consultancy business overseas'

**To contact the Bureau:**

**The British Consultants Bureau,**

**Tel: 0171 222 3651, Fax: 0171 222 3664**

21

# 3. YOUR COMPETITORS

- who are they?
- which products and services compete directly with yours?
- does your product or service differ from those of your competitors?
  - in what way?
  - how different?
  - on price?
  - packaging?
  - presentation?
  - use of local language?
  - colour range?
  - comprehensive user instructions?
  - product description?
  - any other characteristics? ie. weaknesses
  - quality of product?
- how does the competition supply the market?
  - through agents?
  - distributors?
  - stockists and retailers?
  - to end-user industrial or consumer?
- are modifications necessary to your products to enable you to compete?
  - if so, what is necessary?
  - is the modification cost effective?
  - would re-design be more effective?

---

HOW CAN YOU FIND OUT?
- by attending Overseas Trade Fairs appropriate for your product or service range
- by making enquiries whilst you are on holiday abroad and are on the spot to make enquiries and assessments

- by using the MARKET INFORMATION ENQUIRY SERVICE (MIES) through your local G.O. Export Regional Office. See Section 1.2
- by researching the DTI EXPORT MARKET INFORMATION CENTRE (EMIC) (at DTI, Ashdown House, 123 Victoria Street, London. Tel: 0171 215 5444/5, Fax: 0171 215 4231) collection of foreign trade directories, and specialised industry sector directories for finding names and addresses of potential manufacturers, agents and importers, mail-order and trade fair catalogues etc.
- by using the EXPORT MARKETING RESEARCH SCHEME (EMRS) to provide in-depth information on specific overseas markets related to your product or service prospects (see Section 1.5)
- use of the **B–C Net** database through the **European Information Centres** (App. F2) or other **B–C Net** access centres (App. F3)
- by using other research organisations and consultants, the specialist country information libraries and services
- by contacting other exporters with knowledge and experience in particular overseas markets
    - contacts provided through Trade Associations
    - through Exports Clubs (see App. A)
    - through UK Chambers of Commerce (see App. D)
    - through Business Links offices (see App. I)
    - through DTI Regional Office contacts (see App. C1)
- by attending market related Seminars arranged by
    - DTI Regional Offices
    - British Overseas Trade Board TRADE ADVISORY GROUP Seminars
    - Chambers of Commerce
    - Export Clubs
    - Trade Associations
- by using your Bank/a Bank Trade Enquiry Service
- DTI Country Desks at 66-74 Victoria Street, London (see Appendix C3)

- contact with overseas Chambers of Commerce Offices in UK (see Appendix E1)
- contact with British Chambers of Commerce overseas (see Appendix E2)
- use a Company Information Report Service to obtain background information on your competitors
- for contact addresses (see Appendix C5.4, page 326)

---

## SINGLE MARKET COMPLIANCE UNIT

Barriers to prevent free trade within the EU countries are illegal

Any evidence of illegal trade barriers in Europe should be reported to this Unit

Whilst gathering evidence may be difficult, you can discuss what information you have with Unit officials

---

Contact:

**Single Market Compliance Unit**
**DTI,**
**123 Victoria Street,**
**London, SW1E 6RB**

**Tel:  0171 215 6730**
**Fax: 0171 215 5989**

# 4. RESEARCH WHILST ON HOLIDAY ABROAD

For those wishing to:
- Sell into shops and stores
- Supply specific industries with equipment, with spares, components, consumables etc
- Develop new areas of interest for their products

For smaller businesses, **'research whilst on holiday abroad'** can provide a good and very cost effective 'visit' to an overseas market

Much useful information can be gained by spending some holiday time assessing the local potential for your products or services

On-the-spot assessment can be most useful

It will certainly add an additional dimension to any written report

Make the most of every opportunity

---

What information?
- look for users or stockists of your product types
- types of outlet
- note prices
- assess quality aspects
- presentation and packaging
- note if Quality Standards or Patent Registration or Trade Mark claims are specified on packaging
- buy examples to measure against your own products

If you think you can compete, ask to meet the potential buyer
- explain what you can provide
- ask to be allowed to quote
- try to get information on their present suppliers
- be prepared to quote prices in buyer's currency – see Section 11

These are but a few of the points which can be considered, there are others depending on the types of products, the target market sector, or the services you have to offer

25

HOLIDAY RESEARCH will not be everyone's cup of tea, but it can be a useful and cost-effective way of using a little of one's holiday time, and it will provide an insight into market potential and may lead to profitable opportunities in the holiday market

# 5. MARKETING RESEARCH

For most product areas/industries in a target market; for the launch of new products into an overseas market, and particularly those of a 'consumer' nature to be offered through retail outlets; for the introduction of services both professional and industrial, a SPECIFIC MARKETING RESEARCH REPORT could provide much useful in-depth information and advice to guide you in assessing the potential for your goods and/or services, your competitors presently serving the market, and the most effective way of trading into the target overseas market

The DTI EXPORT MARKETING RESEARCH SCHEME is Grant-aided for approved research projects, and is managed by:

> The Association of British Chambers of Commerce,
> 4 Westwood House, Westwood Business Park,
> Coventry, CV4 8HS
> Telephone: 01203 694484          Fax: 01203 694690

---

Research Projects can be undertaken using approved Consultants, or by using an 'in-house' researcher

Up to three research projects may be eligible for grant-aid, with a maximum of two in a year

Details of grant support available will be provided by the ABCC address shown above

Grant support cannot be given for marketing research projects already commissioned, already underway, or completed

Companies (not Divisions within Companies) who have less than 200 employees are eligible to apply for the Scheme's grant support if their products are mainly of UK origin, and are exportable from the UK. (May 95 – The eligibility criteria are currently under review)

UK Trade Associations conducting research on behalf of their members are also eligible to apply, and there is a requirement for the Report to be made available to all members of the association

ABCC is also able, under the Export Marketing Research Scheme, to provide free professional advice to any company seeking to research overseas markets. International marketing research training courses are held regularly – contact ABCC, Coventry, 01203 694484

---

There is a Buyers' Guide to Industrial Marketing Research Consultancies, published by the Market Research Society (Business & Industrial Group) and available from ABCC Coventry (Price £20)

---

A **Research Project** should be based on 'Desk Research' initially and followed up with 'Field' research in the market as appropriate

Research should embrace the following points:

- Background to the target overseas market
- the size of the market and assessing the demand for your product
- if there are competing products, what are they,
  - who is the competitor and where are they serving the market from – see Section 1/3/1
- any tariff and/or import restrictions
- any import duties and/or taxes on your product types
- movement of goods to the market and distribution considerations
- identification of technical standards required by the importing country
- target customers and techniques for reaching them
  - size and location
  - financial standing and ability to pay for goods
  - credit terms/payment terms to be provided in relation to normal market practice
  - availability of export credit insurance on the potential/target customers (through ECGD, Trade Indemnity etc)
- market considerations
  - literature/packaging in local language/dual language etc
  - style of packaging/presentation of goods
  - sales support displays/literature/advertising

– currency to be used for invoicing goods from UK – see
  Section 11
   – to make it easier for the buyer to buy from you
   – pricing and whether discounts expected as market norm
– any adverse considerations envisaged/encountered
– whether Trade Fair exhibiting necessary/advisable to support
  product launch

This is not an exhaustive list of points to be considered during a
Marketing Research Project, and there will be other points which
may be identified as relevant during the course of the research

Ensure that all relevant information is recorded for future
reference

---

### Overseas Status Report Service (OSRS)

When you are introduced to, or approached by, a foreign company
you will need to find out if good business can result, and whether a
continuing relationship is in your best interests. An Overseas
Status Report can help you decide whether an overseas agent or
distributor is right for you

– report on an overseas company prepared by Diplomatic
  Service staff
– gives details of overseas companies' business activities
– you get up-to-date information from staff with local knowledge
– helps you to decide if company is right for you to do business
  with. Saves travel and other costs

Contact your Regional G.O. Office – see Appendix C1

## 6. THE IMPORTANCE OF LANGUAGES AND BROCHURES IN THE BUYER'S LANGUAGE

There is no doubt that a working knowledge of one or more European languages will be extremely useful when trying to sell abroad

Brochures and literature should be multi-lingual (English, plus one or more translations alongside)

EU law requires all packaging and labelling to be in the language of the country where the goods are to be sold

---

If you have employees with a language at GCE 'O' and/or 'A' levels, or GCSE, encourage them to develop business language capability

- useful for incoming telephone calls from abroad
- translation of incoming letters, although anything other than 'simple' translations will demand professional attention, particularly relating to technical matters
- useful for contacting the overseas buyer in case of need, particularly telephoning the customer
- gives a good impression when overseas visitors call to see you

---

Under EU Product Liability, Product Safety and Consumer Protection laws, there are important obligations on producers of goods which demand that all Instruction manuals, Instruction notes, Product labelling, are in the language(s) of the country into which products are to be sold, including for certain markets, in dual languages – or multi-languages – (ie English/French, English/Spanish, English/French/German etc)

ALL SAFETY LABELLING should be in the Buyer's language

---

Use recognised translation services to assist:

- Chambers of Commerce can assist with identifying the appropriate language translation agency

- Language for Export Centres are available at some locations (Contact G.O. Regional Office (Appendix C1) or Chamber of Commerce for further information/contact numbers etc). See page 329

Language training courses can be arranged for individual or group tuition

Consult the specialist country sections established at certain Universities. For contact addresses, see Appendix G

- Banks may also be able to assist with translations
- Universities have language training facilities and there are language agencies in most areas
- Most universities have students from overseas countries who can be particularly helpful to businesses
- See page 55/6 for details of the UK Overseas Students organisation, known as AIESEC UK

## 7. FINDING A REPRESENTATIVE ABROAD

Having decided that an Agent and/or Distributor in a target market is desirable or essential, how do you find the right one?

There are a number of services designed to assist this selection process

- The DTI EXPORT REPRESENTATIVE SERVICE (ERS) will provide a list of potential agents/distributors or joint venture partners for your consideration
  - this listing has been checked and recommended by the UK Diplomatic Service staff overseas
  - only experienced and reliable business people will be listed
  - a detailed report of their activities will be provided
  - the names shown will have been approached and expressed an interest in your products
- CHAMBERS OF COMMERCE can also assist in the search for the right representative
- BANKS can also make enquiries
- EUROPEAN INFORMATION CENTRES can use their BC-Net database across 200 EIC's spread across the European countries – see Appendix F2
- INDEPENDENT CONSULTANCY firms may also be able to assist, particularly where they are employed to undertake Marketing Research projects

Ensure you have a status report on the financial background of the potential agents/distributors

One or more meetings will be necessary to discuss arrangements and the basis upon which your interests will be represented – see Section 2

**Don't be rushed, and ensure agreements are approved by your Solicitor**

# 8. USE OF OVERSEAS TRADE FAIRS

Trade Fairs offer a ready-made shop window for goods and services

They are extremely useful for assessing what competition there might be for your products and/or services in world markets

They also provide opportunities for component suppliers to identify potential users of their products, and to open discussions and seek follow-up meetings

Many trade fairs are truly international, attracting buyers from around the world

Lists of Trade Fairs in the UK and Abroad are available from the G.O. Regional Offices, Chambers of Commerce, Business Link Offices, and Trade Associations

The DTI offers subsidised support for participation in certain approved overseas trade fairs

Participation in overseas trade fairs can be by way of individual stand, or group participation with trade association or Chamber of Commerce stands

The temporary export of goods, stands and technical equipment can be covered for Customs purposes by CARNETS – see Section 21

There are also 'all-British' exhibitions and trade fairs organised with DTI support, including specialist sector 'in-store' promotions

The DTI normally provide an Interpreter where there is group participation at a trade fair/exhibition in a non-English speaking country

Attendance at overseas Trade Fairs/Exhibitions can be publicised through the BBC WORLD SERVICE broadcasting – see Section 1.12.2

Publicity support for attendance at certain events may be provided through the services of the Central Office of Information (COI) (contact G.O. Regional Office for details)

DTI supported participation will require:
- company representatives and exhibits to arrive at least 24 hours before the exhibition opens to allow for setting up
- the stand to be staffed at all times the trade fair is open by personnel who have full knowledge of the products and services on offer, and can deal with business enquiries

For further details of Trade Fairs in overseas markets, contact the Regional G.O. Office – see Appendix C1

Exhibiting abroad needs careful preparation if it is to be successful for you

# 9. VISITING THE OVERSEAS MARKETS

Much will depend on WHAT you propose selling and HOW it will best be sold

If it is to one, or a small number of customers, the requirement to spend time in the market, and the frequency of visits, could be different to that required for visiting multiple customer locations

Researching a market may well require several days' presence in the market

Customers abroad like to see the supplier taking an interest in the market, with planned visits

Day or two- or three-day trips may suffice once main contacts have been established

With an Agent in the market, an annual or semi-annual visit may often suffice. However, much recent research emphasises the importance of visiting the market and developing personal lines of communication towards successful market entry

The DTI 'HINTS TO EXPORTERS VISITING' series of booklets is produced for a large number of individual markets

 – they have much useful information on the country

 – information on travelling within the country, climate, currency, local expectations for trading and payment terms, protest instructions, and a host of other useful notes

 – available from DTI Export Publications Office. See App. C5.1

---

VISITING THE OVERSEAS MARKET IS IMPORTANT

For some countries a Visa and inoculations will be required – make enquiries in good time

You might be required to visit your customer at short notice to clarify requirements, discuss potential orders etc

 – IF YOU WANT THE ORDER BE PREPARED TO MEET THE BUYER'S REQUIREMENTS

Travel with organised TRADE MISSIONS can be a very cost effective way of visiting your customers – see below

---

**OUTWARD TRADE MISSIONS**

Organised by Chambers of Commerce, Export Clubs, Export Associations, and Trade Associations

The DTI Seconded Export Promoters are actively involved in leading and supporting Outward Missions to the particular markets for which they have responsibility for promoting UK export activity

– Export Promoters can be contacted through the DTI Country Desks (see Appendix C3 for contact numbers)

Destination countries outside Europe attract DTI financial support

Group travel with other exporters, many of whom have experience in the destination market(s)

All organisational matters done by the Sponsoring organisation

Normally three visits to a market receive financial support, except to Japan where five visits are permitted with support

Secretarial support provided by the Sponsor organisation throughout the Mission, with telex, fax and telephone availability

Pre-Mission briefing on the target market, and briefing on arrival by British Embassy Consulate commercial staff

You can benefit from the market experience of the Mission leader and others

Assistance in arranging visits/appointments during the Mission

Mission brochure listing all participating businesses, mailed out to the market in advance of arrival of Mission

Travelling and hotel costs on group basis are usually lower than could be achieved by a lone traveller, and particularly so when the DTI financial subvention is paid after the return of the Mission

---

For further information on planned Missions, contact the Regional Government Office, Exports Section – for contact numbers, see Appendix C1

OR your local Chamber of Commerce – see Appendix D

OR your Business Link Office, see Appendix I

OUTWARD TRADE MISSIONS to European countries are
organised by some Chambers of Commerce, Export Clubs/
Associations, Trade Associations

Some Outward Missions attract sponsorship from other
organisations, such as local authorities, development
corporations etc,

The DTI Seconded Export Promoters will also be able to advise on
proposed Missions to the particular country for which they have
responsibility for promoting UK export activity

---

TRADE MISSIONS ARE AN IDEAL INTRODUCTION TO AN
OVERSEAS MARKET, WITH THE BENEFITS OF TRAVELLING
WITH OTHER BUSINESS PEOPLE, OFTEN WITH EXPERIENCE IN
THE MARKET

---

Support for missions is provided by DTI and contact should be
through the Country desk – see Appendix C3

---

### LARGER GROUP TRADE MISSIONS

UK Exporting companies now have the opportunity of joining
large-group Trade Missions (upwards of 50 participants),
targeted at non-European markets where there is perceived to be
very good potential for UK goods and services

DTI Seconded Export Promoters lead missions, often with
support of a government Minister

– Contact with Export Promoters can be arranged through the
   respective DTI Country Desks – see App. C3 for contact
   numbers

Whilst these draw participants from a wide cross-section of
industries, they are focused on the large value contract
opportunities, particularly where potential for the use of UK new
technology or to secure major new project contracts is identified

Target markets and dates of ALL proposed Trade Missions
supported by DTI travel grant are advertised well in advance

---

## PROGRAMME ARRANGING SERVICE – PAS

Assistance with arranging a programme of appointments to potential customers

Programme of visits complete with directions, addresses, telephone numbers etc, for each appointment

Information on local etiquette, business practices and public holiday interference if any

Advice on local travel and geography

**At least two months notice of your intended visit is required – programme of appointments arranged provided approximately one month ahead of visit**

---

## IN-MARKET HELP SERVICE – IMHS

Assistance in devising a programme for your visit to a market, to follow up on contacts identified through use of other DTI services

Planned and pre-arranged visit programme

A DTI local expert to accompany you on visits and help with understanding local business and social cultures

The DTI local expert will give an independent assessment of your business discussions and advice on how best to proceed on next steps

Help to introduce you to agents, distributors, professional advisers and other organisations relevant to your needs

---

**To take advantage of PAS or IMHS, you will have to have used either:**

| | MIES | – Market Information Enquiry Service |
| or | EMRS | – Export Marketing Research Scheme |
| or | ERS | – Export Representative Service |

| MIES | – see Section 1.2 |
| EMRS | – see Section 1.5 |
| ERS | – see Section 1.7 |

---

Contact:   DTI Regional Office (Appendix C1)
or local Business Link office (Appendix J)

---

# RECOVER THE VAT PART OF YOUR COSTS OF TRAVELLING AND OBTAINING SERVICES IN EUROPE

**VAT on business expenditure in Europe, other than that incurred in the country where a business is registered for VAT purposes (ie UK), can be recovered in most instances**

**VAT paid on business expenditure abroad, such as:**

- travel, including meals and accommodation, fuel
- hire cars in certain countries
- business entertaining
- trade fairs, conferences, exhibitions
- marketing, consultancy and lawyers' fees

**can be reclaimed and there are businesses available to prepare and submit the claim on your behalf to the Tax authority in the country in which the VAT was paid**

- **you must obtain an original VAT invoice for all expenditure**
- **use a copy invoice for your internal accounting records** (advise your Accountants)

---

See page 321 for VAT Recovery firm addresses.

# 10. USE OF BUSINESS LINK SERVICES

Business Links provide access to a full range of information and advice for businesses, under the style of

ONE STOP SHOPS FOR BUSINESS

Business Links are a partnership with TECs (Training & Enterprise Councils), Government Office/DTI Export and other Services, Chambers of Commerce, Enterprise Agencies, Local Authorities, and other local bodies

Availability of information, advice and counselling will include:

- Exporting
- Business start-up
- Technology and innovation
- Marketing
- Design
- Standards – BSI and TQM
- Finance
- Patents, trade marks and copyright
- Grants and support schemes

plus other areas

- Counsellors are available for discussions on all aspects of exporting

---

New Business Links are being established and the list at Appendix I, is correct up to 1 May 1995

---

- THEY WILL BE THE LOCAL FOCUS POINT FOR BUSINESS INFORMATION, FOCUSED ON MEETING THE NEEDS OF BUSINESSES IN THEIR CATCHMENT AREA

---

- **TRAINED AND EXPERIENCED STAFF AVAILABLE TO ASSIST BUSINESSES**

- MANY WILL HAVE AN **EXPORT DEVELOPMENT COUNSELLOR**, available to assist businesses into export, or to assist those already exporting to become more successful
  - Export Development Counsellors are experienced exporters, providing their knowledge of selling into overseas markets to assist other less experienced business people
  - Export Development Counsellors will visit businesses to assess their needs
- No charge will be made for the initial EDC consultation
- Many Chamber of Commerce export services will be delivered through the Business Link network
- EACH BUSINESS LINK WILL BE ACCREDITED TO ENSURE STAFF ARE FULLY TRAINED, AND THAT ALL SERVICES MEET DEFINED QUALITY STANDARDS
- **BUSINESS LINKS ARE A STRATEGIC NEW DEVELOPMENT TO ASSIST ALL BUSINESSES TO MAXIMISE THEIR ACTIVITIES AND OPPORTUNITIES, PARTICULARLY THOSE AVAILABLE IN OVERSEAS MARKETS**

# USE OF EUROPEAN INFORMATION CENTRE SERVICES

There are over 200 **EUROPEAN INFORMATION CENTRES** throughout Europe

All are linked by computer databases

Provide an Information Service for small and medium sized businesses

They can assist with:

- information on EU programmes, legislation and finance
- advance notice of public tendering opportunities and advice on the preparation of applications
- researching new markets
- verifying product standard requirements

- information on trading procedures in the EU countries
- assessing business expansion opportunities
- identifying prospective business partners through use of the BC-Net programme for
  - identification of potential agents
  - identification of suitable partners for technology transfer and technology co-operation and development
  - formation of joint venture operations

Industrial Sector Guides are available relating to individual industry sector European law matters

---

USE OF

**EUROPEAN DOCUMENTATION CENTRES (EDCs), EUROPEAN REFERENCE CENTRES (ERCs) & EUROPEAN DEPOSIT LIBRARIES**

---

**EDCs** are mainly located in Universities

**ERCs** are based in academic institutions and have small collections of EC documentation

**EDLs** maintain a comprehensive collection of EU official documentation

---

They are intended to stimulate awareness of and interest in European Union matters

They receive all major official EU publications

There are study facilities to enable visitors to seek information from official publications

Staff will attempt to answer all EU-related enquiries, or direct enquirers to the appropriate source of information

Many produce guides and current awareness bulletins on EU matters

---

See Appendix F for list of

**EUROPEAN COMMISSION OFFICES**                    **F1**

**EUROPEAN INFORMATION CENTRES**                   **F2**

**EUROPEAN DOCUMENTATION CENTRES** ⎫
**EUROPEAN REFERENCE CENTRES**        ⎬ **F3**
**EUROPEAN DEPOSIT LIBRARIES**      ⎭

# EUROPEAN UNION INITIATIVES TO SUPPORT PROMOTION OF OVERSEAS BUSINESS

## EUROPARTENARIAT

A business promotion initiative within the European Union, designed to assist small and medium sized businesses from all around the European Union, and beyond, to forge business relationships

To foster business between countries and regions by bringing together etablished businesses within European member countries, with a view to setting up partnerships

## INTERPRISE

Events similar to the Europartenariat in structure and objectives, but limited in range to, usually, three countries or regions, and sometimes a limited range of market sectors

HOW CAN YOU USE THESE INITIATIVES?

- to gain access to potential business partners from European countries, and European neighbours
- facilities for discussion available at all events
- entry to event by catalogue
- access to additional information on participants attending from other EU regions, or from the targeted area outside the EU

Information on UK business participation in
**EUROPARTENARIAT**, and **INTERPRISE** initiatives can be
obtained from:

> The Association of British Chambers of Commerce,
> 4 Westwood House,
> Westwood Business Park,
> Coventry, CV4 8HS
> Tel:  01203 694484
> Fax: 01203 694690

## 11. EXPORT BUYING OFFICES IN THE UK

There are a number of Buying Offices based in London and the South East, seeking to encourage and promote **exports of CONSUMER GOODS** from the United Kingdom

They represent the leading department stores, importers and manufacturers in nearly every country of the world

They will advise manufacturers on the suitability of their goods for sale in overseas markets

Manufacturers are expected to quote their keenest prices allowing trade and cash discounts

Their terms are ex-works or FOB prices in sterling or any selected currency

NO COMMISSION IS PAYABLE TO MEMBERS OF THE EXPORT BUYING OFFICES ASSOCIATION

DOCUMENTATION AND SHIPPING ARRANGEMENTS are normally handled by the Buying Office – the Supplier is relieved of these requirements

---

British Manufacturers of CONSUMER GOODS and Giftware can supply into overseas markets through the Export Buying Offices based in the UK

More information and the names of Buying Offices

– addresses and contact names

– merchandise handled

– markets supplied to

can be obtained by Fax from:

> Export Buying Offices
> Association (EXBO)
> Londwood Cadogan Pier,
> Chelsea Embankment,
> London, SW3 5RQ
>
> Fax: 0171 351 9287

See also Section 1.14

# 12. OVERSEAS PUBLICITY SUPPORT

### 'NEW PRODUCTS FROM BRITAIN' SERVICE

A Service to help you test and promote your products overseas in magazines and journals through editorial features

Can help to generate interest in your product in the overseas market

News story about your product written by a professional journalist appointed by the CENTRAL OFFICE OF INFORMATION (COI)

The story will be targeted at the appropriate publications in the selected market(s)

Can be used as a market research tool and to augment promotional campaigns

Cost effective way of bringing your product to the attention of potential buyers

Feedback on product potential and possible sales opportunities identified

The exporter will be asked to check the English text for factual accuracy

Translations where appropriate carried out by COI staff, or translated overseas

The story relies on its 'news value' for publication

- there is no guarantee of publication
- editors are always seeking 'newsworthy' contributions for their publications

Allow at least 8 weeks' preparation-to-publication time

A report on action taken will be made to you

A charge is made for this service

---

Contact your Regional G.O. – see Appendix C1

---

47

## BBC WORLD SERVICE BROADCASTING

The BBC World Service offers a FREE Publicity Service for British manufacturers and service industries

If you have a good new story to tell . . . tell the BBC World Service

Tell them about interesting new developments,

– innovative products and services

– export orders won

– visits to target areas in sales missions or to trade fairs

– joint venture participation

– training initiatives

– IF IT HAS NEWS VALUE tell the BBC World Service

Specialist writers will put the message across to overseas audiences in a manner and language they will understand

Enquiries resulting from such radio publicity will be passed on to you

---

The BBC broadcasts in English, Arabic, Bengali, Bulgarian, Burmese, Chinese (Cantonese and Mandarin), Czech, Slovak, Finnish, French (to Europe and Africa), German, Greek, Hausa, Hindi, Hungarian, Indonesian, Nepali, Pashto, Persian, Polish, Portuguese (to Europe, Latin America and Africa), Romanian, Russian, Serbo-Croat, Sinhala, Slovene, Spanish (to Latin America), Swahili, Tamil, Thai, Turkish, Urdu and Vietnamese.

---

Don't be shy about your new ideas and achievements:

Contact:

> EXPORT LIAISON
> BBC WORLD SERVICE,
> BUSH HOUSE,
> Strand,
> London, WC2B 4PH
> Tel:    0171 257 2039/2321/2471
> Telex: 265781 BBC HQ G
> Fax:    0171 240 4635

# 13. TRADE ENQUIRIES ABROAD THROUGH YOUR BANK

Most Banks are able to make enquiries on your behalf abroad, and may be willing to circulate your literature

– They use their own branches overseas, or their close relationships with Overseas Correspondent Banks

– They will ask whether they have any customers who might be interested in your products

– The Correspondent Bank will be asked to circulate details of your requirements in its trade publications and circulars to branches of the bank

– There is no guarantee that such enquiries will bring results

– Banks charge for this service

– Responses will take time

---

TO USE THE SERVICE

– Contact your Bank or a Bank offering an Enquiry Service

– You must provide them with information on what type of approach you wish to be made and on your requirements

---

– You may find that the UK office of an Overseas Bank can assist in a particular targeted market because of their local knowledge and contacts

## 14. THE SERVICES OF EXPORT HOUSES AND CONFIRMING HOUSES

There are a number of EXPORT HOUSES which can assist UK businesses into overseas markets:

- they will act as Agents and/or Principals
- they can represent manufacturers or service providers in overseas markets, seeking opportunities for sales to be achieved
- export documentation preparation can be handled by agreement
- their knowledge of markets/market areas/specific industries etc can be a particular benefit
- UK exporter is paid by the Export House
- exporter's credit risk is with the Export House, and is not spread over a number of individual buyers
- the Export House will purchase goods outright and on-sell for their own account, or they will handle sales on an agreed commission basis

CONFIRMING HOUSES

A Confirming House will act on behalf of an overseas buyer, and place orders to meet specific requirements

- it acts as the Buyer's Agent in the UK
- the UK manufacturer or service provider will be paid by the Confirming House against production of correct documentation
- the exporter's credit risk is with the Confirming House and not the overseas buyer to whom the goods are shipped or services provided
- the overseas buyer will pay the Confirming House for its services in procuring goods

Contact address for more information:

The Secretary,
British Exporters Association,
16 Dartmouth Street,
London, SW1H 9BL
Tel: 0171 222 5419,
Fax: 0171 222 2782

This was formerly The British Export Houses Association, and it can provide more information on how Export and Confirming Houses can assist UK exporters of goods and services, into successful selling in overseas markets

Its Directory lists Export and Confirming Houses, product interests, territorial market interests, and services provided

# 15. UK UNIVERSITIES CAN HELP EXPORTERS

**Many of the UK Universities have specialist departments which can provide very real support and information for UK exporters**

**These specialist departments often relate to specific industrial sectors, to environmental studies of and in overseas countries, and to developments in the application of technology**

**Database information is available which can enable UK businesses usefully to avoid duplicating research work and process/product information already undertaken, and provides a fast track to obtaining up-to-date data**

**Project work is also undertaken on commercial terms by most Universities, and can be very cost-effective**

**UK EXPORTERS CAN ACCESS THIS INFORMATION BY CONTACTING THE APPROPRIATE 'INDUSTRY CONTACT' shown at Appendix G1**

**or from the specimen University specialisms listed in this section**

---

Practical assistance which might be available:

- language training
- technical translations, particularly from those with specialist country sections, and provision of interpreters
- advice on cultural etiquette, local customs, business practices, briefings
- information on socio-economic and geographic factors of overseas markets
- loan of graduates to assist with specific research projects to assess export potential
- access to country library facilities
- consultancy services relating to Single European Market matters, including European law
- overseas project work undertaken by University staff can provide useful additional information for UK exporters

– a wide range of courses with relevance to various aspects of exporting

---

For further information of what the Universities can do to help UK exporters, contact:

> The Senior Administrative Officer,
> Industrial Liaison,
> CVCP,
> 29 Tavistock Square,
> London, WC1H 9EZ
>
> Tel: 0171 387 9231
> Fax: 0171 388 6256

See Appendix G1 for list of Universities

---

### Some University specialisms

| | |
|---|---|
| Aberystwyth | – development of crops to |
| Univ. Coll. of Wales | suit overseas climates |
| Bangor | – research projects to |
| Univ. Coll. of N. Wales | study tree growth in rain forests |
| Bradford | – European/Latin American Research Unit providing commercial briefings on L.A. business and trade |
| | – European Briefing Unit |
| Buckinghamshire Coll. | – interactive video-disc on |
| 01494 464535 | business opportunities in Spain |
| Cardiff | – test facility for solar |
| Univ. of Wales Coll. | energy equipment |
| | – export finance course |
| Durham | – East Asia Centre (joint with Newcastle) |
| | – Small Firms Export Programme |
| East Anglia | – management of land resources in Africa |

53

| | |
|---|---|
| | – national recovery plans for poor countries |
| Exeter | – European Legal Studies, centre of excellence on European law |
| Glasgow | – European Contracts Information Service |
| | – Veterinary Research School |
| Heriot-Watt | – technical translations and interpreting in West European languages, Russian & Arabic |
| | – water sanitation systems for arid zones |
| Leeds | – Arabic language courses |
| | – Chinese culture and commerce |
| | – computer based market intelligence resource planning for European expansion |
| Leicester | – Textiles research |
| London School of Oriental & African Studies | – specialist staff available for Japanese, Chinese, Korean, South-East Asian, African and Middle Eastern languages |
| London, Kings College | – total immersion and semi-intensive French courses |
| London, Imperial Coll. | – animal cooling systems etc |
| Loughborough | – The Water Engineering and Development Group research and training in planning, provision, operation and maintenance of water supplies in Third World arid zones |
| Manchester Business Sch. | – evaluation of overseas market potential |
| Newcastle | – East Asia Centre (joint with Durham) |

| | |
|---|---|
| | − library of Japanese science and technology periodicals and company reports |
| | − European financial analysis course |
| Nottingham | − engineering, law, pharmaceuticals and other specialist areas related to European ways of doing business |
| Salford | − mini-electric power stations work in Sri Lanka |
| Strathclyde | − technology transfer European network to help small to medium sized enterprises with technological and marketing aspects related to Europe |
| | − database of financial assistance schemes in EU countries |
| Sheffield | − Japanese Business Services Unit |
| | − Asia–Pacific Business Services Unit |
| Swansea | − maximising food production |
| Ulster | − languages and translations |
| | − Transatlantic Business Project for the American market |

This is not an all-inclusive list of specialisms, but more a selection, to illustrate the fact that UK Universities can offer real help in specialised sectors to UK exporters

---

## ASSISTANCE FROM OVERSEAS STUDENTS

Overseas students attending UK Universities may be available for short placements in businesses, to assist with particular projects akin to their studies, or to advise on local cultural and other aspects of their own country as a potential overseas market for a UK exporter.

---

## The overseas student body in the UK is AIESEC UK

- there are 30 branches covering most UK Universities
- they welcome opportunities to place overseas students with UK businesses
  - insight into their own home market culture, particularly for consumer products
  - research projects relating to their own country
  - assistance with translations

UK businesses can help overseas students understand UK business culture and operations

---

**AIESEC UK** Headquarters are located at:

> AIESEC United Kingdom,
> 2nd Floor,
> 29–31 Cowper Street,
> London, EC2A 4AP
>
> Tel: 0171 336 7939
> Fax: 0171 336 7971

See Appendix G2 for list of **AIESEC UK** University branches

## 16. ROYAL MAIL INTERNATIONAL SERVICES FOR EXPORTERS

## ROYAL MAIL INTERNATIONAL AND DIRECT MAIL

### BENEFITS OF DIRECT MAIL

Direct Mail has grown dramatically compared with more traditional advertising media. This is due not only to the great leaps forward in computer science and database technology, but also, importantly, to the considerable benefits of the medium:

– Results can be measured exactly

– It is extremely flexible – you can control the volumes of mail sent, where it is sent and when. You can tailor the message and language to suit the target audience

– It is cost-effective – particularly in comparison with other media

– It is an ideal vehicle for targeting, database building and communicating directly with customers

– **It is a truly world-wide medium**

---

### USES OF INTERNATIONAL DIRECT MAIL

These are many and varied:

– As a substitute for a sales force, for example mail-order

– Generate new business and to cross-sell new products and/or services

– To reinforce customer loyalty

– As a market research tool (postal questionnaires)

– To test new markets

– To support agents and distributors abroad

---

## ROYAL MAIL INTERNATIONAL SERVICES

Royal Mail offers a range of international services to suit direct mail needs, from mailshots and responses, to fulfilment and delivering lightweight samples and mail-order goods. General services cover letters and small packets, with a choice of airmail for speed or surface mail for economy

THE FOLLOWING SERVICES ARE ALSO AVAILABLE FROM POST OFFICE COUNTERS:

– Swiftair – the express airmail service
– International Recorded
– International Registered
– Advice of Delivery

---

A number of account and contract services providing beneficial rates are also available for customers with regular or large volumes of mail, as well as **Response Services,** to encourage prospects to reply to mailings at no cost to themselves, and **International Door to Door,** which can be especially helpful when good mailing lists are hard to come by.

---

## ROYAL MAIL INTERNATIONAL – OTHER SUPPORT:

RMI provides a number of additional support services for exporters:

– **'Marketing Without Frontiers'** – 200 pages of step-by-step advice on international direct marketing, from running campaigns and finding mailing lists, to export finance and country profiles (video also available)
– **'The DIY Guide to International Direct Mail'** – provides advice on how companies can 'do their own' mailshots if they cannot afford the services of a direct marketing agency to implement campaigns on their behalf
– **'RMI Service Guide'** – information on how to send mail abroad, with advice on packing and mailing requirements for over 200 destinations (available on IBM PC-compatible floppy disk or in book form)

- **'RMI Business Travel Guide'** – over 400 pages of important facts on every country in the world, including information on exchange rates, visa requirements, import regulations, climate and local etiquette
- **'Business Portfolio Club'** – a quarterly magazine covering updates on RMI services and information on exporting and overseas markets

---

For further information on RMI services or to obtain order forms for the above guides, which are subject to availability, simply contact your **Royal Mail Business Service Centre on 01345 950950**

# 17. SELLING FOOD FROM BRITAIN

**'FOOD FROM BRITAIN' is a bureau** which was formed under The Agricultural Marketing Act 1983 to improve the marketing and promotion of British food overseas, and the promotion and development of Speciality foods

Primarily funded by HM Government to support British businesses in the food industry

The organisation includes the **'BRITISH FOOD EXPORT COUNCIL'**

**There are FOOD FROM BRITAIN offices in six European countries (Belgium, France, Germany, Italy, The Netherlands, Spain), and one in North America to assist UK exporters of Food products**

**See Appendix C5–6 for contact addresses**

---

Assistance includes:

- development and promotion of British food and drink products throughout the world
- targeted advice and information on overseas markets and niche opportunities
- UK Supplier-meets-international-buyer events
- participation in Food from Britain stands at international food exhibitions
- participation in dedicated 'Food' export Trade Missions
- regional seminars around UK to assist in highlighting valuable export opportunities

---

Services offered

- market opportunity analysis
- strategic planning for market entry
- distributor selection and monitoring
- buyer contacts with leading retailers and caterers
- merchandising and in-store promotions
- guidance on labelling and packaging
- advertising and media relations planning

- food sector written reports
- legal advice

---

There are good opportunities to sell British food in overseas markets
All 'food' sector businesses should contact the **Food from Britain Bureau** for advice and guidance

# Use of Agents and Distributors in Overseas Markets

On 1 January 1994, a new law covering AGENCY AGREEMENTS between organisations and/or individuals in the EU countries came into effect. The legislation applies to all agency contracts in operation on or after this date

**Under EU Agency Law, an Agent has a right to a written agreement**

Agents and Principals are required to undertake broad reciprocal obligations to each other

An Agent has an obligation to look after his Principal's interests, act dutifully and in good faith, and comply with the Principal's reasonable instructions

A Principal should act dutifully and in good faith towards the Agent

The possible appointment of an Agent, or Agents, and/or Distributors is of importance when considering how to sell, or how your products and/or services might best be sold in overseas markets. Any such appointment must be made with the utmost care, preferably after a trial period, and after checking the legal aspects, and for a definite albeit renewable period of time

BUT THE APPOINTMENT OF AGENTS AND/OR DISTRIBUTORS SHOULD NOT BE CONSIDERED AN ABSOLUTE PREREQUISITE

– Some products can be sold and some market sectors penetrated on a direct basis without the services of an Agent
– Much will depend on the type of market, and to whom you will be targeting sales

Your market research findings and other information should point you in the most appropriate direction and advice from other contacts could also be useful in making assessments and decisions

How is the target market served now, and by your competitors?

Will the appointment of Agent(s) and/or Distributors give you an edge over the competition?

Will economies of scale in transporting products to a central distribution point be an advantage or a disadvantage?

THESE ARE POINTS WHICH REQUIRE THOROUGH CONSIDERATION AND EVALUATION BEFORE YOU SIGN ANY AGREEMENTS TO REPRESENT YOUR INTERESTS ABROAD

IF AN INTERESTED PARTY OFFERS YOU AN AGENCY/ DISTRIBUTORSHIP AGREEMENT, DO NOT SIGN IT IMMEDIATELY; RETAIN IT AND DISCUSS IT WITH YOUR COMMERCIAL LAWYER

The DTI EXPORT REPRESENTATIVE SERVICE is available to assist businesses to find an agent or distributor in an overseas market

ERS can be used to find replacement agents or distributors, if the existing party's agreement has been or is being terminated, or where a new product line is not covered by an existing agreement

---

**'Local Factors' in Representation selection for Export Markets**

Points to consider:

- Knowledge of and track record in the industry or market sector you'll want him to sell into
- Does he handle other products which might compete with yours?
  - if he does, will he relinquish those interests in favour of yours?
  - he could effectively keep you out of the market by not promoting and selling your products and/or services
  - is he aware of competitive products in the market?
- Is he financially stable?
  - who are his bankers?

- ask your Bank to make an enquiry to establish his financial standing and reputation
- seek a status report through your DTI Regional Office using the OSRS – Overseas Status Report Service
- seek a business intelligence report from one of the names shown in on page 326
- What area is the potential representative to cover?
  - the whole territory
  - specific industries or market sectors
  - a clearly defined area
- Can he provide Trade References?
- What will his responsibilities be?
  - securing orders?
  - negotiating terms and prices?
  - providing market reports and up-dates relevant to your products, customers and the industry sectors served?
  - chasing late-payers and protecting your interests?

---

AND ADDITIONALLY FOR DISTRIBUTORS
- ABSOLUTELY VITAL TO ENSURE FINANCIALLY SOUND
- Do they have adequate secure warehousing and handling facilities?
- Good distribution channels are essential
- Agree payment and stocking terms
- Will they handle Warranty Claims and/or replacement of faulty goods?

---

- Under EU product Liability laws, Product Safety and Consumer Protection are important matters for all producers of products and, in certain instances, others involved in the chain of supply of those products into European countries. This is an area of trading which requires careful consideration, and it is therefore advisable for businesses to discuss their trading terms and conditions of supply with their commercial lawyer

65

- Whilst there is an obligation for Producers to place only safe products on the market, there is also a new duty of care on Distributors to comply with general safety requirements and to monitor the safety of products they place on the market
- In the event that products are found to be defective, there is now an obligation on Distributors and Producers to withdraw defective products from sale, and recall such defective items from users

THE IMPLICATIONS FOR YOUR COMPANY OF THESE NEW EU LAWS ON DISTRIBUTORSHIP AGREEMENTS SHOULD BE DISCUSSED WITH YOUR COMMERCIAL LAWYER

---

Under Product Liability, Product Safety and Consumer Protection laws, there are important obligations on producers of goods which demand that all Instruction manuals, Instruction notes, Product labelling, are in the language(s) of the country into which products are to be sold

---

**AGENCY or DISTRIBUTION AGREEMENTS**

**Do not sign any agreements offered to you until your lawyer has considered them and given approval for signature. Do not prepare agreements without discussing the wording and format with your lawyer**

The following points should be included (not necessarily in this order):

1. Names, Addresses (Registered Head Offices) of Parties
2. Territory to be covered and whether exclusivity is given
3. Products involved – schedule separately (this permits additions or deletions to be recorded without requiring a full new agreement) making reference to any warranty matters
4. Pricing policy – permitted negotiation terms
5. Payment terms  –  Agent            – commission terms and
                                                     when due
                              Distributor     – period of credit allowed
                                                     – method of payment

66

6.  Sales Targets and Performance Assessment criteria, including market reports etc
7.  Advertising and Sales Promotion Responsibilities and Support by you and the Agent/Distributor
8.  Reference to any Trade Mark representation/usage
9.  Representation of competitor/other product ranges
10. Product awareness training responsibilities
11. Sales to third parties (if appropriate)
12. For Distributors – stock levels
    – supply and distribution frequency to market
    – fate of termination stocks
13. Period of Agreement/Period of Notice
14. Immediate break clauses
15. Long term break clauses
16. Operative law
17. Arbitration clauses (if appropriate)
18. Any other responsibilities – ie chasing debts etc

CONSULT YOUR LAWYER, AND ENSURE HE PREPARES AGREEMENTS OF THIS AND LIKE TYPE

This is a series of points suggested for inclusion in such agreements and it is in no way an exhaustive or fully comprehensive list

TAKE FURTHER LEGAL ADVICE ON THE COMPOSITION OF SUCH AGREEMENTS

**PAYMENT TERMS FOR AGENT**

Your agent will normally sell on your behalf to customers, and in return will expect to receive an agreed percentage commission on the price achieved

– the basis of payment can vary:
  – calculated on monthly or quarterly sales volumes and paid in the following month

67

- calculated on a basis which is set out in the Agency agreement

Remember to include your agent's commission terms in your selling price calculations

---

**If you wish to terminate an Agency agreement, the Agent is entitled to 'reasonable notice' to terminate if there is no agreed notice period written into the agreement, and a sum of compensation may be due to the Agent unless the Agent is in breach of the Agency agreement. It is important that all Agency agreements operative within the EU countries are discussed fully with a lawyer**

---

## AGREEMENTS WITH DISTRIBUTORS

The distributor will normally buy on his own account and earn his income from the mark-up he adds, or from an agreed margin within a price structure

It may help the distributor to stock your range of products if you consider placing stock on a Consignment basis

- this allows him to maintain higher stock levels than he might otherwise be able to
- it reduces his risk
- you should mark all invoices/agreements to indicate you retain title to the goods until you have been paid (Romalpa clause)

For consignment stocking arrangements, you should ensure there is clarity about when you will be paid, and ensure there are monitoring procedures in place to minimise your risks

You should also assess most carefully the financial standing and reputation of the potential distributor

---

Remember, it is easy to sign an agreement, it can be very expensive and difficult to get out of it

You should use a lawyer with commercial/ international experience.

# Credit Risk Insurance

Credit Risk Insurance on your overseas buyers should be considered

**All businesses insure their premises, machinery, equipment, work-in-progress, stock, vehicles, and staff**
**TOO FEW BUSINESSES CONSIDER INSURING THEIR MOST VULNERABLE, YET MOST VALUABLE, ASSET – THEIR DEBTORS – THE MONEY OWED TO THE BUSINESS – THE MONEY WHICH IS REQUIRED FOR FUTURE TRADING!**

There are a number of providers:

NCM (formerly ECGD short term up to two years)

TRADE INDEMNITY PLC (short to medium term cover)

COFACE (short to medium term cover)

HERMES (short to medium cover)

NAMUR (short to medium cover)

ECGD (medium to longer term – **Credit periods two years upwards**)

There are a number of Insurance Broking Firms with specialist Credit Risk Insurance sections

Brokers are able to assess the credit risk requirements of a business, and obtain premium quotations to suit the requirements of the business you transact

They have connections with most, if not all the Credit Risk Insurance providers

A review of your risk exposure situation could be beneficial to your business

---

These organisations provide Credit Limit approvals on overseas buyers so that, within the specified limit for each buyer, goods may be shipped without delay in the vast majority of cases

Whole or an agreed proportion of turnover covered

Insurance against a wide range of risks

- insolvency of the buyer
- buyer's failure to pay within six months after the due date for goods accepted
- buyer's failure or refusal to accept goods despatched which comply with the contract

Country Risks:

- difficulties and delays in transferring funds from the buyer's country for political reasons
- action by a foreign Government which prevents performance of the contract, either wholly or in part
- covered for war, civil war and similar risks outside the UK which prevent performance of the contract, where the cause of loss is not normally commercially insurable
- cancellation or non-renewal of an export licence or the imposition of new restrictions on exports to the buyer's country after date of contract
- for public buyers, failure or refusal to fulfil any terms of the contract

---

The Insurer will agree the % level of loss cover provided when assessing your Credit Risk Insurance requirements

Whilst insurers generally provide up to 90% of loss cover a lower agreed percentage, to cover, say, manufacturing costs and perhaps a proportion of the profit margin, could result in lower premiums

70

Insurers will also discuss 'excess' loss situations – the insured
business will stand losses up to an agreed figure, and the Insured
will pay out all sums in excess of the agreed figure

---

NOTE:    i.  NCM (Nederlandsche Credietverzekering
Maatschappij), the Dutch credit risk insurers, took
over the former ECGD short-term credit insurance
service on 1 December 1991

      ii.  Whilst the overall Credit Risk Insurance points are
general, there are minor differences between what
the insurers offer

     iii.  There are other insurers offering insurance of
credit risks

See Appendix C4 for contact addresses

# When You Travel Abroad, Go Prepared

1. Know what limitations, if any, there are to your own authority whilst abroad
   - to negotiate contracts/contract terms/sale of goods
   - to negotiate prices
   - to agree credit terms
   - to agree payment terms                (See Section 5)

2. Know what the cost of giving extended credit period is, in case the buyer demands/you have to agree, extended credit terms to win the order               (See Section 10)

3. If extended credit is likely to be required, know what the various methods for financing longer periods of credit might be, appropriate to the markets you are selling into
   (See Section 13)

4. Are you selling in STERLING or in a FOREIGN CURRENCY appropriate for the market into which you're selling?
   (See Section 11)

   - if STERLING, there is no Exchange Risk for you, BUT THERE WILL BE AN EXCHANGE RISK FOR THE BUYER
   - if CURRENCY, know which currency (or currencies) you can quote in
   - BEFORE YOU LEAVE, check the currency conversion rates
     - ENSURE YOU USE A CONVERSION RATE HIGHER THAN THE CURRENT SPOT RATE OF EXCHANGE
     - Agree the currency pricing with colleagues
   - whilst you're away, monitor the Exchange Rates of the currencies you have authority to invoice in, particularly if you are away for more than a few days
   - if necessary, telephone your office to update on rates

5.  SELLING/INVOICING IN A FOREIGN CURRENCY will
    expose your business to a foreign currency risk – BUT
    THAT RISK IS MANAGEABLE

6.  If you secure an order with payment to be made in a foreign
    currency, consider telephoning your office, so one of your
    colleagues can consider eliminating the foreign exchange
    risk by one of the methods available          (See Section 12)

7.  Take with you a pro forma setting out the terms you require
    for payment under a Letter of Credit – this will assist the buyer
    in instructing his bank to open the Letter of Credit, and it
    may make the terms of the Letter of Credit easier to
    comply with, without diminishing the buyer's expectations
                                              (See Section 14.5.2)

8.  If you require a Letter of Credit to be Confirmed by a UK Bank,
    ask your Bank if it has any arrangements to Confirm Letters
    of Credit issued by your buyer's bank, or other banks in the
    buyer's country

---

GO PREPARED TO DO BUSINESS – KNOW THE TERMS YOU CAN
SELL ON

---

The DTI Hints to Exporters booklets provide a great deal of useful
information on the conditions to be found in a country, including
trading conditions (issued for most countries). These are
available from:

>   DTI Export Publications
>   PO Box 55
>   Stratford-on-Avon
>   Warwicks. CV37 9GE
>   Tel: 01789 296212

# Obtaining Payment – Summary of Methods

**Obtaining payment** – the most important aspect of exporting. Whilst trading on a 'payment with order' basis, or payment prior to delivery, has distinct advantages for the exporter, not all buyers will agree to such terms. To secure the order you may have to accept payment on other terms, and this section explains the alternatives available

See Section 13 for alternative methods of Financing export turnover that are directed to ensuring payment is received

# 1. PAYMENT WITH ORDER, OR PRIOR TO DELIVERY

MAKE IT SIMPLE – give instructions to your customer to transfer funds DIRECT INTO YOUR BANK ACCOUNT

- this will save time
- avoid waiting for cleared funds
- reduce bank charges
- avoid the possibility of an overseas cheque being returned to you unpaid
- avoid cheques being lost in the post

IT WILL ENSURE YOU ARE PAID

---

GIVE YOUR CUSTOMER THE FOLLOWING INFORMATION ON YOUR INVOICE

- YOUR Bank name and branch address
- YOUR Bank's Sort Code number
- the name of YOUR business account
- YOUR account number

ASK YOUR CUSTOMER TO INSTRUCT HIS BANK TO TRANSFER FUNDS DIRECT TO YOUR BANK ACCOUNT

- by SWIFT bank-to-bank transfer, OR
- by Telegraphic transfer,
- QUOTE THE TERMS (period of credit etc) AND THE DATE WHEN YOU EXPECT TO BE PAID

---

BY BANK DRAFT

- A Bank Draft in Sterling payable in the UK, can be paid direct into your Bank Account
- A Draft drawn in a foreign currency can be:
  - Paid into a currency account
or – proceeds collected by your Bank

76

or – your bank may agree to 'negotiate' the draft, that is, to advance you the amount of the draft less a commission, and the bank will then proceed to collect the value of the draft

– Your Bank will inform you if they wish to retain recourse to you for the monies they have advanced, or have credited to your currency account

– There will be a clearance period for the Draft, which could be as long as one month if payable abroad

CAUTION – There have been many instances where bogus bank drafts, purporting to be issued by Banks, have been received by UK businesses with the express intent to defraud

– When you receive a Bank Draft pay it into your bank **without delay, and allow sufficient time for it to be cleared before you supply any goods**

---

It should be noted:

Cheques and Bank Drafts payable abroad may be paid and funds remitted to the payee's bank, or presenting bank, but in certain countries, local law may allow recourse to the payee/presenting Bank for a number of years after presentation, if fraud is known or suspected, or for other reasons which may be specified in the appropriate local law

---

BY CASH – STERLING NOTES – BEWARE OF LARGE SUMS BEING OFFERED

BY CASH – FOREIGN CURRENCY NOTES

– Foreign notes are a convenience currency, and the Bank will quote a rate for conversion into sterling, or an 'adjustment rate' to transfer the value into a currency account

– Beware of large sums being offered

– BEWARE OF THE POSSIBILITY OF FORGED NOTES

– DO NOT SUPPLY GOODS UNTIL YOU HAVE CLEARED THE QUESTION OF VALUE WITH YOUR BANK

CHEQUE – If in **Sterling** and payable at a UK Bank, it will have to be cleared in the usual way, and this can take up to 4/5 **working** days

– A **Sterling** Cheque drawn on a UK Bank can be cleared by Special Presentation
  – your bank will advise you
  – a small fee will be payable for this service
  – clearance is usually one working day, with telephone follow-up by the Bank to confirm payment made
  – without telephone follow-up, bank will advise when cleared funds can be expected

– A **Sterling** Cheque drawn payable at a Bank outside the UK,
  – will take longer to clear and to receive funds into your account
  – can take up to one month to clear
  – ask your bank to send the cheque for Collection

YOUR BANK MIGHT BE PREPARED TO ADVANCE FUNDS TO YOU WHILST THEY COLLECT THE CHEQUE PROCEEDS

---

CHEQUE – **In a Foreign Currency** will require collecting

– Your bank may agree to 'negotiate' the cheque, giving you the sterling value, but retaining recourse back to you until the Bank has received good value for the cheque (a period of one month is generally applied)

– Can be credited to a currency account

– If the cheque is not honoured by the Bank upon which it is drawn, it will be returned, and your Bank may then ask for the repayment of sterling value advanced when they negotiated the cheque

– If the Bank agrees to negotiate a currency cheque, it is making an advance to you, and you will have to agree a 'Negotiations' facility with the Bank, as part

of the total advances package the Bank agrees to
make available to your business
- DO NOT accept foreign cheques from other than the
drawer
- If the payee of a foreign cheque is other than your
business name, BEWARE and consult your Bank
- Foreign cheques will require endorsement on
the reverse

## 2. PAYMENT BY LETTER OF CREDIT

Irrevocable Letter of Credit

- Should always be irrevocable
  - An Irrevocable Letter of Credit **cannot be cancelled, nor the terms varied, without the agreement of all parties to it** including the Exporter (the Beneficiary)
- The buyer will have to approach his Bank with a request to open a Documentary Letter of Credit
- You can send the buyer a Suggested Format which will help him and his Bank to open the Letter of Credit in your favour – see Section 14.5.2
- The buyer's Bank will open a Letter of Credit through a Bank in the UK, and you will then receive the definitive Letter of Credit
- You can ask for the Letter of Credit to be opened at your own Bank, or other Bank of your choice, but the option of which Bank is to be used in the UK lies with the buyer's Bank
- Always ask for the Letter of Credit to be payable in the UK
- The Letter of Credit will stipulate which documents you have to produce to evidence the supply of goods or services, and you have to comply with these requirements
- If there are any errors, or requirements specified in the Letter of Credit that you cannot meet, or will have difficulty in meeting, consider seeking an amendment to the Credit without delay
- A Letter of Credit is an undertaking to pay upon production of the documentation specified and evidencing that all requirements have been met, i.e. shipment within the time specified etc
- Use the Letter of Credit CHECKLIST when you check the terms of the Credit – Section 14.6

ACCURACY IN PREPARING THE REQUIRED DOCUMENTATION IS ABSOLUTELY VITAL IF YOU ARE TO OBTAIN PAYMENT UNDER A LETTER OF CREDIT

- The Letter of Credit will specify when payment will be made:
  - Payment at Sight – on presentation of correct documentation at the paying Bank

- Payment after 'X' days –
  - This is referred to as a 'Term Credit'
  - Documents are presented to the paying Bank, and the Draft (Bill of Exchange) will be 'accepted' (signed by the Bank) and a maturity date specified, this being the date when payment will be made
  - If no Draft (Bill of Exchange) is required, then the documents will be accepted, an acknowledgement given to you, and a date specified when payment will be made – this is referred to as a Deferred Payment Credit
  - The Bank may be prepared to pay you the sum due when you present the documents, less a charge for interest for the period to the given maturity date when payment would normally be made (known as discounting)
- Payment only after the funds have been made available to the Bank to whom you have presented documents

# 3. PAYMENT BY CONFIRMED IRREVOCABLE LETTER OF CREDIT

- Detail as set out in Section 5.2
- Procedure for establishing a 'Confirmed' Irrevocable Letter of Credit the same as detailed in Section 5.2
- If your requirement is a 'Confirmed' I/L/C you should instruct the Buyer accordingly
- Your instruction should be:

  Please arrange for the Letter of Credit to be 'Confirmed' by a UK Clearing Bank (you can nominate a Bank if you wish)
- The 'Confirming Bank' takes over responsibility to pay you when correct documentation is presented within the validity of the Credit
- You may have to be satisfied with a 'Confirmation' added by the London Office of the Issuing Bank. This may not give any added 'strength of Confirmation' to the original Letter of Credit. You could be paying out Confirmation fees and receiving no added security of payment. If in doubt, consult your Bank
- Confirmation is security against the failure or default of the Issuing Bank. If there are payment problems with the Overseas Issuing Bank and their London office has confirmed the Letter of Credit, will the London Office of that Bank be able to continue operations?
- A Bank can, if it so wishes, refuse to add its Confirmation to another Bank's Letter of Credit
- A 'Confirmation Fee' will be charged by the Confirming Bank
- For 'high-risk' countries a Confirmation Fee may be higher than that applicable to less risky areas
- Confirmation Fees are payable by the UK Exporter, unless otherwise indicated in the Letter of Credit

FURTHER INFORMATION ON LETTERS OF CREDIT IS CONTAINED IN SECTION 14

**Strength of a Confirmation**

CONFIRMATION of a Letter of Credit, by a major bank adding its CONFIRMATION to a letter of credit issued by another bank, means that the confirming bank undertakes the obligation to pay when the specified documents are presented and meet all the terms of the Letter of Credit

The CONFIRMING Bank puts its strength behind the Letter of Credit

CONFIRMATION added by the London Office of the ISSUING BANK may not give added strength of Confirmation to the Letter of Credit

CONFIRMATION is added security against the failure or default of the Issuing Bank

THERE IS NO HARD AND FAST RULE

IF IN ANY DOUBT, DISCUSS THE SUBJECT OF CONFIRMATION OF LETTERS OF CREDIT WITH YOUR BANK'S INTERNATIONAL DEPARTMENT. THEY WILL ADVISE YOU

# 4. PAYMENT BY USING BILL FOR COLLECTION

- Bill of Exchange drawn on the Buyer

  See Section 16.2
- Usually accompanied by other Documents

  See Section 16.3–7
- You prepare the documentation and hand in to the Bank
- Complete the Bank's Bill for Collection Form
- The Bank sends the Documents to the Buyer's Bank, or (if you do not give Bank details) to a convenient branch of the Bank's Correspondent Bank
- The Bank receiving the 'Collection' will notify the Buyer that they have received a Bill of Exchange and Documents
- If the Bill of Exchange is a 'Sight' Bill, payable when the Buyer 'sights' the Bill and Documents, he will be asked to make payment immediately
- If the Bill of Exchange is a 'Term' Bill, payable at a future date after a given Term, then the Buyer will be requested to 'Accept' the Bill of Exchange
- If the Bill is Paid, or Accepted, the accompanying documents will then be handed to the Buyer
- An Accepted Bill is usually retained by the Overseas Bank until the maturity date, and they will then ask the Buyer to pay
- If the Buyer refuses to 'Pay' or 'Accept' the Bill, the Overseas Bank should notify the UK Collecting Bank, take Protest action if specified by the Exporter, and continue to seek the Buyer's agreement to pay or accept the Bill

  Protest – see Section 18
- Even though the Overseas Bank may be your Buyer's Bank, when they receive your Collection they are acting on your behalf and must therefore protect your interests
- **Settlement** – Settlement by Telegraphic Transfer, or Urgent SWIFT Transfer will ensure speedy transfer of funds to your account

- Do complete the Collection Form carefully, and complete as many of the boxes as possible
- If you have any queries on what information is required, ask your Bank for guidance
- If shipment by sea, you should present a full set of Bills of Lading as part of the documentation, or if one or more originals have been sent direct to the buyer (or your Agent), you should advise the Bank handling the collection what has happened to the various originals (full set of Bills of Lading usually consists of three originals)

---

### Italy

Specifically for Italy, there is a method of obtaining payment by using BANKER'S RECEIPT - RICEVUTA BANCARIA in place of a Bill of Exchange for collection

The procedure of 'banker's receipt' is extensively used in Italy in dealings between suppliers and their clients

The 'banker's receipt' (ricevuta bancaria) **is like** a bill of exchange or draft, drawn by the supplier on his client and remitted to his bank for collection at the due date

Such document, evidencing credit, **is not** a bill of exchange or draft, and does not come under the Law relating to a bill of exchange

'Banker's receipts' cannot be accepted, discounted or protested

'Banker's receipts' issued abroad are not subject to stamp duties in Italy (bills of exchange attract stamp duty)

A 'banker's receipt' must bear the date when payment is due, it constitutes an order for collection of funds to be carried out by a bank

You will be required to detail:

> Invoice No(s), Invoice amount, due date for payment, buyer's name and address, buyer's bankers

A 'banker's receipt' can be issued for single invoices, and a number remitted for collection as a single item

You should obtain your customer's agreement to settlement by 'banker's receipt' (ricevuta bancaria), and obtain your customer's banker's instructions for submission of these collections – This should be done through your own Bank's International Branch

---

'Banker's Receipts' should be remitted for collection of funds through your bank, in the same way as a Bill for Collection

Supplies of printed 'banker's receipt' forms can be obtained either through your own bank's International Branch, or your customer's bank

Do not send the receipt to the buyer, since possession of it could be used to claim that payment had already been made. The collecting bank in Italy (usually the buyer's bank) will not release the receipt to your buyer until they have received payment on your behalf

# 5. OPEN ACCOUNT TRADING

- **Least secure method of payment,** but most common, relying on the buyer to pay you on an agreed basis
- You must set out your payment terms clearly on your invoice to the buyer
- If you allow the buyer a period of credit before payment is due, the terms should be stated on your invoice, and it is suggested you also add: WE THEREFORE EXPECT TO BE PAID ON (you calculate the date and quote it)
- Specify how you wish to be paid, ie
  - By urgent SWIFT TRANSFER, direct from the buyer's bank to your Bank and into your account
- the name, address and Sort Code of your Bank branch, and your Account Name and Number
- You supply the goods or services required
- You invoice the buyer and prepare any other documents that are required to support the entry of goods to the overseas market
- You send the documents direct to the buyer
- The buyer should then pay on the basis of what terms you have agreed with them, and on the agreed date – they should honour your payment instructions – these should be quoted on your invoice
- Allow up to one week for the funds to arrive in your Bank but much depends on the instructions your buyer gives to his Bank – it is essential you give clear and precise instructions for payment to the buyer, so that delays can be minimised
- Monitor the arrival of funds, noting remittance date, which will show if the buyer is taking extra credit days before instructing his Bank to pay
- If there are delays, take them up with your Bank who will clarify the position

**Note:**    The Bank to Bank transfer of funds by SWIFT is a far superior method of payment, it is more secure and far

speedier than being paid by foreign cheque or
foreign draft

The need for correct documentation is just as important as with a
Letter of Credit, because errors of substance not only give the
customer an excuse for delaying payment, but they can also
create problems with his country's import authorities and might
delay the issue of exchange control permission where this is
applicable

---

If OPEN ACCOUNT trading is the norm for your business, you are
advised to consider CREDIT RISK INSURANCE OF YOUR
DEBTORS, so that in the event of a non-payment by a Debtor, you
should be in a position to claim a substantial portion (a pre-
agreed portion) of the unpaid debt from the insurer

(See Section 3)

WHEN TRADING ON OPEN ACCOUNT TERMS, IT IS VITALLY
IMPORTANT THAT ALL INVOICES AND OTHER
DOCUMENTATION SENT TO THE BUYER, **ARE ABSOLUTELY
ACCURATE AND CONTAIN ALL THE CORRECT INFORMATION
RELATING TO THE TRANSACTION**

## 6. AVALISED BILLS OF EXCHANGE

CAN BE USED VERY EFFECTIVELY TO PROVIDE A BUYER WITH
90 DAY OR LONGER PERIODS OF CREDIT

- A BILL OF EXCHANGE, ACCEPTED BY THE BUYER, AND
  AVALISED BY THE BUYER'S BANKER

  - Formalities can be completed either BEFORE SHIPMENT,
    with the agreement of the BUYER and his BANKER, which
    gives security of getting paid, before the goods are
    despatched,

  OR after the goods have been despatched as an Outward Bill
  with documents for collection and avalisation

---

CAN BE USED SINGLY or IN A SERIES OF AVALISED BILLS
DRAWN PAYABLE AT AGREED INTERVALS – SAY 90 or 180 DAYS
– CAN BE USED TO PROVIDE LONGER PERIODS OF CREDIT

(See Section 13.4 FORFAITING)

See Section 13.4 (p. 150) for specimen Avalised Bill of Exchange

---

- An AVALISED Bill of Exchange is a guarantee of payment
  because the avalising bank is a party to the arrangement
- This method can be used for large value transactions
- To obtain security for multiple payments
- To provide your business with finance during a manufacturing
  period
- To provide the buyer with lower interest charges for the period
  of credit he requires
- Can be payable in STERLING or FOREIGN CURRENCY
- Interest costs can be included in the value of the Bill of Exchange

---

You will need guidance on how to draw up the Bill of Exchange, or
a series of Bills of Exchange if more than one payment date is
agreed

Your Bank will be interested in discussing the use of Avalised

Bills of Exchange, and will quote terms for 'FORFAITING' the Bills
(Discounting before the maturity date(s))

(See Section 13.4 FORFAITING)

**DISCUSS THE POSSIBILITIES WITH YOUR BANK'S
INTERNATIONAL DEPARTMENT**

# 7. BARTER TRADE

There are various alternatives under the term 'Barter Trade', including:

– Barter

– Counter-trade

– Counter-purchase

– Off-set trade

BARTER TRADE CAN PROVIDE OPPORTUNITIES FOR GOOD AND PROFITABLE BUSINESS

– The exporter does not become involved in the 'barter' sale, this is handled by a specialist Barter Trade Agent

– Various methods of taking goods in total, or part payment for the goods you supply to a foreign buyer

– There are Agents who specialise in this type of transaction, and they can advise on the procedures and measures to be considered, and should be consulted before any commitments are made

– These Agents can arrange the disposal of 'bartered' goods subject to them being paid an agreed commission on the value

– Commission rates and any discounts are predetermined, and can often be included in the price (either in full or in part) you quote to the buyer

– Barter discussions often commence with full or high value, but every attempt should be made to negotiate the percentage value down – the Agent will advise

---

DO NOT DISMISS BARTER AS A METHOD OF PAYMENT – IT CAN BE PROFITABLE

IT MAY BE THE ONLY WAY TO OBTAIN BUSINESS

---

CONSULT

– The Department of Trade & Industry Regional Office (See Appendix C1)

- The British Exporters Association (See 1.14)
- Obtain copy of BOTB COUNTERTRADE GUIDE FOR
  EXPORTERS from DTI

# 8. OTHER METHODS OF OBTAINING PAYMENT

There are other methods of obtaining payment and these are summarised below:

## CASH ON DELIVERY

- Certain Road Carriers and/or Freight Forwarders offer a CASH ON DELIVERY SERVICE, primarily into European markets
- Ascertain the Charges for this service before use
- Precise instructions as to amount to be collected, and whether charges are to be collected also
- Ensure the Carrier offering this service has an effective and speedy method of providing your business with the funds collected

## BY CREDIT CARD

- For modest amounts, or for Mail Order sales, payment by Credit Card – VISA – MASTERCHARGE – or by Charge Card – AMERICAN EXPRESS – DINERS CLUB – can be an effective method
- For Overseas-issued Credit Cards, check with your Credit Card Company/a UK Credit Card Company, that they can collect the debit charge on an overseas card
- NOT ALL CREDIT CARDS/CHARGE CARDS have international availability
- CHECK WHAT CHARGES WILL BE MADE ON CREDIT/CHARGE CARD TRANSACTIONS, BEFORE ACCEPTING SETTLEMENT BY THIS METHOD

## BY STERLING OR FOREIGN CURRENCY NOTES

- Small value transactions (say less than £100 value), can be settled by currency notes

- *BUT THERE ARE CONSIDERABLE DANGERS IN ACCEPTING OTHER THAN VERY MODEST SUMS IN CURRENCY NOTES*
- *CHECK WITH YOUR BANK BEFORE AGREEING ANY SUCH TRANSACTIONS*

# 9. FACTORS WHICH MAY DELAY PAYMENTS TO YOU

- the Buyer may use YOUR INCORRECT INVOICES or other documents as an excuse to delay payment
- Buyer/Remitter has insufficient funds to make the payment from his account when due
- Remitter gives incorrect or incomplete instructions to his bank
  - Ensure your Customers have your
      Bank name and address and sort code
      Correct title and Account number of your account
- Funds are not sent by SWIFT or Telegraphic Transfer
- Routing of funds through remitter's Bank branch and its International Centre can delay transfer
- Cut-off times
  - In some countries in Europe and elsewhere, a system of Cut-off times is applied
  - this can delay transfer of funds by one business day
  - it means that if instructions for a transfer are not at the Bank processing centre by a given cut-off time, the transaction will be deferred to the next banking day
- Routing of funds through an Intermediary Bank
  - If the Remitter's Bank and your own Bank do not have accounts with each other, a third intermediary bank will be used to effect the transfer
- Value dating
  - The paying bank will require cleared funds onto its account from the remitter's bank, to enable it to credit your account
  - Payment in a currency other than the remitter's or the recipient's currency might cause a value dating delay
- Failure by the Seller to clearly define the period of credit allowed to the Buyer, and the date when payment is expected
- UK Bank delays
  - These should not occur

– If they do, enquire into the causes and ensure they don't
   recur

If a transfer into your account is delayed, the causes can be
ascertained

If a Buyer states funds have been transferred, ask for the
reference number applied to the transfer by his Bank, and the
transaction can be checked by your bank. The actual date of
transfer by the remitter's bank can be determined

YOUR ADVICE FROM THE BANK OF INCOMING FUNDS WILL
HAVE A REFERENCE NUMBER AND THIS INCLUDES THE DATE
YOUR BANK IS GIVEN GOOD VALUE BY THE REMITTING BANK

---

BE WARY OF THE FOLLOWING:

If you receive what purports to be a BANK DRAFT or BANKER'S
PAYMENT direct from abroad, PARTICULARLY IN RESPONSE TO
A RECENT ENQUIRY or REQUEST FOR YOU TO QUOTE ON A PRO
FORMA INVOICE, consult your Bank and/or your Bank's
International Branch and ask them to obtain payment, and advise,
BEFORE YOU SHIP OR SUPPLY ANY GOODS

If there is any doubt, ENSURE YOU RECEIVE **CLEARED** FUNDS
INTO YOUR ACCOUNT BEFORE YOU SHIP OR SUPPLY ANY
GOODS

If a Letter of Credit, or any other document purporting to be a
payment instrument, looks at all questionable CONSULT YOUR
BANK'S INTERNATIONAL BRANCH FOR ADVICE

DO NOT SHIP OR SUPPLY GOODS UNTIL YOU ARE SATISFIED
YOU WILL BE PAID, subject of course to the production of any
specified documentation, complete and correct and meeting all
the stated requirements

DO NOT TAKE SHORT CUTS – You might not receive payment

---

Your own Bank's International Branch will present documents
under a Letter of Credit to the paying Bank on your behalf. They
should control the transaction, making such representations as
appropriate if payment/acceptance is delayed

96

# Summary of Delivery Terms

## ALSO KNOWN AS SHIPPING TERMS

The International Chamber of Commerce issues Standard
Delivery/Shipping terms under the title of **INCOTERMS**

The last issue was INCOTERMS 1990, and a booklet is available
from the ICC, or most local Chambers of Commerce

(See page 321 for ICC address)

---

INCOTERMS are standard terms in use throughout the world
They clearly indicate the basis for delivery of goods

---

**THE FOLLOWING ARE THE CURRENT INCOTERMS**
**EX-WORKS**

**FOB**  Free on Board
**FOA**  Free on Airport
**CFR**  Cost and Freight
**CIF**  Cost, Insurance and Freight
CIP  Carriage and Insurance paid to
FCA  Free Carrier
FAS  Free alongside ship
CPT  Carriage paid to
DAF  Delivered at frontier
DES  Delivered ex ship
DEQ  Delivered ex Quay
**DDU**  Delivered Duty UNPAID
DDP  Delivered Duty PAID

The 'INCOTERMS 1990' booklet is recommended reading

---

Two abbreviations not to be confused with shipping terms are:

FCL  – full container load
LCL  – less than container load (groupage container)

The Incoterms 1990 booklet explains the responsibilities of the exporter and buyer in relation to the shipping/delivery terms and insurance obligations

# Handling Export Enquiries

**Replying to an Enquiry from Abroad**

- Read and understand the enquirer's requirements
- If the enquiry is of interest, acknowledge immediately, or as soon as possible

  **by Telex  or Fax  or Telephone  or Letter**
- If it is in a foreign language, have it translated without delay
- Consider if you can supply, and when
- If you require clarification of the enquirer's requirements seek it urgently, by fax or telephone if possible
- When you reply, thank them for their enquiry
- If a first enquiry, tell them about your company
  - how long established
  - range of products
  - your emphasis on service
  - state order and delivery periods applying
  - state what you can supply to meet their requirements
  - if a definitive requirement, state prices
  - state how you would like to be paid, and if you offer credit terms, what they are
    (If you provide a Pro forma Invoice, these details should be included)
  - supply supporting literature if available
- State the capacity of the person signing your reply, ie. Managing Director/Director/Secretary/ Partner etc

REMEMBER TO REPLY PROMPTLY

- A prompt reply gives a good impression of the efficiency of your business

If you are able to reply and meet their requirements, a letter together with a pro forma invoice should be prepared and sent, by fax if possible

- if you offer specific despatch dates, make sure they are achievable after allowing for the potential buyer to take a little time to respond with an order, ie state: you will despatch within 'X' days of receipt of order (or receipt of funds)
- Assure them of your best attention to Quality, Delivery and Service at all times
- Make them feel that you want their business
- If prices vary with differing quantities, state what they are
- Attach relevant literature and show capacity of the person signing both the letter and pro forma invoice
- Make sure the pro forma invoice accompanies your fax or letter

---

- Keep a diary note for an appropriate period, ie 7/14/21/28 days
- If no response received, consider telephoning your potential customer
- By telephoning you are:
  - demonstrating an interest in doing business
  - in the best position to discuss your quotation, any variations or problems
  - to negotiate if necessary on price, quantity, delivery or technical aspects
  - **and in a position to ask for the order**
- If you are not able to telephone, follow up by telex, or by a faxed message, or by writing to the potential buyer

---

REMEMBER – Deal with every enquiry promptly
- If you cannot reply fully immediately, send an acknowledgement
- All enquiries represent business opportunities
- Don't lose business through lack of attention to detail, inefficiency, or slow response to enquiries

100

- DON'T PROMISE DELIVERIES YOU WILL HAVE
  DIFFICULTY IN FULFILLING
- Don't over-sell your capacity to produce or
  provide
- And it is courtesy to attempt, at least to some
  extent, to communicate with an enquirer in
  his/her own language
  - and there is help available through Chambers
    of Commerce and Language Schools

---

Beware of approaches where there is undue haste, requests for
quantities of samples, bankdrafts sent with a request for urgent
despatch of goods by air etc. Fraudulent approaches do occur

# Credit Control Procedures

If you trade on terms which allow the buyer to pay you later than cash-with-order terms you should establish a procedure for assessing the buyer's ability to pay you

- the procedure should be automatic
- effectively establish the buyer's creditworthiness
- be regularly reviewed and up-dated
- delays in receiving payment after the due date should be monitored – delays are costly and reduce profit margins
- credit limits should be decreased as well as increased to reflect the level of trading, and payment record
- effective credit control procedures should reduce the risk of incurring bad debts

ASK ALL BUYERS FOR THE NAME AND ADDRESS OF THEIR BANKERS
There are several ways in which the creditworthiness of a buyer can be established.
They are:

1. **FINANCIAL REPORT:**

   Ask your Bank to make a STATUS ENQUIRY on the Buyer's Bankers **by telex, or fax** – by mail might take too long for business purposes
   The Bank will need to know:
   - Full name and address of the buyer
   - Name and address of Buyer's Banker
   - What you are enquiring for: amount and duration etc

e.g. Whether trustworthy for business on 'X' days credit, and the amount – see below

OR General business standing and for credit up to 'Y' amount outstanding at any one time

REMEMBER
- If you are likely to trade on regular monthly terms you may start to supply a second or third month's supplies before you receive payment for month 1 supply
- **Enquire for more than the value of a single order,** this gives a better indication of the buyer's creditworthiness
- The Bank will charge for status enquiries, but this should be regarded as a necessary charge for the well-being of your business and money well spent if it helps you to avoid trading with risky buyers
- Diary for a reply
- Consider very carefully release of goods before enquiries completed – do not be rushed – seek more secure payment terms – see Section 5
- Your bank relies on the overseas bank to reply
- If you have any doubt about the terms of the reply you receive, discuss with your bank's International Department

---

## 2. CREDIT RISK INSURANCE COVER APPROVAL

**Financial report:**

Export Credit Risk Insurance provides
- a credit limit on approved buyers which allows you to trade on agreed terms
- insurance against risk of non-payment
- in the event of delayed or non-payment by a buyer, recovery support aimed at securing payment
- effective credit control management through the credit limit procedures

---

There are a number of Credit Risk Insurers – see Section 3 CREDIT RISK INSURANCE and Appendix C4 for addresses

## 3.  COMPANY REPORTING AGENCIES

There are several agencies who will provide information
either from their records, or make enquiries on overseas
buyers on your behalf

A report may include:
- details of ownership where known
- last filed balance sheet information
- credit/payment record
- description of business activities
- record of any debentures issued, or charges over assets
  recorded
- details of the principals' other recorded business interests

Agencies will charge for such reports, and charges vary
according to the country of the buyer

Agencies include (See Appendix C5.4 for addresses):

>CCN Systems Ltd.
>
>Dun & Bradstreet Ltd.
>
>Infocheck Ltd.

---

## 4.  BRITISH OVERSEAS COMMERCIAL POSTS

These can provide written reports on businesses in their
respective localities, to include the following points:
- Trading interests and scope of activities
- Capabilities and territory covered
- Other suppliers' represented
- Warehousing and distribution facilities
- Sales force, technical know-how and After-sales support

THESE REPORTS CAN PROVIDE INVALUABLE INFORMATION
ON BUYERS (there is a fee scale for this service)

---

## 5.  OPEN ACCOUNT TRADING – STANDBY LETTERS OF CREDIT

Issued by a customer's bank, these can provide security for Open
Account trading (see Section 15 for use of Standby L/Cs)

105

# Customer Information File

Know your customer

Know who your contacts are

Keep in regular contact by visiting, by telephoning, by fax or by telex

For all new customers obtain the information necessary to complete a Customer Information pro forma

Ensure that all orders are dealt with speedily

If there are any doubts contact your customer without delay by telephone, by fax, or by telex

Keep status reports up to date

Ensure that all personnel within your business, particularly those in sales and sales administration, order taking, controlling customer accounts and payment terms, know of your credit control procedures and what credit limits are approved for each buyer

Effective control of debtors will include regular monitoring of amounts outstanding, and information from payment record and/or Debtor-Age analysis should be used when assessing credit limits

---

IF YOUR TRADING EXPERIENCE WITH A PARTICULAR BUYER IS LESS THAN SATISFACTORY, WITH DELAYS IN RECEIVING PAYMENT, OR IF STATUS REPORTS CHANGE IN TONE, YOU SHOULD CONSIDER SEEKING MORE SECURE TRADING TERMS, – see Section 5 – or, use of a Standby Letter of Credit – see Section 15

Keep your Customer Information File up to date

## CUSTOMER INFORMATION FILE – Suggested format

### CUSTOMER INFORMATION FILE

Name .................................................... VAT No. ....................

Address ..............................................................................

..........................................................................................

Telex .............................. Fax .............................. Telephone ..............................

Name of Bankers ..................................................................

Address ..............................................................................

Account No. ........................................................................

**Contact names**

**Status information sought/obtained:**

| Date | From | | Amount/Term | Reply |
|------|------|--|-------------|-------|
|      |      |  |             |       |
|      |      |  |             |       |
|      |      |  |             |       |

*NCM/TI Credit limit applied for: ...................................................

Amount approved ..........................................................Date

*NCM/TI Discretionary limit for .........................................................

* OR OTHER CREDIT RISK INSURER

Sterling invoicing ..................... OR CURRENCY .....................

**Trading terms established** CIF/CFR/FOB/DDU/DDP/Ex-works/ .....................

**Payment terms agreed**

| | |
|---|---|
| Cash with order ..................... | SIGHT or Term |
| Irrev. Letter of Credit ..................... | ......... days from date of |
| Confirmed I/L of C ..................... | Bill of Lading/Invoice/ |
| Bill of Exchange & Docs ..................... | end of month/fixed date |
| Avalised B of E ..................... | |
| Open Account ..................... | |

Standby Letter of Credit – amount .....................

Issued by ..................... Valid until .....................

| | | | | | | |
|---|---|---|---|---|---|---|
| Date terms last reviewed | | | | | | |
| Any Variance to be reported to: | | | | | | |

Customer Information record should be maintained and amended as required

There is danger in having no up-to-date customer record

# The Cost of Giving Credit

If you don't get paid when the goods are ready for despatch, or when a service has been provided, then it costs your business money, and to many businesses this is an unknown and hidden cost

It is normal practice in business to ask a supplier for a period of credit, and you the supplier will have to decide what period you are prepared to allow the buyer

Credit periods range from a few days to longer periods, i.e. 30/60/90/120/150/180, and for some markets overseas, periods of 360 days are not uncommon

For projects involving major capital expenditure, credit periods often range over several years, but usually there are finance packages arranged as project loans which enable the suppliers to the particular project to be paid within a short period – see Section 13 on Export Finance availability

The Cost of Giving Credit can be ascertained by considering the following points:

1. **Interest cost** – For each period of 30 days credit calculate 1/12th of the interest rate you are being charged by the Bank if you are overdrawn on your business account

   **OR** If your account is normally in credit, you should calculate 1/12th of the Deposit Interest rate you could earn by having the outstanding funds placed on a deposit account for each period of 30 days

   (In practice it is simpler to use the overdraft interest rate to calculate the cost of each period of credit)

   thus for a 180 day period of credit, the calculation would be 6/12ths of the annual rate of interest charged

111

2. **Add** the likely cost of monitoring the outstanding debt
   - time
   - additional correspondence, telephone, telex etc
   - Possible cost of reviewing future business activity if periods longer than the agreed credit period are taken
3. There may be a delay in actually receiving funds after the end of the agreed credit period
   - delay could be due to
      buyer's shortage of funds
      method of transferring funds to you
      shortage of foreign exchange in the buyer's country
   - the delay could be from 3 days upwards
   - ensure you give the buyer your
      Bank name and address, sort code number,
      Account name and Account number
   - you should ask for payment by URGENT SWIFT or by Tele-graphic
      Transfer, or Tested Telex
4. There is a cost if discounts for payment within a given period are offered, and are still taken when payment is received outside the agreed terms
   - To make discounts effective, ensure they are related to the date when funds are received into your account
5. There may be a cost to adjusting a forward contract to allow for later delivery of currency

---

It is advisable to assess the Cost of Giving Credit and try to build this cost, or part of it, into your prices

If extended credit terms are demanded, be mindful of the monthly additional cost, and try to recover all or part from the buyer

- Remember, if the buyer has to pay you on short credit terms, he may have to resort to overdrawing his account, and in some countries this can be far more costly than agreeing to pay you interest for an extended credit period
- So he might welcome the offer of longer credit and pay the interest

DELAYS IN RECEIVING PAYMENT COST YOUR BUSINESS
MONEY, AND YOUR MARGINS FOR PROFIT WILL BE ERODED

---

KNOW THE COST OF GIVING CREDIT

# Invoicing in Foreign Currency

Invoicing your overseas customers in their own currency, or another currency convenient for them, has a number of advantages

MAKE IT EASIER FOR THE BUYER TO BUY FROM YOU
- Use as an effective marketing tool
- Take the currency risk from trading in sterling away from your buyer
- The buyer can see exactly what the cost is
- You can improve your margins by invoicing in currency
- It can be easier to compete against other suppliers
- You will have a Foreign Exchange Risk, but THIS CAN BE MANAGED EFFECTIVELY

IF YOU BORROW FROM THE BANK TO RUN YOUR BUSINESS
- You can borrow an amount of currency to match the funds to be received from the buyer/buyers
- This can reduce your sterling borrowing
- The interest cost of borrowing currency against receivables can be less than sterling interest cost
- Borrowing in currency effectively eliminates the exchange risk for you. See Section 12.2

EVEN IF YOU DON'T BORROW FROM THE BANK TO RUN YOUR BUSINESS
- You can obtain advantage from the interest rate differential (where interest rates for the currency are below sterling interest rate)

- This will improve your margins
- You can eliminate the exposure risk to Exchange Rate movements by arranging a Forward Exchange Rate Contract, or through use of Currency Option Contracts, through your Bank – see Section 12

---

A further suggestion:

The buyer might also be an exporter of goods and/or services, and he might receive a currency other than his own or sterling

It might help the buyer to buy from you, if you were to quote in the 'third' currency – ie the one he receives

You still have a currency risk as with the buyer's own currency which can be eliminated – see Section 12

---

**Calculating your Currency price**

1. **For individual transactions**
   - you will know your Sterling price, and for selling overseas you should ensure any additional costs are taken into account to arrive at a total sterling price
   - you now have various alternatives for determining the appropriate currency exchange rate to use, for example:
     
     i.   you can ask the bank to quote the current 'spot' exchange rate for 'Bank Buys' the appropriate currency
     
     ii.  you can obtain a rate by looking at the *Financial Times* 'Currencies' page, taking the higher figure from the 'Day's Mid High' column – p. 119
     
     iii. you can arrange to eliminate your exchange risk by arranging a Forward Exchange Rate Contract with the Bank, and use the rate quoted – see Section 12.1
     
     iv.  **you should always try to use a rate HIGHER than the current Spot rate**
     
     v.   you could speculate, but this is not advisable
   - multiply your sterling price by the currency rate to give the invoice value in currency

---

116

SEE SECTION 12 for Elimination of Foreign Exchange Risk

---

If you are merely quoting a currency price, use a higher rate than the spot or forward rates, state clearly that the price holds valid to a set date (although this may not prevent orders being placed on the price at a later date

---

NOTE  –  If you have used a rate HIGHER than the Spot rate of exchange, then you will have an additional margin, which can, if you have to improve your competitiveness, be used to give discounts as necessary

---

If you are in a very price competitive position, you can use the Forward Exchange Rate from the Bank as your conversion rate to give you the keenest price possible without incurring loss

---

**Calculating your Currency price**
2. **For multiple sales or price lists**
   – you will know your Sterling price, and for selling overseas you should ensure any additional costs are taken into account to arrive at a total sterling price
   – as sales are likely to be spread over a period of time, you should pitch your currency conversion rate ABOVE the current SPOT rate, as high as possible without becoming uncompetitive
     eg  DM 2.25 spot – use 2.30, or 2.35, or 2.40 (or whichever rate will still allow you to remain competitive)
       (the same principle applies for other currencies)
   – with multiple currency amounts to be received, you should consider the various alternatives for eliminating exchange risk – see Section 12
     These are:
     – Forward Exchange Rate Contracts (Bank buys currency) – see Section 12.1
     – Currency borrowing alternative – see Section 12.2

- Combination of both Forward Exchange Rate Contracts and Currency borrowing (Section 12.2–12.3)
- Use of Currency 'full' Options – see Section 12.3
- Use of a Currency Account where either there are payments to be made in a matching currency, or for collation of smaller currency amounts prior to placing under Forward Exchange Rate Contracts – see Section 12.5
- to remain without exchange risk protection will render your business open to adverse movements in the currency exchange rates
  - CAN YOU AFFORD TO RUN THE RISK?
- it is advisable to protect profit margins against adverse movements in the exchange rate
- it is true that additional profits can accrue from beneficial movement in the exchange rate
- NO-ONE CAN PREDICT EXCHANGE RATE MOVEMENTS WITH ANY DEGREE OF ACCURACY

---

**Monitoring Exchange Rate movements** – using the *Financial Times* Currency Page information to assist in converting your sterling prices into a currency to suit a particular buyer

- An example of the most useful section is shown on page 119

REMEMBER!  –  The Currency tables in the *Financial Times* and other newspapers are *'yesterday's rates'* – they record the movements which took place in the previous business day

---

**POUND SPOT** FORWARD AGAINST THE POUND

| | | Closing mid-point | Change on day | Bid/offer spread | Day's Mid high | low | One month Rate | %PA | Three months Rate | %PA | One year Rate | %PA | Bank of Eng. Index |
|---|---|---|---|---|---|---|---|---|---|---|---|---|---|
| **Europe** | | | | | | | | | | | | | |
| Austria | (Sch) | 17.1350 | +0.0763 | 267 - 433 | 17.1433 | 17.0527 | 17.1307 | 0.3 | 17.1188 | 0.4 | - | - | 115.4 |
| Belgium | (BFr) | 49.9918 | +0.0985 | 713 - 122 | 50.0810 | 49.8520 | 49.9618 | 0.7 | 49.9068 | 0.7 | 49.5468 | 0.9 | 117.3 |
| Denmark | (DKr) | 9.5153 | +0.0159 | 105 - 201 | 9.5319 | 9.4941 | 9.5106 | 0.6 | 9.5293 | -0.6 | 9.5587 | -0.5 | 117.4 |
| Finland | (FM) | 7.4893 | +0.0148 | 798 - 988 | 7.5090 | 7.4450 | - | - | - | - | - | - | 88.4 |
| France | (FFr) | 8.3381 | +0.0244 | 348 - 413 | 8.3508 | 8.3066 | 8.3385 | -0.1 | 8.333 | 0.2 | 8.2837 | 0.7 | 110.5 |
| Germany | (DM) | 2.4296 | +0.0061 | 284 - 307 | 2.4377 | 2.4223 | 2.4284 | 0.6 | 2.4252 | 0.7 | 2.3957 | 1.4 | 126.8 |
| Greece | (Dr) | .372.810 | +0.977 | 556 - 064 | 373.572 | 371.761 | - | - | - | - | - | - | - |
| Ireland | (I£) | 1.0122 | +0.0005 | 114 - 129 | 1.0145 | 1.0112 | 1.012 | 0.2 | 1.0116 | 0.2 | 1.0135 | -0.1 | 105.4 |
| Italy | (L) | 2480.81 | +8.04 | 939 - 223 | 2485.17 | 2472.58 | 2486.91 | -3.0 | 2498.71 | -2.9 | 2553.11 | -2.9 | 74.9 |
| Luxembourg | (LFr) | 49.9918 | +0.5985 | 713 - 122 | 50.0810 | 49.8520 | 49.9618 | 0.7 | 49.9068 | 0.7 | 49.5468 | 0.9 | 117.3 |
| Netherlands | (Fl) | 2.7223 | +0.0066 | 212 - 233 | 2.7283 | 2.7150 | 2.7209 | 0.6 | 2.7175 | 0.7 | 2.6868 | 1.3 | 121.3 |
| Norway | (NKr) | 10.5796 | +0.0241 | 753 - 839 | 10.6037 | 10.5034 | 10.5791 | 0.1 | 10.5824 | -0.1 | 10.5832 | 0.0 | 86.7 |
| Portugal | (Es) | 248.891 | +0.733 | 748 - 033 | 249.285 | 248.002 | 250.621 | -8.3 | 253.801 | -7.9 | - | - | - |
| Spain | (Pta) | 202.480 | +1.023 | 365 - 594 | 202.624 | 201.464 | 202.82 | -2.0 | 207.715 | -10.3 | 206.37 | -1.9 | 86.6 |
| Sweden | (SKr) | 11.6574 | +0.0209 | 484 - 663 | 11.7078 | 11.5830 | 11.6784 | -2.2 | 11.7254 | -2.3 | 11.9134 | -2.2 | 75.9 |
| Switzerland | (SFr) | 2.0138 | +0.0002 | 125 - 151 | 2.0209 | 2.0103 | 2.0108 | 1.8 | 2.0046 | 1.8 | 1.9675 | 2.3 | 123.2 |
| UK | (£) | - | - | - | - | - | - | - | - | - | - | - | 80.2 |
| Ecu | - | 1.2757 | +0.003 | 748 - 765 | 1.2786 | 1.2716 | 1.2756 | 0.0 | 1.2754 | 0.1 | 1.2716 | 0.3 | - |
| SDR† | - | 0.920496 | | | | | | | | | | | |
| **Americas** | | | | | | | | | | | | | |
| Argentina | (Peso) | 1.6186 | +0.0034 | 181 - 190 | 1.6212 | 1.6125 | - | - | - | - | - | - | - |
| Brazil | (Rl) | 1.3809 | +0.0142 | 789 - 828 | 1.3828 | 1.3658 | - | - | - | - | - | - | - |
| Canada | (C$) | 2.1903 | +0.0011 | 889 - 916 | 2.1962 | 2.1823 | 2.1894 | 0.5 | 2.1884 | 0.3 | 2.1871 | 0.1 | 86.6 |
| Mexico | (New Peso) | 5.5387 | +0.014 | 333 - 441 | 5.5444 | 5.5212 | - | - | - | - | - | - | - |
| USA | ($) | 1.6188 | +0.0034 | 184 - 192 | 1.6214 | 1.6125 | 1.618 | 0.6 | 1.6172 | 0.4 | 1.6062 | 0.8 | 61.0 |
| **Pacific/Middle East/Africa** | | | | | | | | | | | | | |
| Australia | (A$) | 2.2011 | +0.01 | 998 - 024 | 2.2051 | 2.1872 | 2.2011 | 0.0 | 2.2024 | -0.2 | 2.2205 | -0.9 | - |
| Hong Kong | (HK$) | 12.5086 | +0.0259 | 051 - 120 | 12.5281 | 12.4611 | 12.5047 | 0.4 | 12.5036 | 0.2 | 12.5107 | 0.0 | - |
| India | (Rs) | 50.7798 | +0.1067 | 611 - 984 | 50.7984 | 50.7610 | - | - | - | - | - | - | - |
| Japan | (Y) | 157.267 | -0.534 | 179 - 354 | 157.940 | 156.840 | 156.837 | 3.3 | 155.882 | 3.5 | 150.947 | 4.0 | 189.5 |
| Malaysia | (M$) | 4.1244 | -0.0041 | 226 - 262 | 4.1326 | 4.1187 | - | - | - | - | - | - | - |
| New Zealand | (NZ$) | 2.6458 | +0.0043 | 436 - 479 | 2.6517 | 2.6364 | 2.6497 | -1.8 | 2.6575 | -1.8 | 2.6798 | -1.3 | - |
| Philippines | (Peso) | 41.1176 | +0.3287 | 837 - 515 | 41.4515 | 40.7837 | - | - | - | - | - | - | - |
| Saudi Arabia | (SR) | 6.0720 | +0.0127 | 701 - 739 | 6.0815 | 6.0488 | - | - | - | - | - | - | - |
| Singapore | (S$) | 2.3783 | +0.0012 | 769 - 797 | 2.3807 | 2.3744 | - | - | - | - | - | - | - |
| S Africa (Com.) | (R) | 5.6970 | -0.003 | 943 - 996 | 5.7078 | 5.6698 | - | - | - | - | - | - | - |
| S Africa (Fin.) | (R) | 6.4105 | -0.0431 | 927 - 282 | 6.5140 | 6.3927 | - | - | - | - | - | - | - |
| South Korea | (Won) | 1294.64 | +4.67 | 423 - 504 | 1296.63 | 1287.90 | - | - | - | - | - | - | - |
| Taiwan | (T$) | 42.2677 | +0.0638 | 524 - 830 | 42.3307 | 42.1185 | - | - | - | - | - | - | - |
| Thailand | (Bt) | 40.3405 | +0.0766 | 224 - 586 | 40.3970 | 40.2000 | - | - | - | - | - | - | - |

†SDR rates for Oct 18. Bid/offer spreads in the Pound Spot table show only the last three decimal places. Forward rates are not directly quoted to the market but are implied by current interest rates. Sterling index calculated by the Bank of England. Base average 1985 = 100.Bid, Offer and Mid-rates in both this and the Dollar Spot tables derived from THE WM/REUTERS CLOSING SPOT RATES. Some values are rounded by the F.T.

The above table is reproduced with kind permission of The Financial Times Ltd.

**Note:**

**Closing mid-point** – The Closing Rate for each currency on the London Foreign Exchange market

**Change on day** – The movement measured against the previous day close

**Bid/offer spread** – The 'points' spread between the forex dealer **bid** (buy) and **offer** (sell) prices

**Day's mid** – **The highest mid point and the lowest mid point** which have been recorded during the day

FOR CURRENCY INVOICING, USE A RATE HIGHER THAN THE **Day's Mid HIGH** – see earlier points in this Section

119

Actual rates quoted by Bank Foreign Exchange dealers as SPOT
or FORWARD rates reflect the 'then' current position at the time
they give the rate

---

The columns headed **'ONE MONTH'**, **'THREE MONTHS'** and **'ONE
YEAR'** show the **FORWARD RATE** applicable for those periods, as
recorded in the London Forex market '*yesterday*' – the actual
Forward Rate will be determined by the Foreign Exchange dealer
when he is asked to quote

THESE COLUMNS **ARE NOT** AN INDICATION OF WHERE 'THE
MARKET' THINKS THE RATE FOR A PARTICULAR CURRENCY
WILL BE IN ONE MONTH'S TIME, IN THREE MONTHS', OR IN A
YEAR'S TIME

---

The Forward Rates are calculated from the Spot rate, using the
INTEREST DIFFERENTIAL BETWEEN STERLING AND THE
OTHER INDIVIDUAL CURRENCIES SHOWN

If interest rates for a particular currency are lower than Sterling
interest rates, then the differential is reflected in a 'Premium',
which is deducted from the prevailing Spot rate, to give the
Forward rate

If interest rates for a particular currency are higher than Sterling
interest rates, then the differential is reflected in a 'Discount',
which is added to the prevailing Spot rate, to give the Forward rate

THE FORWARD RATE WILL BE APPLIED TO A GIVEN
TRANSACTION ON EITHER A FIXED FUTURE DATE, OR
BETWEEN TWO QUOTED DATES

---

Remember, the rates shown in the *Financial Times*, or other
printed rate tables, are 'historical' rates, ie they record what the
rates were in the immediate past

---

**THE ECU – European Currency Unit**

The European Commission formed the European Monetary
System (EMS) and from this emerged the EUROPEAN CURRENCY
UNIT

It is a 'basket' of currencies and each ECU has within it a requisite proportion of the participating currencies, roughly in line with relative Gross National Products (GNPs) of the countries whose currencies make up the ECU

It is an attempt to create a currency within Europe which is less volatile than individual currencies

IT IS A FULLY FLEDGED INTERNATIONAL CURRENCY

THERE IS A SPOT AND FORWARD FOREIGN EXCHANGE MARKET IN THE ECU

See the **POUND SPOT** table for Spot and Forward rates for the ECU on page 119

IT CAN BE BORROWED AS WELL AS DEPOSITED OUT TO FIVE YEARS

IT IS WIDELY USED IN THE BOND MARKET

You can quote and sell in ECUs

You should consult your Bank's International Branch for advice on current exchange rates for the ECU

# Eliminating/Managing Foreign Exchange Risk

## SECTIONAL INDEX

# 1. BANK BUYS CURRENCY RECEIVABLES

Invoicing in a foreign currency can make your products more attractive to an overseas buyer than they would be if you simply offered them a sterling price. Make the buying decision easier for your customer: give him a price in his own currency

There will be a risk, of course. Any movement in exchange rates against sterling could cost you money. Therefore there are well-established mechanisms for eliminating the risk from your transaction. The following checklist will assist you to identify your risk and the risk timescale. It will also advise you about approaching your bank to make arrangements to eliminate the risk of exchange movements

---

### 1. RECEIPT OF CURRENCY EXPORT EARNINGS

WHY YOU WILL NEED THE ADVICE GIVEN HERE

**FROM**   the moment you take an order and agree to be paid in foreign currency you have a currency risk

**YOU**   can eliminate the risk by arranging a BANK BUYS FORWARD CONTRACT

HOW TO CALCULATE YOUR RISK PERIOD

1. Date order taken ............................

2. Manufacturing period ....................days

3. Delivery period ....................days

4. Credit period ....................days

5. Date when buyer expected to pay ............................

6. Transmission time for funds
   ie telegraphic transfer/urgent, swift
   (up to 7 days), standard transfer
   (up to 21 days) ....................days

7. Expected arrival of currency proceeds
   Earliest date ............................

   Say one month period to ............................

It is advisable to allow a period between two dates for the actual receipt of currency

---

## ACTION TO TAKE

IF you wish to eliminate your currency risk, telephone the bank and ask them to arrange a BANK BUYS FORWARD CONTRACT (amount of currency)

.................................

(which currency)

.................................

Delivery period from

.................................

to

.................................

---

## WHAT HAPPENS NEXT

A RATE is quoted by the bank
Rate quoted

.................................

Ref. no.

.................................

**NOTE** that once the rate is agreed, this is a firm contractual commitment

---

## FOLLOW-UP

CONFIRMATION of the deal will be sent by the bank to you within a few days
- **YOU** must check the details carefully
- **THE BANK** will require your confirmation on the copy dealing form which they will supply

**Note:**      You sell the foreign currency, THE BANK BUYS IT

There is an alternative to a Bank Buys forward contract – see 12.2

## CURRENCY RECEIVABLES DELAYED

If currency receipts are delayed beyond the final date of a Bank Buys Forward Contract, there are two main courses of action. They are:

1. Arrange with your Bank to 'Extend' or 'Roll-over' the Forward Contract to a later date, by which time you expect the currency to have arrived

   – at the date of extension or roll-over, dependent on what the 'spot' rate of exchange is compared to the original forward contract rate, there will be either a credit or a debit to your account

$\emptyset$ – **if sterling has strengthened** your account will be credited (the bank effectively sells you the requisite amount of currency at the current spot rate of exchange, to fulfil the original forward contract – if the spot rate is 'higher' than the forward contract rate, the 'cost' of buying the currency (Bank Sells Currency) is less than the sterling amount you will receive from the forward contract – your account will be credited with the net amount)

\* – **if sterling has weakened** your account will be debited (the rate at which the bank 'sells' you the currency to fulfil the forward contract will be lower than the forward contract rate, therefore the cost will be higher to buy the currency than you will receive from the forward contract – your account will be debited with the net amount)

   – the 'extension' or 'roll-over' is effectively a new Bank Buys Forward Contract based on the current 'spot' rate

   – if your account has been net credited as above $\emptyset$, add the sterling value of the 'new' forward contract to the amount net credited, to arrive at the full sterling value of the original currency receivables

   – if your account was net debited as above \*, deduct the net debit amount off the 'new' forward contract sterling value to arrive at the sterling value of the original currency receivables

   – any difference in sterling value from a 'roll-over' should be relatively marginal

2. An alternative is to arrange with your Bank to borrow the requisite amount of currency required to fulfil the original forward contract, and then when the currency proceeds arrive later, they repay the borrowing. The sterling proceeds from the forward contract are placed to your normal current account. If you are overdrawn in sterling, you effectively replace sterling borrowing with currency borrowing to the value of the currency you will be receiving

---

THIS CAN BE AN EFFECTIVE WAY OF OVERCOMING THE DELAY IN RECEIPT OF CURRENCY RECEIVABLES, PARTICULARLY IF THE DELAY IS LIKELY TO BE RELATIVELY SHORT

---

Discuss matters with your Bank branch or the Bank's International Office

# 2. CURRENCY BORROWING

WHAT YOU CAN DO INSTEAD OF A BANK BUYS FORWARD
CONTRACT

**IF**      you have a sterling overdraft position it is viable for you
to eliminate the exchange risk by **borrowing an amount
of currency equal to your expected currency export
earnings**

**THE**    currency borrowing alternative gives greater
flexibility, which is particularly useful where you cannot
forecast within, say, a month, when currency proceeds
will be arriving

**WHERE**  there are multiple receipts in the same currency, a
currency overdraft in that matching currency can be
used very effectively. It reduces the administration
which would be necessary in applying the currency
receivables if Forward Contracts were used, reduces
paperwork to and from the Bank, may well reduce the
number of telephone calls to and from the Bank. A
currency overdraft can therefore be a very effective
alternative to the use of Forward Contracts. Costs in
handling currency receivables can therefore be
reduced

---

ACTION

**YOU**    will have to agree with your bank a currency borrowing
facility as part of your total finance package or as an
alternative to sterling borrowing

PROCEDURE

1. The currency equal to your expected currency receivables is
borrowed on a currency overdraft account
2. The borrowed currency is bought from you at the spot rate of
exchange by the bank and you receive the equivalent value in
sterling

3. You use this sterling to repay part or all your overdraft in sterling
4. When your currency export earnings are received they are used to repay the currency borrowing and interest

---

THE BANK WILL NEED TO KNOW

Which currency　　　　　............................

Amount　　　　　　　　............................

Period required　　　　　............................

Source of repayment ............................

It is useful to record expected currency earnings as a way of monitoring receipts

---

A Currency Overdraft used to manage receivables can provide a prime Audit Trail of all transactions in each currency for which it is used

---

As an alternative to a Bank Buys Forward Contract, and Currency Borrowing, there are **Currency Options** –

# 3. CURRENCY OPTIONS

('over the counter options' offered by Banks, rather than 'traded currency options')

An Alternative to Bank Buys Forward Contract, and Currency Borrowing

A CURRENCY OPTION CONTRACT is a further alternative

---

The BANK will quote a rate at which it will agree to BUY Foreign Currency receivables,

– but will also allow the owner of those receivables (the Exporter) the option to ignore the rate agreed for purchase

if the movement in the Foreign Exchange market rates is beneficial to the exporter

This represents a One-Way Risk for the Bank

– the Bank has to perform at the agreed rate if required to do so by the exporter when receivables arrive

– the exporter need not deliver the receivables to the Bank if either he does not receive the funds, or if he prefers to exchange the receivables at a market SPOT rate which will ensure he receives a greater amount of Sterling in exchange

THE BANK WILL REQUIRE THE EXPORTER TO PAY A PREMIUM, calculated to reflect the Risk to the Bank, with the Premium being paid to secure the rate agreement/contract (up-front)

---

A CURRENCY OPTION CONTRACT gives the Exporter the chance to improve his sterling return from the currency receivables

---

The London Foreign Exchange market trades in two types of Currency Option contract expressed as:

– AMERICAN STYLE OPTION   – Exercisable at any date up to a stated Expiry Date

– EUROPEAN STYLE OPTION   – Exercisable on an agreed fixed date

130

**The Bank will require to know:**

The AMOUNT of a SPECIFIC CURRENCY it will be required to BUY

The FINAL DATE (American Option) or the FIXED DATE (European Option)

**The Bank will quote** the rate it will offer:

AND THE PREMIUM IT WILL REQUIRE TO WRITE THE CONTRACT, usually expressed as a percentage of the value

Written Confirmation of the Contract will follow when the Bank has received the Premium required

---

The effective rate for a CURRENCY OPTION CONTRACT can be calculated as follows:

1. **Divide** Currency amount by the agreed rate = sterling value (X)
2. **Deduct** the sterling value of the Up-Front Premium paid to the Bank to secure the Currency Option Contract from the Sterling Value (X)

   This will give the Net Sterling Value of the Currency amount
3. **Divide** the Currency amount by the Net Sterling Value to give the **Effective Rate** for the transaction (this will be a higher rate than the agreed contract rate)

---

To calculate the exchange rate level to which the currency/ sterling rate would need to move effectively to recover the amount of the premium in full, as follows:

4. **Add** the sterling value of the Up-Front Premium to the sterling value (X). See above
5. **Divide** the Currency amount by the total sterling amount (4) to give the exchange rate at which point the sterling value of the currency at the agreed rate, AND the sterling value of the Up-Front Premium would be recovered in full

If the exchange rate for Spot transactions at the point when the currency actually arrives is below the agreed rate under the Currency Option Contract, then the Spot rate should be used, and a proportion of the Up-Front Premium will have been recovered

There are a number of other currency hedging 'products' available from some banks, including the following:

CYLINDER OPTIONS – Two currency option contracts, one written by a Bank for its customer, the other in reverse, written by the customer for the Bank (This is a product confined to larger organisations)

---

## AVERAGE RATE OPTIONS

These can be useful where there are more than two currency receivable amounts due at monthly or other intervals

An Average Rate Option Contract provides for the Bank to make reimbursement if the agreed AVERAGE RATE has not been achieved as a MINIMUM RATE

---

- You are required to specify:
  - the currency
  - the total amount to be received
  - the approximate value of each receivable amount
  - the number of transactions
  - the first date (approx) and subsequent anticipated dates of the amounts to be received
- The Bank will quote the AVERAGE RATE it will offer, and the PREMIUM it will charge to secure the Averge Rate
- The PREMIUM is payable up-front to secure the Average Rate Option Contract

---

- As currency amounts arrive they are converted to sterling at the prevailing SPOT RATE
- When the final transaction has been completed, you should total the currency amounts received, also total the sterling value received
- Divide the sterling total into the currency total, to determine the AVERAGE RATE achieved

- IF THE AVERAGE RATE ACHIEVED IS WORSE THAN THE AGREED (Ave. Rate Option) RATE, APPROACH THE BANK, THEY WILL CHECK YOUR FIGURES, AND THEN THE BANK WILL REIMBURSE THE DIFFERENCE
- IF THE AVERAGE RATE ACHIEVED IS BETTER THAN THE AGREED RATE, YOU KEEP THE STERLING VALUE ADVANTAGE

---

Average Rate Options therefore give protection against adverse exchange rate movements, whilst also providing the opportunity to benefit from advantageous movements in exchange rates

---

Note:    There are other types of currency contract for use to eliminate exchange rate risk, and as these can vary between individual Banks, you should ask your Bank/a Bank what they have available

# 4. CURRENCY SWOP ARRANGEMENTS

There are occasions when currency receivables will arrive early If there is a Bank Buys Forward Contract with first usage date some while after the actual arrival of currency, the following alternatives are available:

- the currency receivables can be placed on an interest-earning currency deposit account
- the forward contract can be utilised early with the possibility of a penalty charged by the bank to compensate the bank for accepting delivery of the currency earlier than agreed

HOWEVER, if you have a sterling overdraft, and the interest rate charged is higher than the appropriate currency deposit rate, you should ask your Bank's International Branch to quote a rate for a CURRENCY SWOP arrangement

that is:

- the bank will BUY the currency from you at the SPOT rate of exchange and place the equivalent sterling amount into your overdrawn current account
- using the same SPOT rate of exchange, the Bank will agree to sell you the same amount of currency at an agreed future date (the earliest date of the forward contract) to enable you to deliver the requisite amount of currency under the forward contract to fulfil that contract. The SPOT rate will be adjusted to compensate for the interest differential (between sterling and the appropriate currency interest rates) and this second half of the SWOP deal will in effect be a forward contract (bank sells currency)
- whilst the SWOP is in place, you get the use of the sterling to reduce your overdraft, and reduce the amount of interest you pay, and when you are required to fulfil the original forward contract, you receive currency from the end of the SWOP arrangement, deliver, and receive the appropriate amount of sterling
- on the final date of the SWOP, your sterling account is debited with the cost of the requisite currency, and credited with the proceeds of the original forward contract

It can be an interest-cost effective arrangement, particularly where there are five-figure or larger sums involved

Discuss such arrangements with your Bank's International Branch

---

LATE ARRIVAL OF CURRENCY RECEIVABLES – If there are changes to the arrival of currencies, which are covered by Forward Exchange Contracts, discuss extending the contract, or borrowing currency to fulfil the contract, with your bank's International Branch

---

# 5. CURRENCY ACCOUNTS

There are a number of other mechanisms/techniques for
'hedging' risks resulting from trading in foreign currencies

---

Accounts denominated in a specific foreign currency can be
opened with UK Banks

They are useful for the collection of foreign currency receivables
in multiple amounts, and can be used effectively for the collection
of currency prior to exchange under Forward Contracts or
Currency Options

They can be run effectively in an Overdrawn form to provide
elimination of currency exchange rate risk on receivables – see
Section 12.2

They can be used effectively to match and provide currency
amounts for payments from a business

Bank statements are produced in the normal way at intervals to
suit the Exporter's requirements for accounting purposes and
they provide an Audit Trail of transactions

Cheque books are available on currency accounts

---

## CURRENCY ACCOUNTS WITH BANKS ABROAD

Can be useful for the collection of funds from a number of buyers
in the same country

Reduce charges for multiple transfers of funds to UK

Regular transfers to UK bank account on an agreed periodicity
basis

Particularly useful where the overseas Bank used is a branch of
your own UK Bank

Always check the charges tariff for use of such accounts including
transfers **before** opening the account to ensure these are
acceptable (in some countries banks have no maximum charge
for transactions, and the charges on large amounts can be quite
high and out of proportion to the work involved)

Discuss your requirements for a currency account overseas with your Bank as it can make the necessary introduction

---

**FINANCIAL FUTURES** – Exchange Rate and Interest Rate Contracts

These are sophisticated instruments and are not normally available to all but the largest of currency users

You should discuss these techniques/products with your Bank's specialist departments

# 6. PAYMENTS TO BE MADE IN A FOREIGN CURRENCY

BACKGROUND

**IF**      you are making payments in a foreign currency

**FOR**    services, to agents, for off-shore non-UK trade, to subsidiaries abroad, or for imports

**FROM**  the moment you order you are at risk because of the movements in exchange rates

**YOU**    can eliminate this risk by arranging a **bank sells** foreign currency forward contract

---

HOW TO CALCULATE YOUR RISK PERIOD

| | |
|---|---|
| Order date | ..................... days |
| Delivery period | ..................... days |
| Credit period commences at date | |
|         of bill of lading | ........................... |
|         or of invoice | ........................... |
|         or of delivery | ........................... |
|         or (other considerations) | ........................... |
| Add no. of days credit granted to you | ........................... |
| Date when payment is due (earliest) | ........................... |
| Amount of latitude (if any) | ........................... |
| Estimated date of payment | |
|         *or* dates between | ........................... |
|         which payment will | |
|         be made | |
|         starting from | ........................... |
|         to | ........................... |

FOR PAYMENTS TO AGENTS OR TO SUBSIDIARIES

**YOU**    can also book a forward exchange contract to eliminate risks on exchange rates

**YOU**　　will need to know when the payment will be made, in which currency, and the amount

---

## ACTION TO TAKE

IF you wish to eliminate your currency risk, telephone the bank and ask them to arrange a BANK SELLS Forward Contract (amount of currency)

..............................

(which currency)

..............................

Delivery period from

..............................

to

..............................

or fixed date

..............................

---

## WHAT HAPPENS NEXT

A RATE is quoted by the bank
Rate quoted

..............................

Ref. no.

..............................

**NOTE** that once the rate is agreed, this is a firm contractual commitment

---

## FOLLOW-UP

CONFIRMATION of the deal will be sent by the bank to you within a few days
- **YOU** must check the details carefully
- **THE BANK** will require your confirmation on the copy dealing form which they will supply

# Export Finance Alternatives

## SECTIONAL INDEX

# 1. EXPORT FINANCING CYCLE

- There are a variety of ways in which you can provide credit (delayed payment terms) to a buyer or buyers
- These are categorised in this section

---

DO NOT REFUSE TO SELL BECAUSE THE BUYER ASKS FOR CREDIT PERIODS LONGER THAN YOU NORMALLY EXTEND – THERE ARE MECHANISMS AVAILABLE TO HELP YOU FINANCE THE LONGER CREDIT PERIODS

---

- Your Bank's International Branch will discuss the various alternatives and advise in what form the Export Financing might be arranged
- Export Finance can be arranged with the backing of an NCM or TI Comprehensive Short Term Credit Risk Insurance policy, or ECGD Supplier Credit Risk insurance
- discuss possibilities with your bank

---

KNOWING WHAT ALTERNATIVES THERE ARE AVAILABLE FOR PROVIDING CREDIT TERMS TO YOUR BUYER, WILL HELP YOU TO SELL PROFITABLY AND EFFECTIVELY

---

The various Export Finance 'products' are normally available for use once shipment has been made and documents are produced

Pre-shipment finance for the period up to shipment/production of documentation is usually done by way of overdraft or loan, and you should discuss requirements with your bankers

On 1 December 1991 the original ECGD credit risk business was split. NCM, the Dutch credit risk insurer took over ECGD short-term credit risk insurance (up to two years), with two years and beyond requirements remaining with ECGD, London

Trade Indemnity plc and other insurers also provide credit risk insurance (See Appendix C4)

## EXPORT FINANCING CYCLE

Purchase of raw materials
and Stock purchase

Manufacturing period            – The whole of this period is

Goods held in stock                generally financed by use

Sale/Despatch/Shipment             of own funds or overdraft
period

Documents assembled

Credit period provided          – financed by use of own funds
to buyer                           or overdraft until payment
                                   received

**OR**

– EXPORT DEBTS SWITCHED
  TO ONE OF THE
  ALTERNATIVES FOR
  FINANCING THE CREDIT
  PERIOD UNTIL PAYMENT
  RECEIVED

As soon as documents are available, a switch to a form of export
finance can be made. You will receive either the full value of the
shipment, or an agreed financed portion (with the balance of
proceeds later) into your current account, and the export debt will
be carried by whichever form of export financing is arranged

REMEMBER TO DISCUSS USE OF THE VARIOUS FORMS OF EXPORT
FINANCING, AND THE SPECIFIC REQUIREMENTS OF ANY OF YOUR
CUSTOMERS, AND MAKE THE NECESSARY ARRANGEMENTS
**IN ADVANCE** OF ACTUAL USAGE

## 2. FINANCING RELATED TO METHODS OF PAYMENT

**Post-shipment Short-term Finance for Exports**

| Method of Payment | Method of Financing |
|---|---|
| **CASH WITH ORDER** IRREVOCABLE LETTER OF CREDIT PAYABLE AT SIGHT | – **None required**<br>– Normally payment is made on presentation of documents, or within a few days, and **own funds or overdraft** is the most effective way of covering the position until payment is received |
| **IRREVOCABLE LETTER OF CREDIT** PAYABLE 'X' DAYS AFTER SIGHT, OR AT A GIVEN FUTURE DATE (Term credit)<br><br>(Note: A sight or term credit Confirmed by a First Class UK Clearing Bank, adds strength to the credit) | – Once documents specified in the Letter of Credit are presented to the Advising Bank correct and in order, the Bank will either accept the Draft (Bill of Exchange), or acknowledge receipt of documents. Either way they will state the date when payment will be made<br>– Banks are normally willing to **Discount** the Draft, or **advance funds** against the documents<br>– You will receive the face value less discount charges ie interest etc<br>– You can await funds at the future date and continue to finance this period by using either your **own funds or by way of overdraft** |

144

| Method of Payment | Method of Financing |
|---|---|
| **BILLS FOR COLLECTION** Bill of Exchange and documents sent via your Bank to the Buyer's Bank abroad for Collection A BILL OF EXCHANGE CAN BE **'AVALISED'** BY A BUYER'S BANKER TO GIVE ADDED SECURITY, AND THIS SHOULD ALLOW THE **AVALISED BILL** TO BE FORFAITED – see Section 13.4 | – **Own funds or Overdraft** – **An advance against Bills/Negotiation** – Certain Bills may be **discounted with or without recourse** to your company, but dependent on the standing of the buyer – **Forfaiting** – without recourse financing – **NCM or TI-backed Finance** – your Bank may have a scheme to join in your credit risk insurance policy, and then advance against your overseas buyers – **Insured Export Finance,** using your Bank's own credit risk insurance policy |
| **OPEN ACCOUNT** | – **Own funds or Overdraft** – **NCM/TI-backed Finance** (as above) – **Factoring debtors** – **Invoice discounting** |

YOUR BANK WILL DISCUSS THESE ALTERNATIVES WITH YOU, AND YOU CAN SEEK THE VIEWS OF OTHERS IF YOU WISH

# 3. FINANCING ALTERNATIVES

**SHORT TERM** – Up to 180 days

| | | |
|---|---|---|
| 1. | **Use own funds** | – cheapest and convenient |
| 2. | **Use overdraft** | – in sterling or currency – convenient |
| 3. | **Term Letter of Credit** | – very common |
| 4. | **Forfaiting** | – using 'Avalised' Bills of Exchange |
| | | – without recourse to the exporter |
| 5. | **Factoring/Invoice Discounting** | – financing book debts |
| 6. | **Short-term NCM/TI-backed overdraft** | – covers whole or part export turnover, convenient |

7. If you're paid by the buyer with his own cheque, arrangements can be made to **Negotiate** such items with your Bank

---

**SHORT-TO-MEDIUM TERM** – Up to 2 years

1/2/3/4/5/6 as above

8. **Supplier Credit** guaranteed by ECGD

**MEDIUM-TERM** – Around 2 years and up to 5 years
3/4/8 as above

9. **Buyer Credit** guaranteed by ECGD. See Section 13.10

---

**LONGER TERM** – Beyond 5 years (usually major projects)

4/8 above – possible, subject to detailed negotiations with banks

9. as above

---

**OTHER FORMS OF FINANCE CONVENIENT FOR THE EXPORTER**

10. **Lines of Credit between Banks** – the buyer effectively borrows from the Overseas Bank which is party to the Line

of Credit, with the funds loaned by a UK Bank to the Overseas Bank. The UK Bank pays the exporter on behalf of the Overseas Bank and the buyer. See Section 13.9

11. **World Bank** financed schemes – payment usually by World Bank

12. **International Aid Packages** – payment made from Aid Monies allocated to specific projects/purchases

---

**STRATEGIC FINANCIAL SUPPORT** (Major strategic projects)

13. **A.T.P. support** – Aid and Trade Provision considered for major projects only

---

**You can contact the DTI:**

Tel: 0171 215 6314

# 4. FORFAITING

**FORFAITING**

- This is the term used to 'discount' or 'forfait' bills of exchange
- In most instances the Bill of Exchange will require a 'Pour Aval' clause added and signed by the buyer's bank

---

**Suggested procedure:**

- Ask the buyer to arrange for his Bank to 'Avalise' Bills of Exchange
- You draw a term Bill of Exchange on your buyer (ask the Forfait Dept. of your Bank for guidance in preparing the Bill of Exchange) and submit this through your Bank for Collection
- Your buyer 'Accepts' the Bill of Exchange payable at a determinable future date
- Buyer's bank adds a 'Pour Aval' clause and also 'Accepts' the Bill of Exchange
- The 'Avalised' Bill of Exchange is returned to the exporter's Bank, and this is now available for 'Forfaiting' (discounting)
- If 'Forfaited', you will receive the face value of the avalised bill of exchange less forfait charges (interest cost)

---

- There is no recourse to your business
- If the buyer is a 'substantial' organisation a Pour Aval clause may not be required (your Bank's Forfaiting Department will advise on this aspect in advance of you submitting the Bill of Exchange to the buyer)
- Forfait financing can be cheaper than normal overdraft interest cost
- Interest cost can be built into the face value of the Bill of Exchange
- For credit periods over a 180 day period two or more avalised bills of exchange might be appropriate (discuss with your Bank's Forfaiting Department)

148

– Sterling or Currency availability

The interest cost of 'forfait' finance can be cheaper for the buyer than his using an overdraft in his country to pay you earlier – interest costs in some countries are higher than for sterling, or other currencies

Bills can be prepared, accepted and avalised before goods are shipped, but your buyer's agreement will be required

---

FORFAITING – THE BENEFITS

1. Without recourse to the Exporter once the Bank has purchased the debt
2. No contingent liability on the exporter's Balance Sheet
3. Forfait finance available in sterling or major currencies
4. Financing of a wide range of goods with no restrictions on country of origin
5. After forfait the exporter has no foreign exchange or interest rate exposure
6. Bill(s) of Exchange can be prepared and accepted by the Buyer, and 'avalised' by his Bank before the shipment of goods (subject of course to the Buyer's agreement)
7. Interest cost can be built into the value of a Bill(s) of Exchange if required
8. The interest cost of 'forfait' finance can be cheaper for the buyer than his using an overdraft to pay you earlier
9. Interest Rate commitment is available

---

CONSTRAINTS

1. Not used for Open Account trading
2. Minimum value of Bill(s) might be applied by some forfait financing banks/financial institutions
3. Minimum credit period requirements might also be applied – consult your Bank

## SPECIMEN AVALISED BILL OF EXCHANGE

The brief 'Pour Aval' clause signed by your Buyer's banker, is shown in this example of an Avalised Bill of Exchange

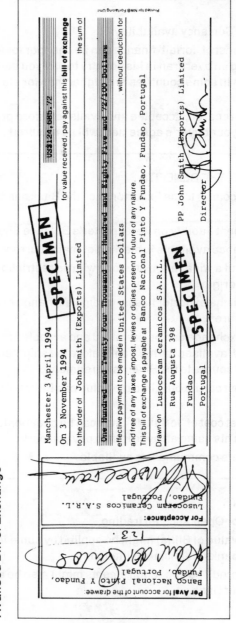

Example reproduced by kind permission of National Westminster Bank Plc.

## FORFAITING

Ask your Bank for an illustrative quotation by fax

You will have to tell them:

1. Your name as seller
   - telephone and contact name
   - fax number
2. Name of Buyer
   - address
   - country
3. Contract/Sales value and currency
4. What goods or services
5. Terms of Payment:
   - % for financing
   - credit period required
   - type of debt instrument offered
     - Bill of Exchange/Promissory Note/Bank
       Guarantee/Deferred Payment/Letter of Credit
6. Name of Avalising Bank or Guarantor
7. Is interest to be built into the face value of the debt
   instrument(s)?
8. From when finance will be required/availability date of bills

---

The Bank or Financing organisation may have other questions

Ask for a written response by fax

---

You can use the written response quotation as the basis for
offering the buyer credit terms to meet his requirements

# 5. FACTORING

## FACTORING

– This is the term used to 'sell' your debtor receivables, with the management of collections being undertaken by the factor (see Invoice discounting below)

– Your business will normally be paid on an agreed date

– It is possible to arrange a 'pre-drawing' immediately, or soon after the invoice is drawn on the buyer

– UK debtors AND/OR Overseas debtors can be Factored, subject to agreement with the Factoring Company

– Sterling or Currency debts eligible for factoring

– 100% bad debt risk cover provided

– Can be used to finance rapidly escalating turnover

– Postponement of any 'Floating Charges' affecting Debtors may be required (Factoring Company will advise)

## INVOICE DISCOUNTING

– Very similar to 'FACTORING', with similar features and benefits, but at lower cost because the discounting house does not involve itself in the collection of payments

– Invoice discounting provides finance for an agreed period of time – normally to the end of the period of credit you allow the buyer

# 6. INFORMATION REQUIREMENTS

– Contract finance/Individual sales contracts
– Information required to enable a Bank to consider what the best way of providing finance for exports might be:

---

Your business name ................................................................
         address ......................................................................
........................................................................................................

Contact name ............................ Tel No. ...............................
Telex ........................................ Fax .....................................

---

Buyer ...............................................................................................
Address in full ...............................................................................
........................................................................................................
Buyer's Bank .................................................................................
Address ..........................................................................................
........................................................................................................
Is Buyer: Private company ...........................................................
         Government buyer ........................................................
Is Buyer end user .................... If Gov't, which Dept ..................
If buyer not end user, who is? .....................................................

---

Contract/Order value/Currency ....................................................
CIF/CFR/FOB etc .................... Tender/Contract .....................
Description of Goods/Services ....................................................
........................................................................................................
Unit prices .....................................................................................
........................................................................................................
New/Re-conditioned/Secondhand .............................................
U.K. Content ............................................................................%
Do you have Cr. Risk Ins. cover? .................................................

Pre-shipment risk .......................................................................

No. of shipments/delivery period ...............................................

INSTALLATION PERIOD ..........................................................................

---

Period of Credit sought ................................................................

Payment terms offered ................................................................

Any security offered by Buyer (ie Gov't guarantee/ Bankers
guarantee/Bankers Aval/ ..........................................................)

---

ARE YOU AWARE OF ANY OFFERS OF CREDIT MADE BY
COMPETITORS?

(This information is particularly useful if periods of credit longer
than say 5 years have been offered by overseas competitors)

---

Any other information:

---

When All, or **even part** of this information is available, telephone
your Bank's Export Finance Department to obtain a quotation

– They will consider the alternatives and suggest how you might
  proceed to offer finance as part of your tender/price package

---

Note  –  Interest charges can be included in the value of the
          Bills of Exchange which will be required to ensure full
          future repayment – you would be paid the net amount
          after interest has been deducted from the face value
          of the Bills

      –  your bank will advise

---

**DON'T LEAVE YOUR APPROACH FOR A FINANCING PACKAGE TO
THE LAST MINUTE – ALLOW TIME**

154

# 7. INFORMATION A BANK SHOULD PROVIDE

The Bank you approach will reply:
- Possibly seeking additional information or clarification
- Will indicate their interest in providing a finance package to support you
- Will quote the terms which you then quote to the Buyer
- Will state how long the offer of finance will be available to you, and whether there will be a Commitment fee charged by them
- You can ask the Bank for a written Commitment to ensure the availability of the finance package for a given period
- This will fix the amount and the interest rate quoted. A Commitment fee will then be payable to the Bank
- If there is any information which becomes available after the Bank has quoted a Finance package, which has any bearing on the contract, its duration, terms, you should advise the Bank immediately
- When you receive the Contract/Order you should advise the Bank immediately

# 8. ECGD 'SCF'

SUPPLIER CREDIT FINANCE FACILITY (SCF)

The main features of the new SCF are:

- Finance will, in most cases, be made available to the exporters without recourse
- Exporters are free to select which contracts to submit to ECGD for approval for financing
- Optional pre-finance insurance cover may be requested from ECGD on a contract-by-contract basis at the same time that approval for financing is sought
- Financing provided by a Bank under the MGA is essentially by the purchase of the principal value of accepted bills of exchange or of promissory notes. ECGD will normally require that such bills or notes be guaranteed by a third party acceptable to ECGD (normally the buyer's banker or other surety)
- All approvals for SCF business have been centralised at ECGD's London Headquarters
- A fast and efficient service to exporters is promised

---

Contact your Bank's Export Finance Dept for further information, and discuss with them the possibility of financing your contracts under this type of facility

Ask for an indication of the possibilities and costs

# 9. ECGD LINES OF CREDIT

A Line of Credit is a finance arrangement whereby a UK bank will provide a loan facility to an overseas bank, to finance UK exports into the recipient country

- there are two distinct types of Lines of Credit:
  - **SCFLOC – Supplier Credit Lines of Credit**
    - used where one buyer is purchasing a range of goods and services
  - **GPLOC – General Purpose Lines of Credit**
    - available for use by individual buyers, subject to the overseas borrowing-bank's approval

---

- they are available for the sale of UK capital and semi-capital goods and/or services into designated countries
- **they give the UK exporter the benefit of cash terms, whilst providing the buyer with an agreed time to pay**
- minimum contract value can be as low as US$25,000 or £15,000

---

- the UK exporter can suggest to his prospective buyer that an approach be made to the named overseas bank to request finance be made available to the Buyer, from the Line of Credit
- the UK exporter can contact the UK bank providing the finance and advise details of the proposed transaction

---

**The UK exporter can obtain details of Lines of Credit which are available, by contacting ECGD – 0171 512 7238**

**THIS IS USEFUL INFORMATION TO HAVE PRIOR TO AN OVERSEAS VISIT, AND COULD HELP YOU CLINCH A SALE**

# 10. ECGD BUYER CREDIT

**Finance lines made available by UK Banks to a specific overseas buyer of UK capital goods, or as a Project Line of finance, and guaranteed by ECGD**

**Only available for the larger contracts**

**Contact ECGD for information:**

**0171 512 7238**

# Letters of Credit

* See Section 15 for Use of Standby Letters of Credit

# 1. INTRODUCTORY NOTES

Documentary Letters of Credit are an internationally accepted
method of arranging for the payment of goods and services

They are issued subject to the:

UNIFORM CUSTOMS AND PRACTICE FOR THE ISSUANCE OF
DOCUMENTARY CREDITS, publication UCP 500,

issued by the International Chamber of Commerce, Paris

This is a common set of guidelines in use in, and recognised in all
but a small number of countries worldwide

---

Copies are available direct from the

> International Chamber of Commerce United Kingdom,
> 14–15 Belgrave Square, London, SW1X 8PS
> Tel No. 0171–823 2811
>
> or from Chambers of Commerce,
> Bank International Branches and booksellers

---

Note:  DOCUMENTARY CREDITS and LETTERS OF CREDIT are
the same

The Buyer applies to his Bank to open a DOCUMENTARY
CREDIT

The seller receives from an Advising Bank the LETTER
OF CREDIT

---

If you are expecting to receive a Letter of Credit, do not ship goods
until after you receive it

– if you do, you may not be able to meet the documentary
requirements, and may not then get paid when you should

# 2. DEFINITION

Definition of a Letter of Credit –

'A written undertaking given by a Bank on behalf of a Buyer to pay the Seller an amount of money within a specified time provided the seller presents specified documents which are strictly in accordance with the terms of the Letter of Credit'

---

BANKS DEAL IN DOCUMENTS AND NOT IN GOODS

The documents specified must conform to the terms of the Letter of Credit, and be presented before the expiry date of the Letter of Credit

---

A Letter of Credit is an IMPORTANT DOCUMENT

It is a CONDITIONAL PAYMENT AUTHORITY

If you ship your goods before the last date for shipment

And produce DOCUMENTS accurately

Which COMPLY FULLY with all aspects of the Letter of Credit

And present these documents to the Advising Bank

You should receive PAYMENT in accordance with the terms of the Letter of Credit

---

If your Documents are not produced accurately, and do not fully meet the terms specified in the Letter of Credit, the Advising Bank will identify the DISCREPANCIES. If these cannot be rectified, there will be a delay whilst the Advising Bank seeks the authority of the Buyer's Bank to pay notwithstanding the discrepancies

THERE WILL THEN BE A DELAY BEFORE YOU ARE PAID

---

ACCURACY IS VITAL

**DISCREPANCIES ARE AVOIDABLE**

DELAYS IN RECEIVING PAYMENT COST MONEY

# 3. PARTIES TO A LETTER OF CREDIT

LETTERS OF CREDIT ARE ISSUED BETWEEN BANKS, OR BY A
SINGLE BANK

The parties are:

| | |
|---|---|
| **THE BUYER** | – The BUYER (the APPLICANT) makes application to his Bank to open a DOCUMENTARY LETTER OF CREDIT in favour of a named SELLER |
| THE BUYER'S BANK | – **THE ISSUING BANK** |
| | – THE ISSUING BANK will open the DOCUMENTARY LETTER OF CREDIT by instructing the SELLER'S BANK, or a Bank in the Seller's country, to advise their (the Buyer's Bank) LETTER OF CREDIT to a named SELLER |
| BANK IN THE SELLER'S COUNTRY | – Becomes the **ADVISING BANK** |
| (possibly the Seller's Bank) | – The ADVISING BANK WILL open the LETTER OF CREDIT by Advising the named SELLER of the terms upon which payment for goods or services rendered will be made to the SELLER |
| THE SELLER | – Is the **BENEFICIARY** |

The ISSUING BANK can also be the ADVISING BANK, if the Buyer
and Seller are in the same country, or if the ISSUING BANK so
chooses to fulfil both roles

If an Advising Bank (other than the issuing Bank) is asked to
advise a Letter of Credit, it can do so without engagement on its
part, but it is required to take reasonable care to check the
apparent authenticity of the Credit which it advises. If the

Advising Bank cannot establish such apparent authenticity, if it decides nevertheless to issue the Letter of Credit, it must inform the Beneficiary that it has not been able to establish the authenticity of the Credit

A Bank requested to advise a Letter of Credit, may refuse to do so, but it has to advise the issuing Bank without delay

**Terminology:**   Irrevocable Letters of Credit are also known as:
             I/L/Cs, ILCs, Doc.Crs, D/Crs, Doc L/Cs, L/Cs etc

# 4. TYPES OF LETTER OF CREDIT

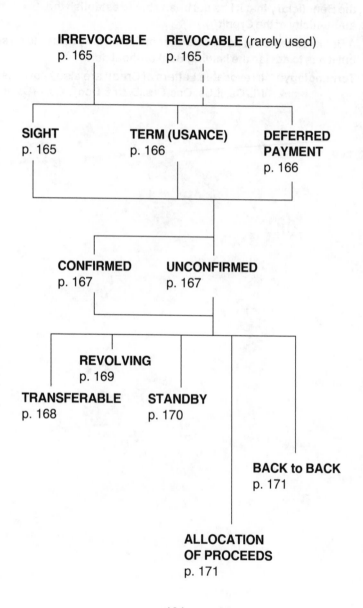

**IRREVOCABLE**
p. 165

**REVOCABLE** (rarely used)
p. 165

**SIGHT**
p. 165

**TERM (USANCE)**
p. 166

**DEFERRED
PAYMENT**
p. 166

**CONFIRMED**
p. 167

**UNCONFIRMED**
p. 167

**REVOLVING**
p. 169

**TRANSFERABLE**
p. 168

**STANDBY**
p. 170

**BACK to BACK**
p. 171

**ALLOCATION
OF PROCEEDS**
p. 171

164

Note:  The following are very rarely used types:

There are RED CLAUSE and GREEN CLAUSE Letters of Credit

RED CLAUSE CREDITS are known as 'Anticipatory Credits' permitting a proportion of the value of the Letter of Credit to be paid to the Beneficiary (Seller) before shipment, on an UNSECURED basis against a receipt

GREEN CLAUSE CREDITS – as for 'Red Clause', but the advance is made on a SECURED basis

---

## TYPES OF LETTER OF CREDIT

**REVOCABLE**       – Terms can be varied or cancelled by the Buyer or his Bank at any time until Payment, Negotiation or Acceptance has been made by the Advising (Paying) Bank

– **TO BE AVOIDED**

**IRREVOCABLE**  – The Terms and Obligations cannot be altered without the agreement of ALL PARTIES to the Letter of Credit (including the Seller)

UCP 500 now states that if a Letter of Credit does not state whether it is Revocable or Irrevocable, it will automatically be considered Irrevocable

---

Letters of Credit will have a number of documentary requirements specified to evidence the shipment of goods, or the provision of services

---

Payment is provided for, either at SIGHT, or after a TERM

**SIGHT**                  – When documents are first presented to the Advising/Paying Bank, and the bank has 'reasonable time' to examine documents

– **Reasonable time is defined in UCP 500, as 'NOT TO EXCEED SEVEN BANKING DAYS FOLLOWING DAY OF RECEIPT OF THE DOCUMENTS' and Banks must decide** whether to take documents up, or to refuse them within this timeframe

---

Payment after a TERM,

**TERM**
- Also referred to as 'USANCE' or 'ACCEPTANCE' Credit
- Payment is made at a date later than the Sight date
- Seller draws a Bill of Exchange (Draft) on the Advising Bank or Issuing Bank or Buyer demanding payment at a future determinable date, ie 30/60/90 days after Sight OR 'X' days after date of Bill of Lading etc
- Documents are prepared and presented as for a Sight presentation to the Advising Bank
- If the documents conform with the specified requirements in the Letter of Credit, the Bank will endorse (Accept) the Bill of Exchange (Draft)
- The Bank will either return the 'Accepted Bill' to the seller, or will retain it until the maturity (payment) date
- The Accepted Bill may be discounted (the value paid to the seller, less an interest charge for 'financing' the bill). This is generally 'without recourse finance'. Not all Banks offer a discounting facility, so the Beneficiary should check with the Bank concerned

---

A DEFERRED PAYMENT Letter of Credit

**DEFERRED PAYMENT**
- Documents only are called for, not a Bill of Exchange (Draft)
- Payment will be made after the TERM specified

166

- The Advising Bank will acknowledge the receipt of documents and advise when payment will be made
- Where the Letter of Credit is Confirmed, the seller can present a Bill of Exchange (Draft) even though not called for under the letter of credit, and request the Bank to 'Accept' it, and if required, request the Bank to consider discounting the accepted draft

---

Letters of Credit are UNCONFIRMED, unless a specific request for the Letter of Credit to be CONFIRMED is made to the Buyer

**UNCONFIRMED**   – The seller is reliant on the issuing bank's undertaking and ability to provide the necessary funds at the time payment is due to be made
                  – If a term Letter of Credit states Bill of Exchange (draft) is to be drawn on the Advising Bank, once the Advising Bank has accepted the Bill of Exchange, it is responsible for payment on the due date

**CONFIRMED**      – Where the Advising Bank adds its 'CONFIRMATION' it guarantees that provided all terms and conditions specified in the Letter of Credit are complied with, payment will be made irrespective of what may happen to the Issuing Bank (buyer's bank)
                  – The CONFIRMATION of a UK Clearing Bank gives the seller maximum security of payment, PROVIDED ALL DOCUMENTS COMPLY WITH THE TERMS OF THE LETTER OF CREDIT, AND DOCUMENTS ARE PRESENTED BEFORE EXPIRY OF THE CREDIT
                  – A CONFIRMATION by a London Branch Office of the Overseas Issuing Bank may not

167

> give the same strength of Confirmation as a UK Clearing Bank Confirmation
>
> – A CONFIRMING FEE will be due to the CONFIRMING Bank, for adding its strength to the original Credit

---

Although you may ask the Buyer for a Confirmed Letter of Credit, some of the major Banks may not wish their credits to be Confirmed

---

**It should be noted that,** for the purposes of issuing Letters of Credit, UCP 500 states that **BRANCHES** of a bank **IN DIFFERENT COUNTRIES** are now considered to be a different bank – this in no way strengthens the overseas branches of a Bank when it comes to considering Confirmation of a Letter of Credit by an overseas branch of the issuing Bank

---

**TRANSFERABLE** – IRREVOCABLE TRANSFERABLE LETTER OF CREDIT

– The Letter of Credit must state it is TRANSFERABLE

– Allows for ALL or PART of the value to be transferred to another Supplier

– Only the amount and the dates brought forward can be changed

– The other terms of the Letter of Credit cannot normally be changed

– TRANSFERABLE LETTERS OF CREDIT ARE A VERY USEFUL WAY OF SOURCING GOODS FROM THIRD PARTY SUPPLIERS AND ENSURING THEY MEET THE TERMS AND CONDITIONS OF THE PRIME CREDIT

– More than one TRANSFER PORTION can be issued up to the value of the original Credit

but the transferred portion cannot be
transferred again

---

- The prime BENEFICIARY will be notified by
  the Bank when the documents under the
  Transfer portion of the Credit are presented
- He will be invited to substitute such
  documents as will ensure the original terms
  and conditions are fully complied with, to
  enable him to receive his proportion of the
  proceeds from the original Transferable
  Letter of Credit
- The Bank will expect the prime beneficiary to
  provide substitute documents 'ON FIRST
  DEMAND' – ie without delay (the prime
  beneficiary should clarify how long the
  Advising Bank will allow for the substitute
  documents to be presented)
- If substitute documents are not presented
  'On Demand' or within the timescale
  permitted by the Advising/Paying Bank, the
  Seller may not receive his proportion of the
  proceeds. If there is undue delay in
  presentation of substitute documents, the
  Advising/Paying Bank is fully entitled to seek
  re-imbursement from the Issuing Bank of
  the sum it has paid out on the Transferred
  portion of the Letter of Credit
- If terms such as 'divisible', 'fractionable',
  'assignable', 'transmissible' are used, or
  suggested, THEY DO NOT MAKE THE
  LETTER OF CREDIT TRANSFERABLE, and
  will be disregarded

---

**REVOLVING**      – The IRREVOCABLE REVOLVING LETTER OF
                     CREDIT must state it is REVOLVING

169

- It may REVOLVE in relation either TO TIME or TO VALUE
- It may REVOLVE automatically OR the manner in which it is allowed to REVOLVE may be qualified
- The value, once payment has been made, may be automatically reinstated for further shipments to be made, or it may be reinstated for further use on a specified date (eg 1st of each month)
- A Revolving Credit is useful where regular shipments to the same buyer are to be made
- It avoids repetitive single value/shipment Letters of Credit
- It ensures documentation requirements are constant for all shipments

---

**STANDBY**
- See Section 15 for use of Standby Letters of Credit
- To be of value must be irrevocable
- The Credit must state it is an IRREVOCABLE STANDBY LETTER OF CREDIT
- It is used as a form of Trade Debt Guarantee
- It is held as a back-up to allow trading on Open Account terms
- See also Section on Credit Control procedures (Section 8)

---

- Very useful form of back-up to Open Account trading
- Avoids the production of specific documentation normally required for obtaining payment under a Letter of Credit
- If the BUYER doesn't pay the SELLER on an agreed terms basis within an agreed

170

timescale, the STANDBY LETTER OF
CREDIT can be used to obtain payment up to
the specified value

- If the SELLER requires an extension to the
  Expiry Date, or to the amount, the SELLER
  must approach the BUYER in good time
- Also used to secure borrowing by subsidiary
  companies from 'overseas' banks
- More easily realisable as security than a
  guarantee

---

**BACK-TO-BACK** — The Seller's 'Export' Letter of Credit
**CREDITS**         is used to 'Back' a further credit to
                    the Seller's supplier

- The 'Export' Credit cannot be considered as
  security for the further credit
- A TRANSFERABLE CREDIT IS MORE
  READILY ACCEPTABLE AND MORE
  EFFECTIVE FOR SOURCING GOODS FROM
  A THIRD PARTY SUPPLIER

---

**ALLOCATION**      — **Not a type of Letter of Credit,** but a
**OF PROCEEDS**       'convenient mechanism'
(referred to in     — Can be used to 'Allocate' all or part of the
UCP500, as            value of a Letter of Credit
**ASSIGNMENT**      — 'Allocation' of funds to a third party is not
**OF PROCEEDS)**      effective until the prime beneficiary has
                      presenteddocuments which fully comply
                      with the requirements of the Letter of Credit,
                      and the Advising/Paying bank is in a position
                      to make payment
                    — The prime beneficiary requests the
                      Advising/Paying/Confirming Bank to
                      'Allocate' all or part of the proceeds to a third
                      party supplier, or suppliers
                    — The Bank, if it agrees, will issue a 'Letter of

Allocation' to the named third party/each of the named third parties as appropriate
- The Bank will make it clear it has no responsibility to make payment
- That when it is able to make payment to the prime beneficiary, it will then take note of the beneficiary instructions to allocate proceeds

---

ALLOCATION OF PROCEEDS is a convenient mechanism for paying a supplier, once the Bank is in a position to make payment under the Letter of Credit to the prime beneficiary (the SELLER)

---

**UNDERTAKING TO PAY**   – The issue and Confirmation of a Letter of Credit now constitutes a definite undertaking to pay in the cases of sight and deferred payment credits, subject to compliant documentation being presented within the validity of the L/C

---

**AMENDMENTS**   – ACCEPTANCE or REJECTION of Amendments should now be notified to the Advising Bank
- FAILURE TO NOTIFY THE ADVISING BANK OF **REJECTION** OF AN AMENDMENT BEFORE PRESENTATION OF DOCUMENTS WILL, WHEN DOCUMENTS ARE PRESENTED FOR PAYMENT OR ACCEPTANCE, BE DEEMED TO BE NOTIFICATION OF ACCEPTANCE BY THE BENEFICIARY OF SUCH AMENDMENT AND, FROM THAT MOMENT, THE CREDIT WILL BE CONSIDERED AMENDED
- **YOU CAN REJECT ANY AMENDMENT TO AN IRREVOCABLE L/C IF YOU WISH, BUT YOU**

**ARE REQUIRED TO NOTIFY THE ADVISING BANK THAT YOU WISH TO REJECT THE AMENDMENT BEFORE YOU COME TO PRESENT DOCUMENTS FOR PAYMENT OR ACCEPTANCE**

# 5. REQUESTING A BUYER TO ISSUE A LETTER OF CREDIT IN THE SELLER'S FAVOUR

It is advisable to send the Buyer some Suggested Terms which he can then use to instruct his Bank to open a Letter of Credit

You should always seek an IRREVOCABLE Letter of Credit

Ask for the Letter of Credit to be opened immediately, and by TELETRANSMISSION, to avoid unnecessary delays

---

## SUGGESTED TERMS

- These suggestions are for use when a SELLER seeks a Letter of Credit from an intending BUYER
- They may be varied at the discretion of the BUYER and/or his Bank, but by suggesting terms it may lead to a more acceptable and workable Letter of Credit, giving the SELLER the security of being paid, providing all terms and requirements of the Letter of Credit are fully complied with
- The Suggested Terms should be on the SELLER's headed notepaper
- When a pro forma invoice is issued, give instructions on how you require to be paid, and if by Letter of Credit, attach a copy of the Suggested Terms to the Pro forma Invoice

---

ENSURE YOUR REPRESENTATIVES TRAVELLING ABROAD HAVE COPIES OF THE SUGGESTED TERMS TO HAND TO THOSE CUSTOMERS FROM WHOM YOU WILL REQUIRE A LETTER OF CREDIT

The following are suggested terms to be requested by a Seller when calling for payment under Irrevocable Letters of Credit:

**Reference** (your order number)

Payment for the above is requested by means of a Letter of Credit which should include the undermentioned particulars. Please arrange for the Letter of Credit to be in our possession by　　　　　　　　　　(date)

**Type of Credit**

Irrevocable – payable/available for acceptance in the United Kingdom at the counter of a Clearing Bank on whom drafts must be drawn

**Amount**　　　　　　　　\*　(Figures and Currency, eg £5,000 Sterling)

**Advising Bank**

Please instruct your bankers to advise the Letter of Credit covering this transaction through a London Clearing Bank and to make the Credit available for payment/acceptance at the advising bank's counter

**Confirmation**

Authorise/request the advising bank to add its confirmation

**Beneficiary**　　　　　Ø

**Description of goods**

**Despatch/Shipment**　　from　　　　　　　　　to

**Latest Date for Shipment**

**Credit to be valid until**　　　　　　　　　for payment/
　　　　　　　　　　　　　　　　　　　　acceptance in the
　　　　　　　　　　　　　　　　　　　　UK

| | | |
|---|---|---|
| **Partial Shipments** | ☐ To be allowed | ☐ Not to be allowed |
| **Transhipment** | ☐ To be allowed | ☐ Not to be allowed |
| **Shipment on Deck** | ☐ To be allowed | ☐ Not to be allowed |
| **Bank Charges** | ☐ All bank charges for account of opener | ☐ All bank charges outside the UK for account of opener |

\* if an exact amount cannot be stated, the use of a term 'about' may be appropriate (see p. 182)
Ø the exporter

Documents evidencing shipment of goods will also be required, these **may** include:
- Signed Invoices
- Documents evidencing shipment include:
    - Bills of Lading
    - Air Waybill
    - Road Waybill
    - Railway Consignment Note
    - Forwarding Agent's Receipt
    - Parcel Post Receipt
- Certificate of Origin
- Packing list
- Inspection Certificate
- Insurance Certificate (or Policy)
- and there are others which exporters to some countries have to provide

Details of individual country import documentation requirements may be found in Croner's Reference Book for Exporters – see Appendix C5.4

---

You may also be asked to draw a Draft, or Drafts (see Section 16.2) upon either the Buyer, the Issuing Bank, or the Advising/Paying/Confirming Bank

---

Further notes relating to the SUGGESTED TERMS for issuance of a Letter of Credit

**Description of Goods:** Try to keep this as **brief** and **succinct** as possible without going into technical details – eg 'Various electrical goods as per order No .... dated .....'. NB: Invoices submitted under Letters of Credit should commence with a description of the goods exactly as stipulated under the Letter of Credit – spelling mistakes, inexactitudes

176

and all! Once the invoice has been headed up in this way you may continue to describe the goods on the invoice in as much technical detail as you wish. It follows that the more simply goods are described in the Letter of Credit, the less room there is for error in completion of the necessary documentation

**Despatch/Shipment:** To take account of industrial action, dock strikes etc, try to stipulate shipment from any UK Port/Airport to any Port/ Airport in the buyer's country

**Latest Date for Shipment:** Should be established having regard to known production time scales etc., and advice from a Freight Forwarder as to available shipping services to importer's country, adding on a small margin of time for safety

**Validity:** It is usual to request the Letter of Credit to be valid until 21 days after latest date for shipment to allow time for the assembly of necessary documentation etc

**Partial Shipments:** If there is any likelihood of the goods described in the Letter of Credit being shipped on a piecemeal basis then the Letter of Credit should authorise partial shipments

**Transhipments:** If more than one mode of transport will be utilised in shipping goods from the UK Port/Airport to point of destination in buyer's country involving issue of a combined transport document, then the Letter of Credit should authorise transhipment

**Bank Charges:** The question of paying bank charges is often an emotive issue and it is preferable at the outset to establish who is responsible for the costs involved. Whilst

most UK Clearing Banks publish a tariff of
their charges the costs of overseas banks
are unquantifiable and often
considerable

# 6. RECEIPT OF A LETTER OF CREDIT

WHEN YOU RECEIVE A LETTER OF CREDIT
- GIVE IT PRIORITY ATTENTION
- DO NOT LEAVE IT TO BE CHECKED LATER
- ENSURE IT IS CHECKED IN DETAIL
- REMEMBER, IT IS A DOCUMENT WHICH SHOULD LEAD TO YOUR BUSINESS BEING PAID ON TIME FOR GOODS OR SERVICES SUPPLIED
- LACK OF ATTENTION TO DETAIL COULD DELAY PAYMENT AND COST MONEY UNNECESSARILY
- MAKE SURE IT IS SOMEONE'S RESPONSIBILITY IN YOUR BUSINESS TO ENSURE ALL THE REQUIREMENTS SPECIFIED IN THE LETTER OF CREDIT ARE MET

---

The following procedures are suggested for the Control of Letters of Credit

These notes and suggestions are offered to try and overcome some of the discrepancies which are regularly found in documents presented to Banks for payment under Letters of Credit

If discrepancies are found in documentation, delays may occur before you receive the funds from the Paying Bank

**DISCREPANCIES ARE AVOIDABLE WITH CARE AND ATTENTION TO DETAIL**

WHEN YOU RECEIVE A LETTER OF CREDIT, **GIVE IT PRIORITY**

DO NOT LEAVE IT FOR ACTION LATER

---

**CHECKLIST OF POINTS**

When you receive a Letter of Credit CHECK THE FOLLOWING POINTS:
- Is it issued by a recognisable Bank?
- Does it look authentic?

IF IN ANY DOUBT ABOUT THE DOCUMENT YOU HAVE,

179

PARTICULARLY IF THERE ARE SPELLING OR GRAMMATICAL
ERRORS, ASK YOUR OWN BANK'S INTERNATIONAL BRANCH
TO CHECK THE AUTHENTICITY OF THE DOCUMENT AND THE
SIGNATURES OF THE OFFICIALS THEREON

---

## SUGGESTIONS FOR THE CONTROL OF LETTERS OF CREDIT

1.  A Letter of Credit is an important document with a direct
    bearing on the speed with which your Company is paid

2.  **UPON RECEIPT,** take one photocopy and read the original
    carefully, marking the photocopy prominently in red with all
    relevant points:

    (a) Specific description of goods to be used including any
        mis-spellings

    (b) Shipping marks ⎤ If the same date, bring

    (c) Latest shipping date ⎥ forward the shipping

    (d) Expiry date ⎦ date to allow for
        documentation preparation

    (e) Transhipment/Part Shipments prohibited etc

    (f) Any other specific clauses, points etc

    (g) Note whether sterling or foreign currency value

    (h) Insurance requirements etc

3.  Take further photocopies, mark a copy as appropriate in red
    for each department in the Company which is to be
    associated with that shipment and number the copies. It is
    also wise to re-date in advance of the shipment date to allow
    sufficient time before expiry. Copy to the Accounts Dept also

4.  Where appropriate, distribute the copies to the Heads of
    Departments and if necessary arrange for them to return
    copies once requirements have been complied with

5.  When all copies are returned, check that every requirement
    has been complied with. If it proves not to be so, you can then
    return quickly to the appropriate section

6.  Ensure also that if any Departmental Head foresees
    difficulties in meeting the requirements for the order this is
    advised at the earliest opportunity

7.   If an amendment or an extension to the validity of the Letter
     of Credit is required, this should be requested from the buyer
     without delay

8.   Ensure a copy of the Letter of Credit is supplied to your
     Freight Forwarder at the earliest opportunity, in order that he
     can arrange to book space and meet transport requirements
     at the appropriate time. Advise when goods are likely to be
     ready for packing and despatch. The Freight Forwarder will
     also advise on documentary and packing requirements

These Notes are offered as suggestions, to be used to ensure all
requirements under Letters of Credit are correctly identified and
notified to the parties who will be involved. These procedures
should also assist in reducing discrepancies in document
preparation and making it more certain the exporter will be paid
on first presentation of documents to the paying/advising bank

---

IS IT PAYABLE IN THE UK?

– If it is, then once documents which fully meet all the
  requirements specified in the Letter of Credit have been
  presented within the validity, payment should be made within
  'reasonable time'. **Reasonable time is defined in UCP 500 as
  'NOT TO EXCEED SEVEN BANKING DAYS FOLLOWING DAY OF
  RECEIPT OF THE DOCUMENTS' and Banks must decide
  whether to take documents up, or to refuse them, within the
  stated timeframe**

– If it is payable ABROAD, are you prepared to accept it? (If in
  doubt seek advice from your Bank's International Branch)

– Is it available for NEGOTIATION in the UK or Abroad? The UK
  Advising Bank may be prepared to negotiate the documents
  and advance the value, but retain the right of recourse (to
  reclaim the funds) if the Issuing Bank does not reimburse the
  negotiating Bank. Interest will be payable for the period from
  when the advance is made, to the reimbursement date. In many
  instances the Negotiating Bank will know the period before it
  will receive reimbursement

Always ask for a Letter of Credit to be payable in the UK

IS IT IRREVOCABLE? It should be shown as IRREVOCABLE, but if it is not shown thus, then under UCP 500 the Letter of Credit will be considered to be IRREVOCABLE (In simple terms, if the L/C is to be considered as REVOCABLE, then IT MUST STATE THIS)

---

IS IT PAYABLE 'AT SIGHT', or AT LATER DATE (ie 'X' days after sight etc)

- If at a later date, have you agreed to the period of credit?
- If not, contact the Buyer

---

HAS THE ADVISING BANK ADDED ITS 'CONFIRMATION' TO THE CREDIT? (See page 167)

OR HAS IT INDICATED IT WILL DO IF YOU REQUEST IT TO DO SO?

IS YOUR NAME AND ADDRESS CORRECT?

- spelt correctly?
- is it shown as it will appear on your Invoice?

IS THE NAME AND ADDRESS OF YOUR BUYER CORRECT?

- a buyer's name and address as shown on the Letter of Credit should be used for documentation purposes

---

IS IT PAYABLE IN STERLING?          IS THE VALUE
OR A FOREIGN CURRENCY?              CORRECT?

If the term 'ABOUT' is used in relation to the value, a variation up to a maximum of 10% is permitted

- if payable in a foreign currency, do you need to arrange a Forward Exchange Contract for  BANK BUYS the currency to eliminate the potential foreign exchange risk. See Section 12

---

DO THE SHIPPING TERMS AGREE WITH YOUR QUOTATION, OR YOUR NORMAL TERMS OF TRADING?

- if they don't, you could incur additional costs

ARE THE LATEST SHIPMENT AND LETTER OF CREDIT EXPIRY
DATES ACCEPTABLE?

– does the latest shipment date allow you sufficient time to
   assemble or manufacture the goods, for packing, to arrange
   any inspections required?

– is the latest shipment date the same as the expiry date?

   – If it is, then you will need to allow at least 10/14 days after
      shipment to assemble documents to present to the bank. You
      will need to 'bring forward' the date by which you will be able
      to ship the goods, to allow time for documents to be
      assembled

– if you ship the goods before the latest shipment date, the last
   date for presentation of documents will effectively be
   considered as brought forward

   – the period between LATEST SHIPMENT AND EXPIRY DATES
      is normally 21 days, or such other time, either shorter, or
      longer, as specified in the Letter of Credit. This period will be
      applied to the actual date of shipment, to determine the
      period allowed for presentation of documents

ARE PARTIAL SHIPMENTS ALLOWED?

– If not, and they are necessary, you should ask the Buyer to
   arrange for an AMENDMENT to be issued

IS TRANSHIPMENT ALLOWED?

– This point is of particular relevance to your Freight Forwarder
   when arranging the transport and preparing movement
   documents

---

CAN YOU MEET ALL THE DOCUMENTARY REQUIREMENTS
SPECIFIED?

– NOTE THE DESCRIPTION OF GOODS GIVEN IN THE LETTER OF
   CREDIT AND ENSURE THIS APPEARS ON ALL YOUR
   DOCUMENTS EXACTLY AS SHOWN

– if the L/C calls for a certificate or other document to be issued by
   the buyer, (eg Certificate of acceptance, or compliance) and
   this has to be presented before you can receive payment in full

or in part, BE CAREFUL AND DISCUSS THE IMPLICATIONS
WITH YOUR BANK'S INTERNATIONAL BRANCH

- what happens if you can't get the required document?
- you might not be paid the amount due even though the goods
  are with the buyer,
- at least, there could be a delay before you receive the
  document and therefore payment

---

WHO IS RESPONSIBLE FOR INSURING THE GOODS?

- If you are, ensure your Insurance cover is adequate to cover the
  Risks specified – see Section 19
- If the BUYER is to insure, does he require you to advise him by
  telex/fax of the shipping details – name of vessel, date of
  shipment, shipping marks etc?
  - if there is such a requirement specified in the Letter of Credit,
    YOU MUST ENSURE YOU COMPLY WITH IT IN FULL DETAIL
    AND IMMEDIATELY ON DAY OF SHIPMENT or within the
    period specified for such advice to be given. If you do not
    meet this requirement, AND DO NOT PRODUCE A COPY OF
    THE TELEX/FAX MESSAGE CONTAINING ALL THE
    REQUIRED INFORMATION, the Buyer may not be able to
    Insure the goods in good time, AND YOU MAY NOT BE PAID,
    since you may cause a Discrepancy against which the
    Advising/Paying Bank will not make payment without
    receiving the Buyer's/Buyer's banker's authority
- The Uniform Customs & Practice for Documentary Credits, UCP
  500, stipulates that unless otherwise specified in a Letter of
  Credit, insurance value must be a minimum of 110% of value of
  goods – you must ensure this is done
- If 'INSURANCE POLICY' is specified, an Insurance Certificate
  will not be acceptable
- If 'INSURANCE CERTIFICATE' is specified, either a Certificate
  OR INSURANCE POLICY is acceptable

If any of the CHECKLIST POINTS are not acceptable, you should
consider approaching the Buyer without delay, and request that
AN AMENDMENT be issued to correct the unacceptable points

If an Amendment is issued, you cannot be selective:
- You have to accept ALL the points amended OR reject the amendment, perhaps seeking a further amendment
- You should notify the Bank that you ACCEPT or **REJECT** the amendment before you present documents for payment or acceptance – if you don't notify that you wish to REJECT the amendment, when you present documents you will be deemed to have accepted it

---

TRY TO INSTRUCT THE BUYER TO INCLUDE ANY SPECIFICALLY IMPORTANT POINTS RELATING TO THE GOODS AND/OR THE TRANSACTION, IN THE LETTER OF CREDIT INSTRUCTIONS HE GIVES TO HIS BANK TO OPEN THE CREDIT

These can relate to:

shipment dates

expiry dates

goods description – summarised rather than finite detail

price/value

part shipment/transhipment

See Section 14.5 for further detail

---

AMENDMENTS ADD TO THE COSTS – TRY TO HAVE THE LETTER OF CREDIT ISSUED 'RIGHT FIRST TIME'

---

**SCRUTINISE THE TERMS OF A LETTER OF CREDIT ON THE DAY IT IS RECEIVED**

**A LETTER OF CREDIT IS AN IMPORTANT DOCUMENT – DEAL WITH IT PROMPTLY**

---

IF YOU HAVE ANY QUERIES, DISCUSS THESE WITH THE ADVISING BANK AND/OR YOUR OWN BANK'S INTERNATIONAL BRANCH WITHOUT DELAY

185

# The Use of Standby Letters of Credit

## 1. STANDBY LETTER OF CREDIT

The instrument known as a 'Standby Letter of Credit' is afforded the protection of Uniform Customs & Practice for Documentary Credits, UCP 500, issued by the International Chamber of Commerce. Earlier, Standby Letters of Credit had been used occasionally in place of Guarantees in a form preferred by North American Banks. A Guarantee is a legal instrument and enforcement under a Guarantee is therefore subject to various legal requirements. The standard format Letter of Credit is a Conditional Payment Authority from an Issuing Bank to an Advising Bank, authorising the Advising Bank to pay a Beneficiary against stipulated documentation being presented in order to the Advising Bank

A Standby Letter of Credit is a Letter of Credit which can remain dormant in the background as security for the seller (the beneficiary) in case of need. Drawings under this type of Credit are usually made against a signed statement by the Beneficiary that a transaction or undertaking has not been fulfilled, which is accompanied by a draft drawn at sight upon the Issuing or the Confirming Bank, as the case may be. In this context, a Standby Letter of Credit can be held at the disposal of the Beneficiary and may be utilised up to and including the expiry date

In the event that the buyers' obligations are **fully** met, either by means of Open Account settlement or Bills for Collection basis or any other alternative means of settlement, the Standby Letter of Credit stands unutilised and ultimately expires for payment at the counters of the Advising Bank, unless extended upon mutual agreement of the interested parties, such extension being effected by an appropriate amendment

Suggested wording for a STANDBY LETTER OF CREDIT to cover trading debts:

---

- PAYABLE AGAINST SIGNED CERTIFICATE FROM (Beneficiary's name) ......................... STATING THAT THE DRAWING AMOUNT REPRESENTS LIABILITIES DUE TO THEM OF (amount and currency) .......................... FOR THE SUPPLY OF ......................... WHICH HAVE BEEN CLAIMED FROM (Buyer) ............................. AND HAVE NOT BEEN RECEIVED BY (Beneficiary's name) ......................... WITHIN (say 30 days or other period) OF THEIR SAID CLAIM
- COPIES OF UNPAID INVOICES MAY BE REQUIRED TO SUBSTANTIATE THE CLAIM FOR PAYMENT
- The buyer may wish to include other documents in the documentary requirements to be submitted when a claim payment is made under a Standby Letter of Credit
- If there are difficulties in agreeing the documentation requirements for a Standby Letter of Credit, consult your Bank and/or Commercial Lawyer

---

If the buyer calls for a copy transport document to be produced by the exporter when any drawings are made under a Standby Letter of Credit, the special instructions in the credit should state that Article 43 does not apply (this is to allow for the date of a copy transport document to be outside the normal 21 days permitted by this article)

---

You should ask for the Standby Letter of Credit to be IRREVOCABLE and valid for a given period, eg 12 months, longer or shorter period to suit requirements

You should ensure the Standby Letter of Credit is recorded on the Customer Credit Information file and shows the name of the Issuing and Advising Banks, the amount and the validity date (expiry date)

Diarise to review the requirement for a Standby Letter of Credit, say ONE MONTH PRIOR TO THE EXPIRY DATE, and if you wish it to be renewed for a further period, approach the Buyer immediately and ask him to arrange renewal

---

The amount of a Standby Letter of Credit should be sufficient to cover normal trading debts, or an agreed proportion of them, outstanding at any one time

A Standby Letter of Credit can be a useful 'medium' stage, between a normal Letter of Credit and Open Account trading, or trading on Bill for collection terms. It will provide the exporter with security of payment up to the value stated for the period to expiry

# Preparation of Export Documentation

## SECTIONAL INDEX

# 1. INTRODUCTORY NOTES

DOCUMENTS MUST BE PREPARED ACCURATELY
**ACCURACY IS VITALLY IMPORTANT**

Inaccurate documentation could be the cause of your not being paid, or payment could be delayed

– in both instances, delays add to your costs and reduce profit margins

---

Prepare documents progressively
– avoid rushing them at the last minute

---

Allow sufficient time for outside bodies:

– Chambers of Commerce
– Pre-shipment Inspection agencies where specified
– Freight Forwarders and Shipping/Airline/Road Transport operators

to prepare and deliver documents

– ensure you instruct them as to the exact detail you require/the Letter of Credit Advising/Paying Bank require to appear in the documents

DELAYS DO OCCUR – GOOD PREPARATION AND INSTRUCTION WILL MINIMISE SUCH OCCURRENCES

---

SITPRO (The Simpler Trade Procedures Board) advise on simplifying the preparation of export documentation through the use of 'aligned' documentation systems. Prepare one master document for each transaction, and from that master produce all documentary requirements

SITPRO is an independent agency supported by DTI, and located at

Venture House,
29 Glasshouse Street,
London, W1R 5RG
Tel: 0171 287 3525
Fax: 0171 287 5751

**ALIGNED DOCUMENTATION IMPROVES ACCURACY, REDUCES THE OPPORTUNITY FOR ERRORS TO BE MADE, SAVES TIME, AND IMPROVES PAYMENT RECORD**

**COMPUTERISED DOCUMENTATION SOFTWARE WILL IMPROVE EFFICIENCY AND REDUCE COSTS OF PREPARING DOCUMENTATION – A GOOD INVESTMENT, NOT UNNECESSARY COST**

---

CRONER'S REFERENCE BOOK FOR EXPORTERS

This is a *very important* reference book for all exporters

- country-by-country listing
- documentation and other import requirements listed in detail
- shipping requirements
- details of any special requirements for each country
- available on annual subscription which includes automatic supply of monthly updates
- much useful information for every exporter

Can be obtained from:

> Croner Publications Ltd
> Croner House,
> 173 Kingston Road,
> New Malden,
> Surrey KT3 3SS
> 0181 942 8966

# 2. BILL OF EXCHANGE

(Also often referred to as a DRAFT)

Legal Definition of a Bill of Exchange:

'A Bill of Exchange is an unconditional order in writing, addressed by one person (or organisation) (The DRAWER) to another person (or organisation) (The DRAWEE), signed by (or on behalf of) the Drawer, requiring the person (or organisation) to whom it is addressed (DRAWEE) to pay on demand, or at a fixed or determinable future time, a sum certain in money to, or to the order of, a specified person (or organisation) (PAYEE) or to bearer'

---

1. Used as a demand for payment
2. Drawn payable either at **'Sight'**, at a fixed future date or **'TERM'** at a determinable future date:
   - 'X' number of days after, say, date of invoice or date of Bill of Lading
3. The parties to a Bill of Exchange:
   - DRAWER  –  The Exporter or provider of services
   - DRAWEE  –  The Buyer or receiver of services
   - PAYEE  –  The Exporter, or to his order, eg his Bank or a Bank acting on his behalf, who will account for the proceeds
4. A Bill of Exchange is not in itself an authority to the Bank to debit the Buyer's account
5. A Buyer will have to authorise his Bank to debit his account in respect of a Bill of Exchange drawn upon him
6. The Drawee can delay making payment on a Bill, or can delay accepting (signing) a Bill drawn payable in the future (a Term Bill)
7. If a Bill is not paid when due it might be advisable to commence, or instruct the Bank handling the Bill to commence, the first stage of legal enforcement

- to Protest the Bill for non-payment or non-acceptance – see
  Section 18
8. Normally a single Bill of Exchange (either sight or term) is
   used, but there will be occasions when Two Bills for identical
   amounts and terms will be required – A First and Second of
   Exchange – see pages 200/1, 202/3

---

- Bill of Exchange drawn payable at SIGHT – see page 197

---

- Bill of Exchange drawn payable at a future determinable date
  (TERM BILL) – see page 199

---

- A FIRST of Exchange at SIGHT – see page 200
- A SECOND of Exchange at SIGHT – see page 201
  - First and Second of Exchange can be drawn either at Sight or
    Term – see pages 200/1, 202/3

---

FIRST & SECOND OF EXCHANGE
- Often called for under Letters of Credit, and also used when
  Bills of Lading form part of the documentation sent for
  Collection
- If the Letter of Credit specifies 'Drafts', this signifies that two
  drafts, a First and Second of Exchange, will be required to be
  presented
- Documents which include Bills of Lading (which are documents
  of title), are split into two sets, one set being sent off
  immediately to the Bank abroad, accompanied by the FIRST OF
  EXCHANGE

  with the second set of documents, and the SECOND OF
  EXCHANGE, sent off after a short interval to the Bank abroad,
  usually after 3 or 4 days
- The splitting of documents, and the use of Two Bills of
  Exchange is a safeguard against the delay or loss in transit

of one of the sets of documents, particularly where these include Bills of Lading

– Demand for payment or acceptance can be made using either the First of Exchange, or Second of Exchange, and if payment or acceptance is made on one of the two, the second then stands unpaid/unaccepted

Ensure:  – Words and figures agree, and amount and currency agrees with invoice

        – dates are correct and, if term, the correct term

        – it is drawn upon the correct party, eg the buyer OR the Advising/Paying Bank as required OR the buyer's Bank, OR a third party specified

        – it is claused appropriately for presentation under a Letter of Credit

        – it is correctly signed, and ENDORSED ON THE BACK

        – it is drawn for the correct term – sight or usance

---

Note  – A Bill of Exchange can be prepared on plain paper, or company letterhead paper, using the wording shown in the following examples, or some stationers sell pre-printed format bills (as seen in the examples on pages 197, 199, 200/1)

## BILLS OF EXCHANGE

## SIGHT BILL

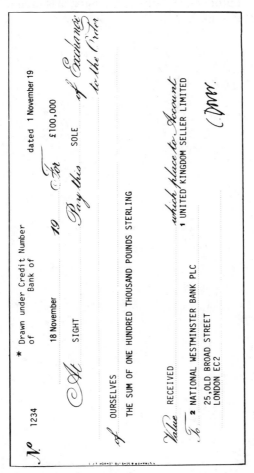

Examples reproduced by kind permission of National Westminster Bank Plc

1. DRAWER – EXPORTER – Also to be endorsed on back of Bill

\* Claused for presentation under a Letter of Credit

2. DRAWEE – The IMPORTER, or his BANK, or a BANK, if drawn to
   meet the requirements of a Letter of Credit

Examples reproduced by kind permission of National
Westminster Bank PLC

TERM BILL – Payable at a future determinable date

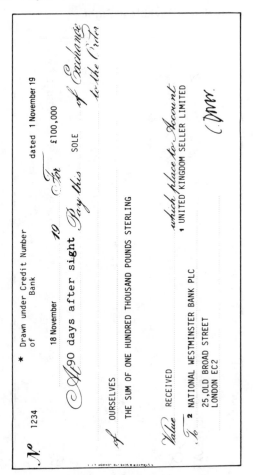

For presentation under a Letter of Credit, the maturity date will be established as (eg) 90 days after the Bank 'sights' documents in ORDER (ie documents fully comply with the terms of the Letter of Credit)

When presented for a Buyer's acceptance, the maturity date will be established as (eg) 90 days from the date the Buyer accepts the term Bill

## BILLS OF EXCHANGE/Cont'd

### FIRST OF EXCHANGE – Payable at Sight

```
* Drawn under Letter of Credit Number
  of
                                              dated      18th November      19.

EXCHANGE FOR   US $100,000.00      pay this FIRST   Bill of Exchange
At   SIGHT                                                      to the Order of
SECOND OF SAME DATE AND TENOR UNPAID
OURSELVES

the sum of  One Hundred thousand United States dollars

for Value Received, which place to the Account

                                              UNITED KINGDOM SELLER LIMITED
To.  Buyer or Bank                                        (Signature)
```

* Claused for presentation under a Letter of Credit

SECOND OF EXCHANGE – Payable at Sight

```
*  Drawn under Letter of Credit Number
of
                                          dated

EXCHANGE FOR  US $100,000.00                    18th November    19

At    SIGHT    pay this  SECOND   Bill of Exchange
FIRST OF SAME DATE AND TENOR UNPAID                    to the Order of
OURSELVES

the sum of One Hundred thousand United States dollars

for Value Received, which place to the Account

                                   UNITED KINGLOM SELLER LIMITED
To   Buyer or Bank                        (Signature)
```

NOTE – ALL DETAILS SHOULD BE IDENTICAL, EXCEPT THE
SECTIONS FIRST/SECOND and SECOND UNPAID/FIRST UNPAID
The Drawer/Exporter should endorse the back of BOTH Bills

## BILLS OF EXCHANGE/Cont'd

FIRST OF EXCHANGE – TERM BILL or TERM DRAFT – Payable at a future date

```
* Drawn under the Documentary Credit of          Bank
  No.                       dated
                       BILL OF EXCHANGE

Amount  F.F.51,204.00        Date  18th November, 19
At 60 days after sight, Pay this FIRST of Exchange,
SECOND OF SAME DATE AND TENOR UNPAID,
to the Order of Ourselves
the sum of Fifty-one thousand, two hundred and four French Francs
for value received             which place to the account of

                                    Joe Bloggs Seller

To.                                    (Signature)
   _____
   _____
   _____
```

* Claused for presentation under a Letter of Credit

Note  –  This example is shown in simple typewritten form

SECOND OF EXCHANGE – TERM BILL OR TERM DRAFT – Payable
at a future date

```
* Drawn under the Documentary Credit of        Bank
            dated
No.
             BILL OF EXCHANGE

Amount F.F.51,204.00          Date  18th November, 19
At 60 days after sight, Pay this SECOND of Exchange,
FIRST OF SAME DATE AND TENOR UNPAID,
to the Order of Ourselves
the sum of Fifty-one thousand, two hundred and four French Francs
for value received         which place to the account of

                                  Joe Bloggs Seller
To._____
    _____            (Signature)
    _____
```

NOTE – ALL DETAILS SHOULD BE IDENTICAL, EXCEPT THE
SECTIONS FIRST/SECOND and SECOND UNPAID/FIRST UNPAID
The Drawer/Exporter should endorse the back of BOTH Bills

# 3. INVOICE

This is the Commercial Document specifying the goods and/or services being supplied

Ensure:

- it is addressed to the correct buyer and correctly dated
- the goods are accurately described with the correct Customs Classification reference numbers for the importing country shown – see Sections 26 and 16.8
- the value is shown correctly, with unit prices etc
- the terms of trading are shown
- the payment terms are specified
  - if a credit period has been agreed ('X' days from a given date, eg date of invoice/date of bill of lading or air waybill), this should be stated
  - STATE ALSO THE DATE WHEN YOU EXPECT TO BE PAID
  - viz – Payment due 30 days from date of bill of lading (state date),

    We expect payment on (quote date calculated)
- state HOW you expect to receive payment
  - viz – Payment by URGENT SWIFT Transfer direct to

    (state your Bank name, address and sort code)

    (state your Account name and Account number)
- show any Import Licence numbers, any relevant pro forma invoice references
- show buyer's order numbers or other references
- show any packing details, shipping marks and other information required, and ensure this information is identical to that shown on other documents, particularly Bills of Lading, Air Waybills etc
- if required to be 'Signed' ensure each Invoice copy is also ORIGINALLY SIGNED – photocopies of signed invoices are not normally acceptable
- if Invoice to be CERTIFIED – ensure the required certifying statement is originally signed on each invoice

 – certain countries will require invoices to be legalised by their
   Embassy/Consulate, for which a charge will be made, and
   there could be a delay whilst this is done
 – legalisation of documents can be done by your Freight
   Forwarder or direct yourselves

---

If for presentation under a Letter of Credit

Ensure:

 – Unless otherwise stipulated in the Credit, invoices must
   appear on their face to be issued by the named Beneficiary
 – Must be made out in the name of the Applicant (Buyer)
 – Whilst UCP 500 states that Invoices need not be signed, unless
   otherwise stipulated in the Credit, IT IS ADVISABLE TO
   ENSURE ALL INVOICES ARE ORIGINALLY SIGNED (some
   Banks will request Invoices to be originally signed, and by
   adopting a policy originally to sign all invoices, you will avoid a
   potential discrepancy situation)
 – your business's name on the Invoice corresponds with your
   name shown in the Letter of Credit
 – THE DESCRIPTION OF GOODS AT THE HEAD OF THE INVOICE
   IS EXACTLY AS SHOWN IN THE LETTER OF CREDIT,
   TOGETHER WITH ANY RELEVANT ORDER NUMBERS, PRO
   FORMA INVOICE REFERENCES ETC
 – price basis and value correctly calculated and does not exceed
   the Letter of Credit value
 – gross and net weights are consistent across all documents
 – may require reference to the Letter of Credit to be shown

---

For buyers in the Single European Market, you should show the
buyer's VAT registration number on invoices. See page 281

# 4. TRANSPORT DOCUMENTS

Your Freight Forwarder should produce such Transport Documents as will be required safely to transport your goods to your Buyer, by whatever mode of transport you specify, or might be most appropriate, or to meet the buyer's requirements specified in a Letter of Credit

If you have a Letter of Credit supply your Freight Forwarder with a photocopy – this will assist them in meeting the requirements specified in the Letter of Credit

– if there are inaccuracies, take these up immediately with the Freight Forwarder

| Transport Documents | Types |
|---|---|
| Bills of Lading | – Marine/Ocean Bills of Lading (pages 207/8) |
| | – Non-negotiable Sea Waybill |
| | – Multimodal Transport Document |
| (usually in sets of three | – Freight Forwarders Bills of Lading* |
| (or more) originals with | – Received for Shipment Bills of |
| additional non-negotiable | Lading* |
| copies) | – Charter Party Bills of Lading* |
| Air Transport Document | – Air Carrier's Air Waybill (page 211/2) |
| | – House Air Waybill* |
| | – Air Consignment Note* |
| Truck | – CMR Note (page 213) |
| Rail | – CIM Consignment Note (pages 213/4) |
| Despatch by Post | – Parcel post receipt (page 214) |
| Despatch by Courier | – Courier Receipt (page 214) |

* If any of these types of transport document are required, they will be specified in the Letter of Credit

Note: CMR – Convention Marchandises Routiers (International Road Consignment note)

CIM  –  Convention Internationale Marchandises (by rail – International Rail Consignment note)

---

All movement documents must indicate:
- the name of the carrier on the FRONT of the document (Front is the side showing details of the goods, vessel and voyage) – (the back of the document is the side showing details of the contract of carriage)
- be signed or otherwise authenticated stating who has issued it, and the capacity in which they act for the named carrier
- Multi-modal transport documents must show the named operator/carrier

---

## MARINE/OCEAN BILLS OF LADING

BILLS OF LADING are TRANSFERABLE DOCUMENTS OF TITLE TO THE GOODS
- they are issued in sets of originals, usually three, but more if requested
- they should have been signed or otherwise authenticated by:
  - the carrier or a named agent for or on behalf of the carrier
  or
  - the master or a named agent for or on behalf of the master
- any signature or authentication of the carrier or master must be identified as carrier, or master
- an agent signing or authenticating for the carrier or master must also indicate the name and the capacity of the party on whose behalf that agent is acting (the carrier or master)
- they are issued when goods/packages/cases/containers are handed over to a Shipper, or Shipper's Agent, for movement to a named destination overseas
- they are also a receipt and evidence of the contract of carriage
- any one of the 'originals' is sufficient to surrender in exchange for the consignment, and once one original has been accepted

by the shipper/shipper's agent at the port of destination, the 'other originals' stand void

(as Bills of Lading are title to the goods they cover, if a single B/L was to be lost, the consignment would have to be warehoused, a duplicate obtained which would cause delay, or an Indemnity to the shipping company given, before the goods would be released. All of this would be a time-consuming and costly exercise, so Bills of Lading are issued in sets of more than one original. It is not wise to enclose a full set of Bills of Lading in one envelope, because of the danger of documents being lost. Banks will therefore split a set into two envelopes, one being posted immediately, the second envelope being held for 2/3/4 days and then posted, to avoid the possibility of both envelopes being in transit in the same bag). However, with the increasing use of Courier handled packages, it is now more common for all documents to be included in a single courier package

- any number of 'non-negotiable' copies will be issued by the shipper on request, and at least three should be requested in case of need

- Most Buyers require 'Shipped On-Board Marine Bills of Lading' since these show the consignment to be shipped

- 'Received for Shipment B/L' do not have the same status, unless a 'Shipped On-Board' notation, the ports of loading and destination, the name of the carrying vessel, and date, are added

- The 'On Board' notation on a Bill of Lading does not have to be signed or initialled

- Bills of Lading with additions 'Loaded On Deck': 'Unprotected on Deck': 'Packing damaged' etc etc are termed 'Claused Bills' or 'Dirty Bills', and they do not have the status of CLEAN SHIPPED ON-BOARD BILLS OF LADING

- 'CLEAN SHIPPED ON-BOARD BILLS OF LADING' are the highest status, indicating the goods have been shipped in good order and without apparent defect

- Bills of Lading are often issued 'TO ORDER', and this makes it necessary for them to be 'BLANK ENDORSED' by the Shipper. The Bills are then 'Bearer' documents, the Bearer being able to

claim the goods. IT IS VITAL THEREFORE THAT PROCEDURES FOR HANDLING BILLS OF LADING ARE PROPERLY REGULATED AND SECURE, ie via Banks
- Once Bills of Lading are with the Exporter, they should be handled speedily. If there is undue delay, they may be termed 'STALE', and not accepted for Letter of Credit purposes

---

A Letter of Credit will specify the status of the Bill of Lading required to be presented to obtain payment

Unless otherwise stated, you will be required to present Marine Bills of Lading in a full set (plus any non-negotiable copies required)

You should ensure the following points are met:
- Issued by a NAMED CARRIER
- they should have been signed or otherwise authenticated by:
  - the carrier or a named agent for or on behalf of the carrier, or
  - the master or a named agent for or on behalf of the master
- any signature or authetication of the carrier or master must be identified as carrier or master
- an agent signing or authenticating for the carrier or master must also indicate the name and the capacity of the party on whose behalf that agent is acting (the carrier or master)
- If issued by a FREIGHT FORWARDER, it should indicate that such Freight Forwarder is acting as the ACTUAL CARRIER, or signed in a capacity as detailed above
- Indicates the goods have been 'loaded' or 'Shipped on Board' a NAMED VESSEL. Ensure the 'On-Board' date is not later than the latest date of shipment stated in the Letter of Credit.

---

- The description of goods, shipping marks, quantities, numbers of cases, weights etc should be consistent with information shown on all other documents
- The Port of Loading and Port of Discharge should be shown consistent with the terms of the Letter of Credit ('Intended' Ports are not acceptable unless the Credit expressly states they are acceptable)

- Ensure the correct 'NOTIFY PARTY' is shown
- If the terms of trading require the Seller to pay carriage, the Bills of Lading must be marked 'Freight Paid'

---

## TRANSHIPMENT

- Unless transhipment is prohibited by the terms of the Letter of Credit, banks will accept a bill of lading which indicates that the goods will be transhipped, providing that the entire ocean carriage is covered by one and the same bill of lading
- Even if the Letter of Credit prohibits transhipment, banks will accept a bill of lading which indicates that transhipment will take place as long as the relevant cargo is shipped in Container(s), Trailer(s), and/or LASH barge(s) as evidenced by the bill of lading, provided the entire ocean carriage is covered by the one and same bill of lading, and/or incorporates clauses stating that the carrier reserves the right to tranship

---

CARE SHOULD BE EXERCISED TO ENSURE THE REQUIREMENTS OF THE LETTER OF CREDIT ARE FULLY MET, OTHERWISE DELAYS IN RECEIVING PAYMENT WILL BE CAUSED

---

## NON-NEGOTIABLE SEA WAYBILL

(can be styled 'Non-Negotiable Sea Waybill for Combined Transport Shipment or Port-to-Port Shipment')

These are issued for port-to-port shipment

- they should indicate the name of the carrier and to have been signed or otherwise authenticated by:
  - the carrier or a named agent for or on behalf of the carrier, or
  - the master or a named agent for or on behalf of the master
- any signature or authentication of the carrier or the master must be so identified
- an agent signed or authenticating must indicate the name and the capacity of the party on whose behalf the agent is agent (ie carrier or master)

- indicates goods have been loaded on board or shipped on a named vessel
- a non-negotiable sea waybill is not a document of title to the goods

---

If for presentation under a Letter of Credit
Ensure:
- if a place of receipt or taking in charge different to place of loading is indicated, the on-board notation must also indicate the place of loading stipulated in the Letter of Credit

---

## MULTIMODAL TRANSPORT DOCUMENT

(can be styled 'Bill of Lading for Combined Transport Shipment or Port-to-Port Shipment')
Issued where at least two different modes of transport are necessary
- the requirements for multimodal transport documents are similar to those for issue of Marine/Ocean Bills of Lading

---

If for presentation under a Letter of Credit
- Even if a Letter of Credit prohibits transhipment, banks will accept a multimodal transport document which indicates that transhipment will or may take place, provided the entire carriage is covered by one and the same document

---

## AIR TRANSPORT DOCUMENT

This is issued for consignments being transported by Air
- it is not a Document of Title
- it is a receipt for goods and evidence of a contract of carriage

---

THE AIR TRANSPORT DOCUMENT should show:
- it is issued and signed by a named Carrier, or be signed on behalf of a named carrier by his Agent
- any signature or authentication of the carrier must be identified

211

as carrier. An agent signing must also indicate the name and capacity of the part (carrier) on whose behalf the agent is acting
- if freight prepaid, or freight collect, and freight charges
- despatch from a named (or nominated) Airport, to a named (or nominated) Airport
- the shipper's name and address
- the consignee's name and address
- the name of any Notify Party required
- Customs reference/status
- correct description of goods, dimensions, commodity code, rate class, chargeable weight, freight rate applicable
- value of goods

---

The date of issuance of the Air Transport Document will be taken as the date of shipment, unless a Letter of Credit specifically calls for an actual date of despatch. If it does, a specific notation is required which will then be deemed to be the date of shipment

---

If for presentation under a Letter of Credit:
Ensure:
- the terms of the Credit relating to the Air Transport Document requirements are met
- if a House Air Waybill, that it is signed as specified above
- consigned to the correct party
- despatch date not later than the latest date for shipment
- even if transhipment is prohibited by the Letter of Credit, banks will accept an air transport document which indicates that transhipment will or may take place provided that the entire carriage is covered by one and the same air transport document
- may require reference to the Letter of Credit to be shown

---

## TRANSPORTATION BY ROAD TRUCK – CMR Note

A CMR Note is an International Consignment Note for carriage of goods by Road

– it is not a document of title and is non-negotiable

It should have the following information:

– Sender's Name, Address and Country

– indicate place of shipment

– Custom's reference and status

– Consignee's name and address and point of delivery

– bear a reception stamp or other indication of receipt by the carrier or named agent for the carrier

– Carrier's name and address

– be signed or otherwise authenticated by the carrier or a named agent for and on behalf of the carrier

– description of goods, number of packages, package markings

– volume and gross weight

– carriage charges if these are to be collected from the consignee

– date and place of issue

– date of issue, or date of reception stamp will be deemed to be the date of shipment

A Letter of Credit will specify the information required to be shown on a CMR Note

---

## TRANSPORTATION BY RAIL – CIM Consignment Note

A CIM Consignment Note is issued for goods transported by Rail

– it is not a document of title and is non-negotiable

It should have the following information:

– name and address of the consignor and consignee

– indicate place of shipment

– name of the destination station

– bear a reception stamp or other indication of receipt by the carrier or named agent for the carrier

- be signed or otherwise authenticated by the carrier or a named agent for and on behalf of the carrier
- description of goods, number of packages, package marks, gross weights
- number of the rail wagon into which loaded
- detailed list of customs documentation necessary for completion of journey
- payment terms for carriage
- MUST BE STAMPED CLEARLY WITH THE DATED STAMP OF THE FORWARDING STATION – Most important

It is the Consignor's duty to complete the CIM Consignment Note

A Letter of Credit will specify the information required to be shown on a CIM Consignment Note

## DESPATCH OF GOODS BY POST

A Parcel Post Receipt should show:
- Post Office date stamp indicating date of despatch
- Name and address of Consignee

For presentation under Letters of Credit, Parcel Post Receipts should also show:
- despatch effected from a Post Office within any nominated area
- date stamp indicating despatch is within the latest date for shipment specified in the Letter of Credit
- amount of postage paid if this is a requirement

## DESPATCH OF GOODS OR DOCUMENTS BY COURIER

A Courier Company Receipt should show:
- Name of the Courier/Service Company
- Be signed, or stamped to indicate receipt, or otherwise authenticated
- Indicates date of pick-up, or of receipt
- Name and address of Consignee
- Indicate package(s) received

For presentation under Letters of Credit, a **Courier Receipt** should also show:
- If a named courier is specified in the Letter of Credit, that it has been issued by the named courier
- The date of pick-up, or of receipt, is within the latest date for shipment, or if for documents, within the period before expiry of the Letter of Credit

**GENERAL NOTES RELATING TO TRANSPORT DOCUMENTS:**

UCP 500 now clarifies certain aspects of transport documentation in relation to acceptance under Letters of Credit, viz:

Unless a Letter of Credit stipulates otherwise, the following will be accepted by Banks:
- Transport Documents issued by a Freight Forwarder as carrier or Multimodal transport operator, and signed as such, or otherwise authenticated
- A transport document (Bills of Lading) which states that the goods **may be carried on deck, provided it does not specifically state that they are or will be loaded on deck**
- Claused 'shipper's load and count' or 'said to contain', or words of similar effect
- Indication that the consignor of the goods is a party other than the Beneficiary of the Letter of Credit
- 'Freight prepayable' or 'freight to be prepaid' or similar words, **will not be accepted as evidence of payment of freight – 'Freight paid' or 'freight prepaid' will be acceptable**
- Transport documents bearing reference by stamp or otherwise, to costs additional to freight, such as costs of or disbursements in connection with loading, unloading or similar operations will be acceptable, unless specifically prohibited in the Letter of Credit

# 5. CERTIFICATE OF ORIGIN

A document stating the origin of goods to be transported overseas

In some countries, Customs Import Clearance cannot be completed without a Certificate of Origin

---

There are two official types:

i. **European Union Certificate of Origin**
   - acceptable in all but Arab League countries, where a certificate of origin is prescribed as a condition of contract or to meet importation requirements

ii. **Arab–British Chamber of Commerce Certificate of Origin**
    See Appendix D1
    - required by the following countries of the Arab League:

| | |
|---|---|
| Algeria | Qatar |
| Bahrain | Saudi Arabia |
| Iraq | Somali Democratic Republic |
| Jordan | Sudan |
| Kuwait | Syria |
| Lebanon | Tunisia |
| Libya | United Arab Emirates |
| Mauritania | Peoples Democratic Republic |
| Morocco | of Yemen |
| Oman | Yemen Arab Republic |

Both are issued by Chambers of Commerce (see Appendix D2–D5)

It is suggested that, where a Certificate of Origin is prescribed either for presentation under a Letter of Credit or to meet contract and payment terms, an Official Certificate of Origin be obtained from a Chamber of Commerce

Technically, a simple requirement for 'A Certificate of Origin' with no other instruction/requirement, can be met by the Exporter preparing his on 'C of O' headed as such

For Egypt, the EU C of O is used, but the documents for attestation are submitted to the Egyptian–British Chamber of Commerce, not the Arab–British Chamber

Application for a Certificate of Origin must be supported by a copy of the Exporter's invoice and documentary proof of origin of the goods if other than manufactured by the Exporter

The following information should be shown:

- full name and address of exporter
- full name and address of buyer (consignee)
- country of origin of the goods – if more than one country of origin, all should be shown, as appropriate against each item
- method of transportation
- description of goods to comply with the letter of credit where appropriate
- number and types of packages, package marking, gross and net weights
- bear the official Chamber of Commerce/Arab–British Chamber of Commerce authentication stamp, be signed on behalf of the Issuing Chamber, and be dated

For presentation under Letters of Credit:

- if required to be legalised or counter-signed by a third party organisation, that this requirement is met
- shipping or other marks, numbers and types of packing cases, weights must be consistent with the information shown on all other documents
- any alterations, additions or amendments must be properly authenticated by the Issuing Chamber/Authority
- may require reference to the Letter of Credit to be shown

# 6. INSURANCE DOCUMENTS

**INSURANCE DOCUMENTS**

See Section 19 for information relating to INSURANCE OF GOODS IN TRANSIT

---

Insurance documents must now appear on their face to be issued and signed by the Insurance Company, or by Underwriters, or by Agents
– Pre-signed open cover certificates or declarations are acceptable, unless specifically prohibited under the terms of the Letter of Credit

---

An INSURANCE CERTIFICATE is acceptable in most instances to evidence the insurance of goods
It should show:
– a date not later than the date of despatch of the goods covered
– the insurance value covered in words and figures and the currency (Minimum 110% of invoice value)
– the method of transportation
– where appropriate, the name of carrying vessel, port of loading and destination
– brief description of the goods and packing
– identifying marks and numbers on packaging
– name and address of organisation with whom any claims should be lodged in country of destination
– categories of risk covered

---

The Seller effecting the insurance should endorse the reverse side of the Certificate to give Bearer status to the Certificate so that any claims can be pursued in the Buyer's country

---

If an INSURANCE POLICY is stipulated, the same information and requirements must be shown therein and endorsement effected

---

The Exporter may be appointed as AGENT FOR THE INSURANCE COMPANY to facilitate the issue of Certificates and Policies without delay. The Insurance Company will instruct the Exporter to ensure compliance with all aspects of Insurance of Goods in Transit

---

For presentation under Letters of Credit:
The following additional points:
- ensure the Insurance Document is issued in the Currency of the Letter of Credit
- for the correct amount, CIF value plus 10% (or such other uplift percentage as specified)
- any alterations, additions or amendments are properly authenticated
- shows the risk cover exactly as specified in the Letter of Credit
- a Policy can be issued and will be acceptable in lieu of an Insurance Certificate, but a Certificate will not suffice where a Policy has been specified
- if cargo is to be loaded on deck, this should be recorded on the Insurance document

---

If an insurance document indicates it has been issued in more than one original, then all the originals must be presented under the Letter of Credit, unless the Credit states otherwise

# 7. OTHER DOCUMENTS

## PACKING LISTS

Should show:
- Name and address of Supplier
- Name and address of Buyer
- Goods description
- Type of packing, number of packages, details of any sequential numbering, and contents of each individual package
- Shipping marks on packages
- Weights, gross and net, and where necessary, of each package

---

For presentation under Letters of Credit:
- Meet any specific requirement for the Packing List
- May require reference to the Letter of Credit to be shown
- All details should be consistent with the information shown on other documents

---

## WEIGHT NOTE or WEIGHT LISTS

Should show:
- Name and address of Supplier
- Name and address of Buyer
- Description of goods
- Gross and Net weights of individual packages
- Weights listed should add up to a stated total

---

For presentation under Letters of Credit;
- Meet any specific requirement of the Credit
- Gross and Net Weight totals should be consistent with such details shown on other documents
- May require reference to the Letter of Credit to be shown

If a Letter of Credit calls for an attestation or certification of weight in the case of transport other than by sea, banks will accept a weight stamp or a declaration of weight which appears to have been superimposed on the transport document by the carrier or his agent, unless the Credit calls for a separate document

---

## CLEAN REPORT OF FINDINGS

This requirement can only be obtained from the Pre-Shipment Inspection Agency nominated in the Letter of Credit

A physical inspection of the goods will be necessary prior to despatch

Contact the Pre-Shipment Inspection Agency in good time: they will give details of their requirements for information

The Agency may also undertake a 'Price Comparison' inspection

See Section 25 for further information on Pre-Shipment Inspection formalities

Normally a Clean Report of Findings will only be made available after the goods have been despatched, and a copy of the movement document has been lodged with the Agency

---

For certain countries the issue of a Clean Report of Findings, after pre-shipment inspection of the goods, will now be made in the destination country. For these countries, the Pre-shipment Inspection Agency WILL RETURN ONE COPY OF THE FINAL INVOICE TO THE EXPORTER WITH A SPECIAL SECURITY LABEL WHICH ATTESTS TO THE ISSUE OF THE CLEAN REPORT OF FINDINGS

IT WILL BE NECESSARY, THEREFORE, FOR LETTERS OF CREDIT FOR THE EXPORT OF GOODS TO CERTAIN COUNTRIES TO PROVIDE FOR A COPY INVOICE WITH SPECIAL SECURITY LABEL AFFIXED TO BE PRESENTED, AND NOT SPECIFY A 'CLEAN REPORT OF FINDINGS' AS A REQUIREMENT

---

If your Letter of Credit specifies a 'CLEAN REPORT OF FINDINGS' will be required, **check with the Pre-shipment Inspection Agency that a CRF will be issued after inspection – IF THE REQUIREMENT**

**HAS BEEN CHANGED TO 'INVOICE WITH SPECIAL SECURITY LABEL' AFFIXED, you should seek an amendment to the Letter of Credit,** to avoid a discrepancy when documents are presented

---

**COPY ADVICES**

INFORMATION TO BE ADVISED TO THE BUYER

in respect of shipping details etc, particularly when the Buyer is responsible for Insuring the goods

- Where there is a requirement of this nature, to be advised within a specific time period (eg within 24 hours), the Letter of Credit should specify what document is required to be produced to evidence compliance with such requirement
- Reference to the Letter of Credit may also be required

---

Other documents may be required for consignments of a special nature, or to meet specific requirements of the Importer, or the Importing Country. The exact nature of such special documents will undoubtedly vary, and it is not possible therefore to cover such uncertain documentary requirements in this text

---

It should be noted that, under UCP 500, if a Letter of Credit contains conditions and requirements for action, and does not specify the documents to evidence compliance, Banks examining documents can now disregard the conditions

# 8. CUSTOMS DOCUMENTS

See Section 26 also

You, as exporter, are required correctly to classify your goods for customs purposes and enter the correct commodity code identified from the 'Tariff' publication

You can allow your Freight Forwarder to complete cutoms forms but you, the Exporter, are legally responsible for classifying your goods correctly

There are a number of other customs forms for use in specific situations

— information on these and their use can be obtained from the Customs & Excise office for your locality (**not** the Customs VAT office)

---

Letters of Credit documentary requirements do not normally include customs forms, but if there is a specialist form specified for certain categories of goods, or required to meet Customs requirements in particular situations, then

— the information on the Customs form should be consistent with all other documentation

You should ensure that the Customs form specified is the correct one for the export of your goods

— if it isn't, contact the Advising Bank for advice

— an amendment to the Letter of Credit might be necessary

## 9. EXPORT LICENCE REQUIREMENTS

See Section 1.2 on EXPORT CONTROL REQUIREMENTS

Export licences are required for certain types of goods and services

Application for an Export Licence must be made prior to the despatch of goods from the UK, and goods must not be moved until the Export Licence is issued by the DTI (Department of Trade & Industry)

If goods which require an Export Licence are exported without, or prior to, issue serious penalties may be incurred by those who are party or accessory to the transactions

---

Export Licence enquiries should be addressed to:

> The Enquiry Unit,
> Export Control Organisation,
> Room 711,
> Kingsgate House,
> 66–74 Victoria Street,
> London, SW1E 6SW
> Telephone: 0171 215 8070

# Presentation of Documents Under Letters of Credit

## SECTIONAL INDEX

# 1. PRESENTATION

IT IS MOST IMPORTANT TO ENSURE A CHECK OF DOCUMENTS TO THE LETTER OF CREDIT IS MADE BEFORE PRESENTATION TO THE BANK

– Check documents are correctly drawn up – see Section 16

– the detail specified for each document should be checked

– the required number of each document is available

– detail is consistent between documents

– carefully collate all documents

PRESENTATION SHOULD BE MADE WITHIN THE VALIDITY OF THE LETTER OF CREDIT (See page 183)

---

When you present documents with the original Letter of Credit to the Advising Bank:

– the Bank is allowed 'reasonable time' in which to undertake a detailed check of the documents you present

– Reasonable time is defined in UCP 500 as 'NOT TO EXCEED SEVEN BANKING DAYS FOLLOWING DAY OF RECEIPT OF THE DOCUMENTS'

– the Advising Bank is responsible to the Issuing Bank for the detailed check of documents, to ensure the BUYER'S INSTRUCTIONS have been complied with before payment can be made, or funds obtained by the Issuing Bank

– **IF DISCREPANCIES ARE FOUND IN THE DOCUMENTS PRESENTED, THE BANK MUST GIVE NOTICE BY TELECOMMUNICATION OR OTHER EXPEDITIOUS MEANS, OF ALL DISCREPANCIES BY THE SEVENTH BANKING DAY FOLLOWING RECEIPT OF DOCUMENTS**

– if the Letter of Credit has been CONFIRMED (see page 167) and documents fully comply with the Credit terms, the Bank will make payment to you, or will ACCEPT THE TERM BILL(S) OF EXCHANGE for maturity at a specified date (and they may be willing to discount the Accepted B of E)

– if the Letter of Credit has not been Confirmed the Advising Bank may have to give notice to the Issuing Bank and ask for funds to be made available to it, before it can pay the exporter, and there may be a delay (The Advising Bank does not normally undertake to make payment, or to accept drafts (bills of exchange) unless it adds its Confirmation to the Credit)

- if the Credit is payable in a foreign currency, advise the Bank whether they pay you the currency, or the sterling equivalent. If you have a Forward Currency Contract with the Advising Bank, give them full details and ask them to place the funds to the Forward Contract. If your Forward Contract is with a Bank other than the Advising Bank (ie your own Bank), instruct the Advising Bank to transfer the currency funds to your own Bank, and you instruct your own Bank to apply the funds to the appropriate Forward Contract, or to a currency account
  - if funds are sterling, ask for transfer direct to your Bank account – whichever Bank
  - payment by banker's payment or cheque is best avoided
- when presenting documents, include a covering letter quoting the name of the person who should be contacted by telephone in case discrepancies are found in the documents including details of who to contact during holiday close-down etc

---

DISCREPANCIES ARE AVOIDABLE –
DISCREPANCIES DELAY PAYMENT
ATTENTION TO DETAIL IS VITALLY IMPORTANT

## 2. IF DISCREPANCIES ARE IDENTIFIED

- you will not be paid, or have drafts accepted immediately
- you should receive notification of ALL discrepancies by telecommunication or other expeditious means BY THE SEVENTH BANKING DAY FOLLOWING RECEIPT OF DOCUMENTS BY THE ADVISING BANK

---

There are the following options:

1.   – if the offending document(s) have been prepared within your office, arrange for replacements to be prepared and forward to the Advising Bank immediately

    – if the offending document(s) have been issued elsewhere, re-possess and contact as follows:

       – if the offending document is the Transport Document contact the Freight Forwarder or Carrier's Agent and ask for corrections to be made, and properly authenticated by stamp and signature 'as Agents'

       – if a Certificate of Origin, contact the Issuing Chamber of Commerce and ask for the necessary amendments to be made

    – if an Insurance Certificate or Policy – if issued by you as Agent for the Insurance Company, cancel and re-issue correctly: if issued by the Insurance Company itself, arrange for authenticated amendment, or re-issue, always ensuring the date of commencement of insurance conforms to the requirements of the Letter of Credit

    – Parcel Post Receipts cannot normally be corrected

    – if the Letter of Credit calls for specific information to be advised to the Buyer by Fax/Telex or other means within a set time period, THE LETTER OF CREDIT SHOULD ALSO SPECIFY BY WHAT MEANS THIS IS TO BE EVIDENCED (see page 222)

      if there is no indication of a documentary requirement to evidence compliance with the action specified, the Banks can now disregard such conditions

IF SUCH A SITUATION OCCURS, CHECK WITH THE
ADVISING BANK HOW THEY WILL INTERPRET THE
INSTRUCTION
- IF SPECIFIC ACTION IS REQUIRED TO BE COMPLETED
UNDER THE TERMS OF A LETTER OF CREDIT, AND THERE
IS A STATED DOCUMENTARY REQUIREMENT TO
EVIDENCE THAT THE ACTION HAS BEEN TAKEN, **THEN IT IS
VITALLY IMPORTANT THAT TIMEFRAMES ARE COMPLIED
WITH** – IF THE REQUIRED ACTION IS NOT TAKEN WITHIN
THE GIVEN PERIOD, THEN A DISCREPANCY MAY OCCUR,
AND SUCH DISCREPANCY CANNOT BE OVERCOME
- ENSURE CORRECTED DOCUMENTS ARE PRESENTED
WITHIN THE TIME ALLOWED FOR PRESENTATION/
VALIDITY OF THE LETTER OF CREDIT

---

2. – if documents cannot be corrected, or if there is insufficient
time remaining within the validity of the Credit to allow
corrected documents to be obtained,
   – the Bank should be asked to telex advise the Issuing Bank
   for permission to pay, notwithstanding the discrepancies
   – there will be a delay before a response is received

---

3. – whilst the Bank may be prepared to pay against an
INDEMNITY signed by you (and probably by your Bank also),
the funds may be reclaimed if the Issuing Bank and/or the
Buyer refuses to accept discrepant documents and
authorise payment

---

4. – the discrepant documents can be sent 'In Trust' to the
Issuing Bank with a request that payment be authorised
   – the Buyer may use the opportunity to refuse payment, or
   attempt to negotiate a reduction in price, or simply to
   delay payment
   – he should not be able to obtain the goods without first
   agreeing to pay or accept/instruct his Bank to accept a

229

Bill of Exchange to obtain the Bills of Lading and other documents – UNLESS OF COURSE GOODS HAVE BEEN CONSIGNED DIRECTLY TO THE BUYER

---

5. –  if the Bank offers to pay 'UNDER RESERVE', they will retain the right to reclaim the funds from you at a future date, if they do not obtain reimbursement from the Issuing Bank

A telephone call or fax by the exporter to the Buyer to advise the nature of the discrepancies may speed the payment/acceptance authorisation

---

IF THERE ARE DISCREPANCIES ON A LETTER OF CREDIT, IT IS IMPORTANT TO IDENTIFY THE CAUSE OF SUCH DISCREPANCIES, WHAT FACTORS HAVE CONTRIBUTED TO THE CAUSE, AND MAKE CHANGES TO PROCEDURES TO ENSURE THE SAME DISCREPANCIES ARE NOT REPEATED

ANY DISCREPANCY IS LIKELY TO DELAY THE PAYMENT OF PROCEEDS TO YOUR COMPANY, AND THEREFORE THERE IS A COST TO DISCREPANCIES, PRIMARILY THROUGH TIME LOST ON MAKING CORRECTIONS, ON RE-WORK, AND LOSS OF USE OF THE FUNDS WITH CONSEQUENTLY ADDITIONAL INTEREST COST IF YOUR COMPANY IS OVERDRAWN, OR LOSS OF USE OF FUNDS WHICH COULD BE RE-USED OR PLACED ON DEPOSIT ACCOUNT TO GAIN SOME INTEREST

---

**ERRORS ERODE MARGINS AND PROFITS**

---

# 3. GENERAL DISCREPANCIES

## COMMON DISCREPANCIES

- Letter of Credit expired (late presentation of documents)
- Late Shipment
- Undue delay in presentation of documents

---

- Documents do not carry reference to Letter of Credit, if this is a requirement
- Detail between documents inconsistent
- Incomplete set of documents presented

## 4. DRAFT/BILL OF EXCHANGE

**COMMON DISCREPANCIES**

– Drawn on the wrong party
– Drawn on the Applicant, **in which case the Bank will disregard and treat as an additional document, with the result that the required Draft was not presented, therefore a discrepancy**
– Not signed
– Not endorsed on the reverse
– Not dated, or incorrectly dated
– Incorrect Tenor
– Incorrect amount
– Words and figures differ
– Not made out in FIRST and SECOND when 'DRAFTS' are called for
– Does not state 'Drawn under L/C No. .............. etc as called for in L/C

---

IT SHOULD BE NOTED THAT UCP 500, ARTICLE 9, STATES: **IF THE CREDIT NEVERTHELESS CALLS <u>FOR DRAFT(S) ON THE APPLICANT</u>, BANKS WILL CONSIDER SUCH DRAFT(S) AS AN ADDITIONAL DOCUMENT(S)**

**CREDITS SHOULD THEREFORE NO LONGER BE ISSUED WITH DRAFTS DRAWN ON THE APPLICANT**

# 5. INVOICES

**COMMON DISCREPANCIES**

- Does not bear a signature if this is specified as a requirement in the Credit
- Not issued by the named Beneficiary
- Wrong amount
- Not issued in correct number of copies
- Made out in the name of the wrong party
- Shows incorrect shipping terms
- Goods Description incomplete or incorrectly stated
- Made out in the wrong currency
- Not legalised when this is specified in L/C, or incorrect number of copies legalised
- Not Certified by Chamber of Commerce when this is specified, or incorrect number of copies legalised
- Detail inconsistent with that shown on other documents

# 6. BILLS OF LADING

**COMMON DISCREPANCIES**

- Not issued to Order and/or Blank Endorsed on the reverse
- Issued to Order of wrong party
- Not signed or otherwise authenticated by the carrier, or a named agent on behalf of the carrier

OR

- Not signed or otherwise authenticated by the master, or named agent on behalf of the master
- The identity of the signature or other authentication as carrier or master not stated, or the capacity of a signing agent not stated
- Incorrect type of Bill of Lading presented, ie Received for Shipment B/L
- Shows Incorrect Port of Shipment
- Shows Incorrect Port of Discharge
- Shows Incorrect Marks and Numbers on packages compared to those shown on other documents or specified in the Credit
- Goods Description incorrect
- Not presented in a Full Set when this requirement is specified
- Shows Incorrect 'Notify Party' or omits Notify Party altogether
- Evidences Shipment on Deck
- Bill of Lading is Claused, ie damage or leaking package specified on Bill of Lading
- Not marked Freight Paid, or Freight Collect, as appropriate
- Unauthenticated amendments

---

**Air Transport document**

- Incomplete/incorrect information shown
- Does not show Flight details
- Not signed by Carrier or the Named Carriers Agents
- Not the original transport document

# 7. INSURANCE DOCUMENTS

## COMMON DISCREPANCIES

- Certificate presented, when Policy is specified
- Not all originals produced (if the insurance documents indicate more than one original issued, all originals must be produced)
- Incorrect amount of cover shown
- A minimum of 110% cover not provided, ie under-insured
- Wrong Currency shown
- Not in Negotiable form
- Not signed by the Insurance Company, or Underwriters, or their Agents
- Not endorsed
- Incorrect Insured Party
- Does not show where Claims are payable
- Dated after shipment date
- Does not show the Risks as called for in the L/C

## 8. PACKING LISTS

**COMMON DISCREPANCIES**

- Insufficient 'packing' information shown
- Shipping Marks, numbers of packages, weights (Gross and/or Net), not shown, or inconsistent with the corresponding information shown on other documents
- Goods Description inconsistent with Letter of Credit

## CERTIFICATE OF ORIGIN

**COMMON DISCREPANCIES**

- Incorrect type presented – Normal type when Arab–British C of O type required
- Detail shown inconsistent with the corresponding information shown on other documents
- Additions or Alterations not authenticated by Issuing Chamber
- Incorrect number of copies legalised where this is called for
- Country of Origin of goods shown differs from the requirement specified in the L/C

## CLEAN REPORT OF FINDINGS FOLLOWING PRE-SHIPMENT INSPECTION

**COMMON DISCREPANCY**

- A Non-Negotiable Report of Findings is presented
- CARE  –  If a Letter of Credit requires the production of a Clean Report of Findings, and the Inspection Agency provides a 'Security Label affixed Invoice' instead, this could give rise to a discrepancy (see Section 25)

236

## OTHER DOCUMENTARY REQUIREMENTS NOT MET

– Not met at all, or not met within a given time stated in L/C
– Requirements specified only partly met
– Information contained in documents is inconsistent with the L/C or between other documents

## SUGGESTION FOR GOOD PRACTICE

When presenting documents under a Letter of Credit, include a Letter to the Bank, setting out **payment instructions**, (particularly if your bank account is not with the bank handling the Letter of Credit), **name of contact, telephone numbers, fax, and any holiday absences/closure of office, with contact numbers,** to be used in case of need

This should ensure there are no delays in advising details of any discrepancies

**Importantly, it should prevent unnecessary delays costing you money, and therefore eroding profit margins**

# Debt Collection and Protest Instructions

Effective Credit Control procedures, the establishment of agreed Payment terms and procedures, and close monitoring of debtor positions should help to minimise the possibility of overdue debts becoming irrecoverable

Accurate invoicing and prompt supply of correct documentation to meet buyer's country entry requirements will help to avoid disputes and delays caused by inaccurate documentation and prevent the buyer using these to extend credit periods by delaying or avoiding payment

Even though a debt may be due, allowance will have to be made for the method of payment agreed and the time factor for transfer of funds

See Sections: Credit Control procedures         Section 8

              Methods of obtaining payment       Section 5

              Preparation of Export Documentation    Section 16

## PURSUING OVERDUE DEBTS

If a buyer regularly delays payment, do the credit and payment terms need revising with the objective of obtaining more secure payment terms? – see Section 5

Check whether the buyer has advised details of any faulty goods, missing goods, damaged goods, or complained of late supply

– were such circumstances advised promptly?

– are matters still under discussion?

Check copy Invoices

– that payment terms were correctly specified, and the date when payment was due was shown – see Section 16.3.1

– were prepared accurately in all respects?

Consider stopping any further supplies until position clarified

Do not leave debts overdue without making early contact with the debtor to ascertain reasons for delay

- if you have an Agent in or covering the debtor's area, use them to approach the buyer, and press for payment without delay
- otherwise, contact by telephone, fax, or telex, and record reasons and comments
- if debtor claims to have made payment, or to have instructed his Bank to make payment, ask for the date, name of Bank, through whom instructions given, and details of any reference numbers etc
- keep up the pressure at frequent intervals, by telephoning, and/or by fax, and/or by telex direct, or via the Agent

If trading on Open Account terms you might (dependent on local country requirements) have to make written demand for payment, by means of a Statement, and Bill of Exchange – see Protest (this section)

Always ask for overdue amounts to be paid by Direct Bank Transfer (URGENT SWIFT/Telegraphic Transfer) to your Bank Account, even though the original payment terms were otherwise

---

## DEBT COLLECTION AGENCIES

Debt Collection procedures vary in different countries

- your Agent should be aware of procedures and requirements
- there are time limitations in some countries
- procedures can be costly

If you don't have an Agent, the following might be able to advise:

- Your Bank's International Branch should be able to obtain appropriate information from either its own Branch in the country, or through an approach to its Correspondent Bank
- the Regional Office of the DTI, using the services of the British Embassy or High Commission in the debtor's country
- your local Chamber of Commerce liaising with a local Chamber in the debtor's country

- your Accountants if they have a network of overseas offices, or have links with a local firm of accountants in the debtor's country/locality

Your agent, or the above contacts, should also be able to identify reputable Debt Collection Agencies and/or legal representatives through whom you can pursue recovery of overdue debts

- anyone acting for you will require copy documentation to support your claim for payment
- you should attempt to ascertain the likely costs involved in pursuing your claim

Debt Collection procedures are not always effective in securing the payment of overdue debts, and can prove to be costly

Monitoring credit periods and payment performance, and taking early action to contact overdue customers and speed up payment, can help to prevent loss situations arising

---

## PROTEST ACTION

Protest action for non-payment of debts, or non-acceptance of term Bills of Exchange, is possible in most countries of the World

- it is generally a pre-requisite to pursuing a debt through court action
- it simplifies court action

The Procedure requires an approved representative:

- either Solicitor, Notary Public, Legal Attorney, or another person where local law so permits, and in some countries there is a procedure known as a Householder's Protest
- to attend the debtor's premises and make demand for payment
- if payment is then refused, the reasons are noted, and a form of words used, ie 'I protest ................' and further demand for payment is made
- a Form of Protest document will be completed and attested, and this, together with the relative invoices, statement, Bill of Exchange, and any other relevant documentation, can then be used to pursue collection of the overdue debt through the appropriate Court

241

In a small number of countries, Protest Action is not possible as there is no provision in local laws

In certain countries, if a Bill of Exchange is dishonoured when due for payment, local laws require Protest procedures to be carried out on the same day as dishonour occurs, and failure to do so might prevent further action to recover the amount overdue

Where method of payment for exports is by way of Bill of Exchange and documents presented through your own Bank, to the buyer's Bank, the Bill for Collection form can be used to give instructions to the buyer's bank/Bank in the buyer's country, to arrange for Protest in the event of non-payment, or non-acceptance

– the bank used will use the appropriate party to make the Protest

Details of protest are often published in local journals and the threat of protest action can be a sufficient deterrent to a defaulting buyer who wishes to avoid being blacklisted in his local community

The effect of Protest action varies according to local law and practice in different countries

---

NCM/TI/ECGD Credit Risk Insurance policy holders are required to take all steps necessary to protect the validity of overseas debts, and the Credit Risk insurer will instruct/advise on procedures to be adopted if a debt becomes overdue

KEEP YOUR CREDIT RISK INSURER INFORMED

# Insurance of Goods In Transit

**IMPORTANT** – You must establish WHO INSURES THE CONSIGNMENT?

THE MOVEMENT OF GOODS SHOULD BE INSURED BY EITHER THE SUPPLIER/EXPORTER, or THE BUYER

THE INSURANCE OF GOODS IN TRANSIT IS MOST IMPORTANT AND SHOULD BE INDISPENSABLE

THERE IS NO GUARANTEE OF RECOVERY OF VALUE AGAINST A CARRIER OF GOODS FOR LOSS OR DAMAGE IN TRANSIT

- If any recovery is made it is unlikely to be for the full value of the consignment lost or damaged
- There are legally defined limits covering compensation claims Carriers are required to pay

DISCUSS THE INSURANCE OF GOODS IN TRANSIT TO FOREIGN COUNTRIES WITH:

|         | – Your Insurance Company, Broker, or Agent |
| ------- | ------------------------------------------ |
| and/or  | – Your Bank's International Branch          |
| and/or  | – Your Freight Forwarder                    |

Your UK Goods in Transit Insurance Policy will require extending to cover Goods in Transit to Overseas countries

WHEN COSTING YOUR GOODS FOR SALE OVERSEAS, INCLUDE THE COST OF INSURANCE IN YOUR CALCULATIONS

REMEMBER YOUR INSURER WILL EXPECT YOU TO ENSURE

THAT THE PROTECTION AND PACKAGING OF GOODS FOR
TRANSIT OVERSEAS IS FULLY CARRIED OUT

- If goods are not packed to prevent damage, your insurance
  cover may not be valid
- Claims for goods not properly and adequately packed may not
  be paid, causing loss

## Who is expected to Insure the goods?

Where insurance is included in the Delivery/Shipping Terms as
shown below, it is the SELLER'S responsibility to insure goods in
transit

| | | |
|---|---|---|
| CIF | Cost, Insurance and Freight | SELLER'S |
| CIP | Carriage and Insurance | RESPONSIBILITY |
| | paid to | TO INSURE |

'INCOTERMS 1990' published by the International Chamber of
Commerce, Publication No 460

Whilst under the Incoterms 1990 shown below the Seller is shown
as having no obligation to insure the goods, clearly the Seller
should ensure the Buyer has, or will insure the goods. If
necessary, and if in any doubt, the seller should arrange for
protection under 'SELLER'S INTEREST COVER'

Shipping Terms:

| | | |
|---|---|---|
| EXW | Ex-works | — SELLER NO OBLIGATION |
| FCA | Free Carrier | — SELLER NO OBLIGATION |
| CFR | Cost and Freight | — SELLER NO OBLIGATION |
| FOB | Free on Board | — SELLER NO |
| FAS | Free alongside Ship | OBLIGATION |
| CPT | Carriage paid to | — SELLER NO OBLIGATION |
| DAF | Delivered at Frontier | |

DES          Delivered Ex Ship
DEQ          Delivered Ex Quay      – SELLER NO
DDU          Delivered Duty Unpaid      OBLIGATION
DDP          Delivered Duty Paid

---

## SELLER'S INTEREST COVER

Whenever the BUYER agrees to insure the goods in transit, the SELLER relies on the BUYER to undertake this responsibility

If the BUYER does not insure the goods in transit,

- OR   if the insurance cover does not adequately reflect the value of the goods being shipped

- OR   if the insurance cover does not fully cover 'All-Risks' likely to be encountered during the transit journey

- OR   if there are exchange control limitations on claims paid

THERE IS, THEREFORE, A POTENTIAL RISK FOR THE SELLER

---

THE SELLER'S INTERESTS IN THE VALUE OF THE GOODS BEING SHIPPED MIGHT BE COMPROMISED IN THE FOLLOWING CIRCUMSTANCES:

- The seller is to be paid on terms OTHER THAN Irrevocable Letter of Credit,

   - OR   Cash received with order

   - OR   other form where payment cannot be influenced by the buyer or non-arrival of goods

TO COVER SUCH EVENTUALITY, the SELLER would be wise to ask his Goods in Transit Insurer to provide

- SELLER'S INTEREST INSURANCE COVER on all consignments where the BUYER is responsible for insuring the goods, and PAYMENT is on:

   - Open Account terms

   - Bill for Collection terms

SELLER'S INTEREST COVER should not be disclosed or made known to the Overseas BUYER, nor his Insurance Company

245

SELLER'S INTEREST COVER can protect any retained interest in the consignment

---

## MARINE CARGO INSURANCE CLAUSES

| INSTITUTE CARGO CLAUSES (A) (For Air shipments, INSTITUTE AIR CARGO CLAUSES relate) | – Offer the widest scope of cover normally available |
|---|---|
| | – Effectively 'ALL Risks' cover |
| | – Covers Total or Partial Loss or damage to cargo |

---

| INSTITUTE CARGO CLAUSES (B) | – Restricted to claims caused by Fire, Explosion, or Perils of the Sea OR Overturning, or Derailment of a cargo on land |
|---|---|
| | – Loss overboard covered |
| | – Drop damage whilst loading or unloading from a vessel covered |

---

| INSTITUTE CARGO CLAUSES (C) | – Minimum protection normally offered |
|---|---|
| | – Restricted to claims caused by Fire, Explosion, or Perils of the Sea OR Overturning, or Derailment of a cargo on land |
| | – DOES NOT COVER CARGO OVERBOARD OR DROPPED WHILST LOADING/UNLOADING |

For a more detailed summary of the Institute Cargo Clauses, consult your Insurer, or Freight Forwarder

---

There is a term GENERAL AVERAGE – this is included in all
Marine Goods in Transit Insurance Policies 'A', 'B' and 'C'
– Does not normally concern the Exporter
– Where part of a ship's cargo is lost or jettisoned overboard to
  secure the vessel's safety, the loss will be covered by the
  Insurers of the other cargo consignments on board and saved
  by the jettisoning
– The Exporter suffering such loss would claim under his Goods
  in Transit Policy in the normal way

---

## Special Clauses

| INSTITUTE WAR CLAUSES<br>INSTITUTE STRIKE CLAUSES | – Provide Insurance<br>only in respect of Actual<br>Damage caused |
|---|---|
| | – Do not provide protection for<br>delays or financial loss which<br>might occur from such action |

---

## INSURANCE VALUE

It is normal practice for insurance values to be up-lifted by 10% (ie
CIF value + 10%), or by a higher margin if this is specifically
required

---

## LOSSES NOT INSURED

| Poor Packing | – Packing should be sufficient to prevent damage in transit in normal transit conditions |
|---|---|
| Inherent Vice | – Conditions which might allow/permit pilferage or directed damage |
| Unseaworthiness | – Of the carrying vessel, where this is known or suspected |
| Delay | – Delays caused by strikes, or any financial loss that may result from strike delays |
| Financial Losses | – Not insured howsoever caused |

247

War & Strikes     —   There are special clauses covering these
                      risks:
                      Institute War Clauses
                      Institute Strike Clauses

---

If your goods are to be stored in a warehouse abroad prior to
actual sale, discuss insurance cover with your Insurer

If your goods are to be TRANSHIPPED EN ROUTE TO THE BUYER,
advise your Insurer of the details

Poor protection and inadequate packing of goods increase the
risks for your Insurer and, if claims result, your insurance
premiums could increase substantially

Use of a good packer, a good Freight Forwarder, and First Class
Shipping Lines where possible, should minimise insurance
premium costs

---

## CLAIM CONSIDERATIONS

When LOSS or DAMAGE has occurred, the Insured has a duty to
take action to mitigate or reduce the loss wherever possible

— This is a legal requirement under the Marine Insurance Act
  1906 (it refers to the duty to act as a prudent uninsured)

— THE INSURED MUST ADVISE HIS BROKER OR INSURANCE
  COMPANY IMMEDIATELY DAMAGE OR LOSS IS KNOWN,
  WITH AS MUCH INFORMATION ON THE CIRCUMSTANCES AS
  IS KNOWN

— the Broker and/or Insurance Company will give instructions to
  the Insured, and these should be followed without delay

— if goods are off-loaded at a port, other than the intended port of
  discharge, the facts as they are known should be reported to the
  Broker and/or Insurance Company without delay

    — failure to advise such facts may result in Insurance cover not
      applying to the off-loaded goods

    — in addition, in such circumstances, every effort must be
      made to have the goods safeguarded in secure
      accommodation

— treat all insurance matters urgently at all times, DO NOT DELAY

---

UNDERSTAND THE CONDITIONS OF YOUR GOODS IN TRANSIT
INSURANCE POLICY

---

Insurance Certificates or copy Policies, required for presentation
under Irrevocable Letters of Credit with other documents, must
be dated/issued not later than the date of despatch from the
seller's premises, OR the shipment date, OR taking in charge
date

The date on an Insurance Certificate/Insurance Policy is not
retrospective

Insurance cover is regarded as effective from the date on the
Certificate or Policy

Insurance Certificates/Policies should be endorsed by the
INSURED to make them a 'Bearer' document, so that any claims
can be made by the buyer in his country

# Moving the Goods – Using a Freight Forwarder

251

## 1. USING A FREIGHT FORWARDER

The role of the FREIGHT FORWARDER in ensuring your goods reach the buyer is a key one

You have to entrust the FREIGHT FORWARDER with your goods, and to take all steps to deliver those goods safely to your customer

It is important therefore that you use a reputable FREIGHT FORWARDER

Many are members of the BIFA (British International Freight Association) which has standards of operation within the freight industry

---

When you receive an order from overseas, if transportation by SEA, AIR, RAIL or ROAD is required, contact a FREIGHT FORWARDER

They will advise on:

– most appropriate route and method of transportation
– shipping/air/rail/road/postal/courier services
– space booking times to ensure goods get moved
– packing and marking requirements
– customs clearance and documentation
– transportation of dangerous goods
– any difficulties likely to be encountered in moving goods
– documentation requirements, including legalisation of documents where this is required to meet importing country requirements
– insurance of goods
– cost of freight
– cost of Freight Forwarder's services and expenses incurred

---

If you have a LETTER OF CREDIT for the transaction, give the FREIGHT FORWARDER a photocopy: this will

- assist the accurate preparation of documents to meet the requirements of the Letter of Credit
- ensure that **accurate documentation**, prepared and presented to the Advising Bank within the validity of the Letter of Credit, should ensure you get paid on first presentation, OR under a Term Letter of Credit, your Bill of Exchange (Draft) is Accepted by the Bank for payment on the later maturity date
- assist the FREIGHT FORWARDER to meet any specific requirements of the Letter of Credit:
    - to use named shipping lines to certain countries
    - labelling and shipping marks
    - 'age-of-carrying-vessel' certificates
    - any other declarations/requirements

---

**Moving the Goods – How To Choose a Freight Forwarder**

There are many reputable and well-known FREIGHT FORWARDERS

Many are nationally known

Equally there are smaller and more local FREIGHT FORWARDERS

---

SIZE OF ORGANISATION SHOULD NOT MATTER
- ATTENTION TO DETAIL
- ACCURACY IN PREPARATION OF DOCUMENTATION
- QUALITY AND SPEED OF SERVICE SHOULD MATTER

---

You can consult:
- another exporting company
- local Chamber of Commerce
- local Export Club
- trade press
- Yellow Pages

OR

BIFA:

>The British International Freight Association
>(Incorporating the Institute of Freight Forwarders)
>Redfern House,
>Browells Lane,
>Feltham,
>Middx, TW13 7EP
>
>Tel: 0181 844 2266
>Fax: 0181 890 5546

BIFA membership requires provision of a High Quality Service

- evidence that experienced qualified personnel are employed within the organisation
- adequate liability insurance cover
- conformity with the Association's Code of Conduct

BIFA members display the BIFA symbol and registered number
In the event of problems or disputes, BIFA will take up complaints

---

Other contacts:

>Freight Transport Association,
>Hermes House,
>157 St John's Road,
>Tunbridge Wells,
>Kent, TN4 9UZ
>
>Tel: 01892 526171
>Fax: 01892 534989

---

AICES:

>Association of International Courier and Express Services,
>Unit 1B, Galleymead Road,
>Colnbrook,
>Berks, SL3 0EN
>
>Tel: 01753 680550
>Fax: 01753 681710

Beware of cheap freight rates
THE ROLE OF THE FREIGHT FORWARDER IS A KEY ONE

---

### LLOYDS EUROPEAN SHIPPING GUIDE

A quarterly publication, provides exporters with comprehensive coverage of shipping lines' services from European ports to destinations worldwide

Listings in destination and alphabetical order include:

– the shipping line
– type of service (eg container or ro-ro)
– frequency and days of service
– name of agent

Headings are in English, French and German

---

**Further details from:**

**Lloyds of London Press Ltd,**
**Sheepen Place,**
**Colchester, Essex, CO3 3LP**
Tel: 01206 772394

## 20.2 PACKAGING REQUIREMENTS

### PACKAGING

Packaging of goods and the medium upon which they are delivered (pallets or outer packaging) are important considerations

Legislation in EU countries is being introduced to enforce the use of bio-degradable materials and/or materials which are recyclable. If packaging materials do not meet this criterion your goods may not be allowed into the buyer's country, or the buyer may be required to return the materials to the supplier at the supplier's expense

A 'green spot' code applies in Germany and is required to be shown on all packaging, and other countries are likely to follow with their own 'green packaging' restrictions

Some countries outside Europe also have restrictions on the materials used to package goods, and may prohibit use of:

– timber with bark remaining

– straw, hay and similar materials

**Restrictions relating to packaging materials are detailed in the country-by-country section of the CRONER 'REFERENCE BOOK FOR EXPORTERS', and it is vitally important that these requirements are fully understood by exporters. See Appendix C5–4 for address**

**Consult your Export packaging company and/or your Freight Forwarder for advice and guidance**

# Temporary Export of Goods

The temporary Export and Re-import of goods must be covered by an ATA CARNET (for use between UK and most other countries outside the European Union)

Goods for exhibition display or required for other marketing purposes, commercial samples, or professional equipment, must be covered by a CARNET to meet strict Customs requirements and avoid the need to complete full Customs Export and Re-import procedures

Goods covered by a CARNET are not liable to import charges in the destination country or countries

If goods are not subsequently re-exported from the destination country after the stated use, Import Duties would be payable

---

**ATA CARNET**

Obtained from The London Chamber of Commerce & Industry and a number of agent Chambers around the UK – there is a charge. See Appendix D1

Security may be required to cover any duty or taxes which may become payable if the export and re-import requirements are not fully met

– to meet this security requirement, your Bank **may be prepared** to join in the Carnet Application Form as Surety for you, in effect as guarantor for any duty which may become payable

Carnet procedures include the issue and subsequent completion of export voucher(s) and re-importation voucher(s) to cover the precise number of countries the goods will enter

Customs authorities in each country of import will set a time limit date for re-exportation of the goods, and if not met, import duties may become payable by the Carnet Guarantor, who in turn will seek reimbursement from the exporter

The following information must be specified:

1. The holder's name and address
2. The name of the Carnet user
3. The period of validity which may not exceed one year
4. The intended use of the goods to be covered by the Carnet
5. The country or list of countries for which the Carnet is to be valid
6. A comprehensive list of the goods covered by the Carnet, including identification of them, marks, numbers, and this information must also be clearly marked on packaging

---

**Export Procedure**

a. **Accompanied baggage** If goods are to be exported in baggage the passenger must allow ample time to ensure they can be presented to Customs at the port or airport of departure

b. **Exports as freight** The exporter must ensure that arrangements are made to produce the goods and the Carnet to Customs prior to departure. Again, plenty of time must be allowed for. In addition, the Carnet number must be inserted on the export loading list.

Note: A Carnet cannot be used for exports by post. The London Chamber of Commerce & Industry will advise which Agent Chambers have the authority to issue ATA CARNETS. See Appendix D1

> London Chamber of Commerce & Industry
> 69 Cannon Street,
> London, EC4N 5AB
> Tel: 0171 248 4444

# Liabilities Under a Bond or Guarantee

Many Export Opportunities come through Contract Tendering which is advertised internationally. Those businesses interested in Tendering or Bidding for the contract will be provided with a set of tender documents specifying the Purchaser's requirements, and inviting price bids to be submitted to a stated authority. Invariably there is a requirement for the party 'tendering' for the contract, to submit either:

— Earnest Money     — a percentage of the tender price paid to the potential purchaser as evidence of the tenderer's seriousness and sufficiency in bidding for the contract

OR — A Bid or Tender Bond — a legal document in substitution for Earnest Money, issued by the tenderer's Banker's

And if the Contract is awarded, for the successful Contractor to provide a 'Performance Guarantee' in substitution for the original Bid or Tender Bond, through his Bankers

---

There are other forms of Guarantee and Warranty which are covered in this section

— ALL BONDS AND GUARANTEES ARE A REAL LIABILITY

— If you are required to provide a Bond or Guarantee OF ANY TYPE, CONSULT YOUR BANK'S INTERNATIONAL BRANCH AT THE EARLIEST OPPORTUNITY

— If you are provided with a specimen form of wording, PROVIDE A COPY TO YOUR BANK'S INTERNATIONAL BRANCH AND ASK FOR THEIR ADVICE

— DO NOT WAIT UNTIL A FEW DAYS BEFORE THE CONTRACT TENDER SUBMISSION DATE

- DO NOT AGREE TO ANY FORM OF WORDING UNTIL YOU HAVE DISCUSSED THE REQUIREMENT WITH YOUR BANK'S INTERNATIONAL BRANCH
- DO NOT SUBMIT BIDS/TENDERS FOR WORK YOUR BUSINESS MAY HAVE DIFFICULTY IN FULFILLING
- **EXPIRY DATES QUOTED CANNOT BE ASSUMED TO BE THE FINAL DATE OF A BOND OR GUARANTEE LIABILITY**
  - CHECK THE POSITION OF THE EXPIRY DATE WITH YOUR BANK; THEY WILL ADVISE WHEN THE EXPIRY IS EFFECTIVE
- Extension of an Expiry Date is not normally provided for in the wording of a Bond or Guarantee
  - Extension is often requested by the Buyer or his Bank, by a telex, requesting extension to a given date, or for a given period, OR TO PAY UP
  - Failure to extend thus requires the Bank TO PAY UP, and they will then debit your account with the amount paid up
- Seek an estimate of the Bank Charges and expenses for the issue of Bonds and Guarantees, both your own Bank's, and those of the Overseas Bank, and seek to include these costs in your contract price

  Note   –   Charges are made relating to the amount and time the liability is outstanding

---

- DO NOT UNDERESTIMATE THE LIABILITY UNDER A BOND AND/OR GUARANTEE ENTERED INTO BY YOUR BANK ON YOUR BUSINESS'S BEHALF
- You will have to arrange a facility with your Bank, **BEFORE** it will agree to issue Bonds and Guarantees on your businesses's behalf – ALLOW TIME FOR THESE DISCUSSIONS AND FOR THE BANK TO CONSIDER ITS DECISION
- REMEMBER, a BOND or GUARANTEE is a CONTINGENT LIABILITY ON YOUR BUSINESS UNTIL YOU ARE NOTIFIED **BY YOUR BANK** THAT THE LIABILITY HAS EXPIRED OR BEEN CANCELLED
- If your overseas Buyer advises you that they have cancelled your Bond or Guarantee, and no longer rely on it

260

- ask them to instruct their Banker to advise your Bank in writing/by telex that the liability can be cancelled
- advise your Bank's International Branch of any communication you receive relating to a Bond or Guarantee liability

Note  – Bonds and Guarantees issued under overseas country laws are more difficult to cancel than those issued subject to English law – your Bank's International Branch will advise on this aspect. For those issued subject to overseas country law, your Bank will be required to 'Indemnify' the overseas issuing Bank – tantamount to the same liability as actually issuing the Bond or Guarantee

---

There are a variety of types of BONDS and **GUARANTEES:**

| | |
|---|---|
| **BID BOND AND TENDER BOND** | – Issued to support an Exporter's 'Bid' or 'Tender' for an overseas supply contract |
| | – An Indication to the overseas Buyer that the 'bidder' or 'tenderer' has serious intent towards winning the contract |
| | – Usually required to be valid for three months beyond the 'bid/tender' closing date, BUT |
| | – **DO NOT ASSUME THE BOND WILL BE LAPSED AUTOMATICALLY** (see later reference to validity dates) |
| **PERFORMANCE BONDS** | – Issued to ensure PERFORMANCE of the Contract by the Exporter/Contractor |
| | – Can cover all types of contract including 'machinery or equipment' performance |
| | – Validity period can vary |

　　　　　　　　　　　　　　　　– Value will be expressed as a
　　　　　　　　　　　　　　　　　percentage of the contract price
　　　　　　　　　　　　　　　　– FAILURE TO PERFORM, EITHER
　　　　　　　　　　　　　　　　　BY THE CONTRACTOR IN
　　　　　　　　　　　　　　　　　COMPLETION OF CONTRACT, or
　　　　　　　　　　　　　　　　　THE FAILURE OF MACHINERY OR
　　　　　　　　　　　　　　　　　EQUIPMENT TO PERFORM TO THE
　　　　　　　　　　　　　　　　　REQUIRED PERFORMANCE
　　　　　　　　　　　　　　　　　LEVELS, MAY CAUSE THE BUYER
　　　　　　　　　　　　　　　　　TO CLAIM AN AMOUNT UP TO THE
　　　　　　　　　　　　　　　　　VALUE OF THE PERFORMANCE
　　　　　　　　　　　　　　　　　GUARANTEE

**ADVANCE**　　　　　　　　　– Gives protection to a Buyer who
**PAYMENT**　　　　　　　　　　may make a payment to the
**GUARANTEE**　　　　　　　　supplier in ADVANCE of the
　　　　　　　　　　　　　　　　　contract being carried out, or
　　　　　　　　　　　　　　　　　machinery/equipment being
　　　　　　　　　　　　　　　　　delivered

　　　　　　　　　　　　　　　　– Can be made Conditional on the
　　　　　　　　　　　　　　　　　Advance Payment actually being
　　　　　　　　　　　　　　　　　received by the supplier (the
　　　　　　　　　　　　　　　　　Advance Payment Guarantee is
　　　　　　　　　　　　　　　　　issued with a non-operative
　　　　　　　　　　　　　　　　　clause, and when Advance
　　　　　　　　　　　　　　　　　Payment is received, the issuing
　　　　　　　　　　　　　　　　　Bank will issue an 'operative'
　　　　　　　　　　　　　　　　　amendment)

　　　　　　　　Note　– The Bank issuing the APG may
　　　　　　　　　　　　　　　　　require the exporter to place the
　　　　　　　　　　　　　　　　　advance funds on a separate
　　　　　　　　　　　　　　　　　account as security for the APG
　　　　　　　　　　　　　　　　　issue (discuss use of the advance
　　　　　　　　　　　　　　　　　funds with your Bank) – do not
　　　　　　　　　　　　　　　　　automatically assume you can
　　　　　　　　　　　　　　　　　have use of the funds advanced

　　　　　　　　　　　　　　　　– Repayment of the advance funds
　　　　　　　　　　　　　　　　　can be demanded if the supplier

fails to commence or complete the contract

**RETENTION BONDS**
- Issued to the Buyer to allow the Buyer to release the final payment to the supplier
- Gives the buyer security for due performance after the supply contract has been completed, for an agreed period
- In the event of non-performance during the agreed period, up to the value of the Retention Bond may be demanded by the Buyer
- Can be issued 'non-operative' until Retention Monies have been received by the supplier (usually received by the Issuing Bank) thereafter an 'operative' amendment is issued

**WARRANTY BONDS**
- Issued to the Buyer to 'warrant' the performance of equipment during a maintenance or warranty period

**GUARANTEES TO OVERSEAS BANKS TO SECURE BORROWING**
- The Overseas Lending Bank will specify the Guarantee format they require to secure the borrowing requirement

- This may be in the form of a Standby Letter of Credit – see Section 15

# Barter Trade/Counter Trade/Off-Set Trade/ Compensation Trade

There is good business to be gained through the types of trade listed in the heading to this section

DO NOT TURN DOWN OPPORTUNITIES BECAUSE PAYMENT TERMS WHICH ARE OTHER THAN PAYMENT IN A CURRENCY (Sterling or other) ARE OFFERED/SUGGESTED

THIS TYPE OF TRADE IS NOT CONFINED TO LARGE DEALS

Often less than 100% of a proposed UK export deal will be suggested for settlement by one of these types of trade

Full-value Barter Trade is not common

UK Exporters should ensure:

- the barter element is kept to a minimum
- they contact 'barter-trade specialist trading houses' for advice on procedures and tactics to use during negotiations, commissions payable for the goods to be sold, and the types of goods to avoid if at all possible. They may also advise on what types of goods are currently being offered
- re-selling commissions/costs are included in the selling price of the goods being exported from the UK where this is possible
- the sale 'contract' is separate from the 'counter-trade' contract where possible

DO NOT TURN BARTER TRADE OPPORTUNITIES AWAY

THEY CAN BE REWARDING

TAKE ADVICE  –  The DTI can provide a brochure and contact names

–  The East European Trade Council, 25 Victoria Street, London, SW1H 0EX – 0171 222 7622 can provide a brochure and advice on request

- Bank International Branches may also be able to provide information and advice and contact names
- If export transaction is insured by NCM/TI/ECGD or other credit risk insurer, you should advise them of the proposed deal, and ensure export insurance cover applies

# Awareness of Exchange Controls in Overseas Countries

Even though the UK has no effective Exchange Control procedures in operation (not to be confused with UK Export Controls – see Section 1.1.1), there are many countries around the world where they are still in operation

They are procedures to control Imports INTO, and Exports FROM individual countries

They are legal requirements and there are penalties for breaching the Exchange Control regulations

Exchange Control procedures vary between individual countries and may cover:

- requirement for Import Licences
- the issue of Letters of Credit
- the transfer of funds
- the availability of foreign currencies
- the use of bank accounts in the country
- the payment of commissions etc
- the import and export of currency notes by travellers
- documentary requirements
- legalisation of documents before payment for goods allowed
- pre-shipment inspection of goods

Advice on Exchange Control procedures should be available from your Bank's International Branch

or from an International Accountancy firm

or the BOTB Hints to Exporter series of booklets

or the Embassy or Consulate of the country in the UK

or the International Chamber of Commerce

or the British Embassy/Consulate Commercial Section in the country concerned

Delays in receiving payment may result from the requirement for the Importer to satisfy his country's Exchange Control procedures

In most instances there are no delays, particularly where a Letter of Credit is received, but the issue of the Letter of Credit might be subject to short delay due to the Importing country procedures

# Pre-Shipment Inspection of Exports

(where this is a requirement for selected markets)

---

DO NOT UNDER-ESTIMATE OR ATTEMPT TO IGNORE THE REQUIREMENT FOR PRE-SHIPMENT INSPECTION OF GOODS TO BE EXPORTED

PRE-SHIPMENT INSPECTION (PSI) REQUIREMENTS HAVE CAUSED PROBLEMS IN THE PAST FOR EXPORTERS

WHERE PSI IS REQUIRED, A 'CLEAN REPORT OF FINDINGS' (or, for certain countries, one copy of your final invoice with Special Security Label added) WILL BE REQUIRED TO PRESENT WITH OTHER DOCUMENTS BEFORE YOU CAN EXPECT TO BE PAID

IF YOU FAIL TO SATISFY THE PSI INSPECTOR, AND THERE ARE UNRESOLVED PROBLEMS REGARDING QUANTITY, QUALITY OR PRICE OF THE SHIPMENT, A 'NON-NEGOTIABLE REPORT OF FINDINGS' WILL BE ISSUED (or your final invoice without the Special Security Label returned by the PSI Agency)

A 'NON-NEGOTIABLE REPORT OF FINDINGS' (or invoice without Special Security label) WILL NOT BE ACCEPTABLE UNDER A LETTER OF CREDIT SPECIFYING A '**CLEAN** REPORT OF FINDINGS' OR INVOICE WITH SECURITY LABEL TO BE PRESENTED WITH DOCUMENTS TO OBTAIN PAYMENT

AN EXPORTER RECEIVING A 'NON-NEGOTIABLE REPORT OF FINDINGS' (or invoice without Special Security Label) WILL HAVE TO RELY ON THE AUTHORITIES IN THE IMPORTING NATION TO AUTHORISE PAYMENT – There are cases where payment has not been released

---

EXPORTERS WHO ARE UNABLE TO RESOLVE DIFFERENCES WITH PRE-SHIPMENT INSPECTION AGENCIES MAY APPEAL IN

WRITING, BOTH IN THE UK AND IN THE IMPORTING COUNTRY –
The PSI Agency will give details of Appeals procedures

PRE-SHIPMENT INSPECTION AGENCIES ARE EMPLOYED BY
OVERSEAS GOVERNMENTS, AND A PSI REQUIREMENT WILL BE
NOTIFIED TO THE SUPPLIER

IMMEDIATELY YOU ARE ADVISED OF A PSI REQUIREMENT
CONTACT THE INSPECTION AGENCY NAMED TO ASCERTAIN
REQUIREMENTS, AND WHAT TIME SCALE IS INVOLVED IN
CARRYING OUT INSPECTION AFTER NOTIFICATION OF THE
EARLIEST DATE GOODS WILL BE AVAILABLE FOR INSPECTION

A PRE-SHIPMENT INSPECTION REQUIREMENT WHEN
SPECIFIED IS UNAVOIDABLE

---

## PROCEDURES

PSI AGENCIES ARE EMPLOYED BY OVERSEAS GOVERNMENTS

To prevent

- over-invoicing
- supply of sub-standard or counterfeit goods
- supply of secondhand for new goods
- substitution of goods or cargo diversion
- supply of obsolete goods for current types
- discrepancies in quantity and quality
- concealed commissions/interest charges
- non-repatriated commissions to third parties
- evasion of customs duties

To conserve Foreign Exchange

Note:   Secondhand and/or reconditioned goods must be
        specified very clearly in all documentation, and
        particularly by the Importer Buyer when he applies for
        the Import Licence issue

---

Notice to PSI Agency

- the Importing Country authorities will normally advise the
  appropriate PSI Agency in the seller's country of the supply
  contract/order placement requiring inspection

- the Seller must approach the PSI Agency for the inspection visit to be arranged
- the Seller will be required to provide the PSI Agency with a copy of the advisory document,
  - Letter of Credit or customer's order etc
- the Seller will be required to advise:
  - the location of the goods
  - when inspection will be convenient
  - who is to be contacted

CHECK ALL DOCUMENTATION REQUIREMENTS WITH THE PSI AGENCY

---

The PSI will cover:      **PRELIMINARY PRICE COMPARISON**

- EVEN THOUGH THE SELLING PRICE HAS BEEN ACCEPTED BY THE BUYER, Price Comparison will still be carried out by the PSI Agency
- the seller may be asked to justify the invoice price if the selling price is not in line with the 'prevailing export market price' as determined by the PSI Agency
- **Sales by international tender**
  - international tenders **may** be subjected to pre-shipment price comparison even after a contract has been awarded on a lowest price basis
  - the date of reference for price comparison purposes would normally be the date of closing of the tender

---

**DOCUMENTARY REQUIREMENTS**

- The PSI Agency will require a Settlement Invoice (often more than one copy) setting out specific information; and may require either an original or copy of the Movement

271

document viz Air Waybill, or Bill of Lading,
or other movement document, as
specified in the Letter of Credit or other
document

---

## FINAL PRICE COMPARISON
- final documents will be compared against
  the initial price comparison and the
  physical inspection report

IF THERE ARE NO VARIATIONS BETWEEN THE CONTRACT/
ORDER DOCUMENTS, THE INITIAL PRICE COMPARISON
DOCUMENTATION AND FINAL DOCUMENTATION, THE PSI
AGENCY SHOULD BE IN A POSITION TO ISSUE THE 'CLEAN
REPORT OF FINDINGS' OR INVOICE WITH SECURITY LABEL so
necessary for the Seller to be paid

---

REMEMBER, IN MOST INSTANCES THE GOODS WILL HAVE
BEEN DESPATCHED TO THE BUYER BEFORE YOU RECEIVE
EITHER A CLEAN REPORT OF FINDINGS, OR A NON-
NEGOTIABLE REPORT OF FINDINGS, OR YOUR INVOICE IS
RETURNED WITH (OR WITHOUT) SECURITY LABEL

---

Sellers should note that if the BASIC PRICE COMPARISON
reveals goods are invoiced BELOW VALUE when compared to the
PREVAILING EXPORT MARKET VALUE in the supplier's country,
THE PSI WILL MAKE NO APPROACH TO THE SELLER
**BEWARE – PRICING ERRORS COULD BE COSTLY**

---

**Physical Inspection of goods** will cover:
- do the goods being supplied confirm to contractural/order
  specifications
- ensure the goods meet national and international standards
- whether the goods are secondhand and/or reconditioned, and,
  if they are, that the buyer's Import Licence and contractual/
  order document so specify

272

- in the event of machinery/mechanical goods ask the PSI Agency if a working-order demonstration will be required
- special sectors; pharmaceuticals, chemicals and related products, canned foods, may be subject to testing – check requirements with the PSI Agency in advance of inspection

---

Immediately a Seller becomes aware from a Letter of Credit, or receipt of customer's order, that a PRE-SHIPMENT INSPECTION is required, CONTACT THE NAMED AGENCY – they will provide instructions and paperwork for completion
EXERCISE CARE

---

**Countries using Comprehensive Pre-Shipment Inspection**

| | | |
|---|---|---|
| ANGOLA | – Banco Nacional de Angola | SGS |

---

| | | |
|---|---|---|
| BANGLADESH | – Government | Bureau Veritas |
| BENIN | – Ministry of Finance | Bureau Veritas |
| BOLIVIA | – Ministry of Finance | SGS |
| BURUNDI | – Banque de Republique du Burundi | SGS |
| BURKINA-FASO | – Min. of Ind. Trade, Mines and Finance | SGS |

---

| | | |
|---|---|---|
| CAMEROON | – Ministries of Finance and Industry | SGS |
| CONGO | – Ministry of Finance | SGS |
| COTE D'IVOIRE (IVORY COAST) | – Ministry of Foreign Trade | SGS |

---

| | | |
|---|---|---|
| ECUADOR | – Government | Cotechna<br>SGS<br>Bureau<br>Veritas |
| ETHIOPIA | – Ministry of Finance | SGS |
| GUINEA,<br>Republic of<br>(Conakry) | – Ministry of Finance | Bureau<br>Veritas |
| GHANA | – Bank of Ghana | SGS |
| HAITI | – Ministry of Finance | SGS |
| INDONESIA | – Ministry of Trade | SGS |
| KENYA | – Central Bank | Cotecna |
| LIBERIA | – Ministry of Commerce | SGS |
| MADAGASCAR | – Government | Bureau<br>Veritas |
| MALAWI | – Government | SGS |
| MALI,<br>Republic of | – Ministry of Finance<br>& Trade | SGS |
| MAURETANIA | – Ministry of Finance | SGS |
| MEXICO | – Controlaria General | SGS<br>Bureau<br>Veritas |
| MOZAMBIQUE | – Ministry of Finance | SGS |
| NIGERIA | – Central Bank | Cotecna |

| | | |
|---|---|---|
| PAKISTAN | – Controller of Customs | Cotecna |
| PHILIPPINES | – Ministry of Finance | SGS |
| PERU | – Government | Cotecna |
| | | SGS |
| | | Bureau Veritas |

| | | |
|---|---|---|
| RWANDA | – Banque Nationale | SGS |

| | | |
|---|---|---|
| SENEGAL | – Government | SGS |
| SIERRA LEONE | – Ministry of Trade | Bureau Veritas |
| SURINAM | – Ministry of Transport, Trade and Industry | SGS |

| | | |
|---|---|---|
| TANZANIA | – Bank of Tanzania | Cotecna S.S.I. & Assoc. |
| TOGO, Republic of | – Ministries of Trade & Finance | Cotecna |

| | | |
|---|---|---|
| UGANDA | – Bank of Uganda | SGS |

| | | |
|---|---|---|
| ZAÏRE | – Banque du Zaïre | SGS |
| ZAMBIA | – Bank of Zambia | SGS |
| ZANZIBAR | – People's Bank | SGS |

For the following countries, the issue of a Clean Report of Findings, after pre-shipment inspection of the goods, will now be made in the destination country. For these countries, the Pre-Shipment Inspection Agency will return one copy of the final invoice to the exporters with a Special Security Label, which attests to the issue of the Clean Report of Findings

Countries using this method of attestation include:

CAMEROON
CONGO
COTE D'IVOIRE
EQUADOR
GHANA
INDONESIA
MALAWI
MAURETANIA
PAKISTAN
PERU
THE PHILIPPINES

Note:    The list of countries requiring an Invoice with Special Security Label, in place of a Clean Report of Findings is likely to change, and exporters receiving a Letter of Credit with a CRF specified should contact the Pre-shipment Inspection Agency **as soon as the Letter of Credit is received**, to confirm the exact requirements. If the requirement specified has changed from a CRF to an SSL Invoice (as can sometimes happen) you are advised to contact your customer and seek an amendment to the Letter of Credit, to avoid a discrepancy when documents are presented

The change from a Clean Report of Findings to an Invoice with Special Security Label affixed in no way reduces the need to comply with all pre-shipment inspection requirements

# Customs Formalities

**ALL GOODS EXPORTED FROM THE UNITED KINGDOM MUST BE IDENTIFIED BY A 'COMMODITY CODE', AND THIS SHOULD BE SHOWN ON ALL CUSTOMS AND TRANSIT DOCUMENTS**

EXPORTERS ARE LEGALLY RESPONSIBLE FOR CLASSIFYING THEIR GOODS CORRECTLY, even though a Freight Forwarder or other party may prepare documentation on the exporter's behalf, and could be penalised if goods are wrongly classified

HM Customs & Excise receive a steady stream of EUR 1s returned by overseas authorities requesting verification that the goods qualify for importation into the buyer's country at a reduced or nil rate of duty. The EUR 1 movement certificate is the passport to such relief, but there are dangers if goods are incorrectly classified. If they are, the overseas customs authority will raise a duty charge on non-qualifying goods on your customer and he will be required to pay the duty. Overseas authorities may also look back through earlier records and, if previous cases are identified, back duty will have to be paid by your customer. In addition UK customs may impose penalties

Exporters should obtain Customs Notices
– 827 (EC Preference Procedures),

- 828 (covers rules of origin EFTA/EEA),
- 829 (other preference-giving countries)

from your local Customs & Excise Advice Centre.

Procedure to determine status of goods is:

- establish the Tariff Heading (4 digit commodity code) of the goods
- refer to the Tariff Heading in Notice 828 or 829 as appropriate

Goods must fully meet all conditions to qualify for preferential status

## CUSTOMS FORMS SHOULD BE COMPLETED WITH ABSOLUTE ACCURACY

---

Customs & Excise offices, Freight Forwarders, can assist with establishing the correct classification, and a copy of the Commodity Code 'Tariff' booklet can be obtained from Customs & Excise offices, or access to a copy can be obtained through local reference libraries, European Information and/or Documentation Centres, and Chambers of Commerce

Freight Forwarders will assist with the accurate preparation of Customs Movement Certificates where these are required for movement of goods to countries outside the EU

## 1. TRADE WITHIN THE EUROPEAN UNION

NO CUSTOMS DECLARATIONS OR CLEARANCE IS REQUIRED
FOR GOODS TRADED WITHIN THE EUROPEAN UNION (EU)
MEMBER STATES

---

A new system for collecting statistics on the trade in goods
between EU countries is known as INTRASTAT

- it is a community-wide system
- requirements are similar in all EU countries
- businesses not registered for VAT, and private individuals who
  move goods within the EU have no obligations under Intrastat
- only the supply of goods between EU countries is covered
- supply of services is excluded
- it does not cover trade with countries outside the EU

---

**HM CUSTOMS & EXCISE OFFICES WILL SUPPLY AN
EXPLANATORY BOOKLET – 'A GENERAL GUIDE TO INTRASTAT'
on request**

---

There are a number of other Customs forms for use in specific
situations, EUR 1, and for postal consignments up to £1850, an
 EUR 2

# 2. TRADE WITH REST OF THE WORLD

For exports of goods to countries outside the EU, but to countries which have preference trade agreements with the EU, the following arrangements apply:

− An **EUR 1** Customs form is required for goods shipped to:

- − **EFTA** (EUROPEAN FREE TRADE ASSOCIATION) countries, viz ICELAND, NORWAY and SWITZERLAND
- − and to other countries covered by Trade Agreements, viz CYPRUS, ISRAEL, MALTA
- − for a number of former Eastern European states where special trading agreements have been signed
    - − Customs & Excise offices will advise which countries have these trading agreements

Note:     Special arrangements are being proposed for some EFTA countries to be accorded special status for trade with EU member states

− An **EUR 2** form is required for postal consignments up to £1850 in value

---

For exports to Turkey an **ATR** form is used, to determine the status, rather than the origin of the goods

---

# 3. VAT REQUIREMENTS

**All goods sold are subject to UK VAT charge except in the following circumstances:**

- for sales to buyers in EU member countries, if the BUYER'S VAT REGISTRATION NUMBER is shown on the Exporter's invoice, VAT is not chargeable
- for sales to buyers in countries OUTSIDE THE EU, invoices can be Zero-rated, and UK VAT is not chargeable

---

- for sales to PRIVATE BUYERS IN THE EU MEMBER COUNTRIES, UK VAT is chargeable

---

ALL VAT REGISTERED BUSINESSES MUST COMPLETE TWO BOXES ON THEIR VAT RETURNS
- showing the value of goods supplied to other EU countries, and the value of goods acquired from other EU countries

---

EXPORTERS ARE REQUIRED TO MAINTAIN ADEQUATE RECORDS TO ENSURE THAT ALL VAT AND INTRASTAT STATISTICS ARE ACCURATELY AND CORRECTLY RECORDED

# 4. PROCESSING OF IMPORTED GOODS FOR EXPORT

If you Export products which have been processed from goods imported from outside the EU, there are arrangements which might entitle you to claim import duty relief

- This is known as Inward Processing Relief
- For agricultural products you may also be eligible for relief of CAP (Common Agricultural Products) levies and other CAP charges
- YOU MUST APPLY BEFORE YOU IMPORT OR BUY THE GOODS

---

Customs requirements can change from time to time and at short notice, and **ALL exporters are advised to contact the HM Customs & Excise office for their locality** prior to the movement of goods, particularly if re-exports or temporary exports are involved

- they will provide booklets setting out the regulations for export of goods to other European Community countries, and to countries outside the Community

The 'Tariff' may be available at some main reference libraries or at most Customs & Excise Offices (not VAT Offices), or it can be purchased from HMSO at addresses in the phone book, or direct by post from:

> HMSO Publications Centre,
> PO Box 276,
> London, SW8 5DT

(the cost of the Tariff includes amendments which are generally issued monthly)

---

Specific country requirements are detailed in Croner's Reference Book for Exporters. (Contact address, see Appendix C5–6)

# Appendices

# UK EXPORT CLUBS

Over 70 Export Clubs and Export Associations meet regularly during the period September–June each year

New and inexperienced exporters, and those looking to become exporters, will find a warm welcome awaits them

---

Export Club objectives are:
- to stimulate interest and activity in export trade
- to provide businesses and individuals with a forum for the interchange of knowledge on all matters relating to export trading
- to encourage that interchange through lectures, debates, discussions, sponsored meetings, visits or other activities
- provide the opportunity for informal discussion
- encourage ACTIVE EXPORTING

---

Export Clubs/Associations have an active part in supporting UK businesses

Regular meetings feature one or more speakers on subjects of interest to the membership

Many Export Clubs are associated with their local Chamber of Commerce which provides for close liaison on all matters 'export'

Clubs also have the support of experienced exporters, who are always willing to offer advice and information

The DTI Overseas Trade Services and the Institute of Export are active participants and supporters of Export Clubs and Associations

---

Contact your local Club – see Appendix A2 for contact list – or write to: Harry Twells, Chairman, The Export Clubs Advisory Committee, c/o Joint Directorate, Kingsgate House, 66–74 Victoria Street, London, SW1E 6SW

# QUICK CONTACT GUIDE TO EXPORT CLUBS

## SCOTLAND

Ayrshire Export Club  G. H. Snider  01355 230325

Dumbartonshire Export Club  W. Cooper  0141 951 2121

Dumfries & Galloway Action Export  I. Clarke  01387 245000

Edinburgh & Lothian Export Club  M. Beaton  0131 225 5851

Fife Export Club  A. Russell  01592 754411 x 6276

Lanarkshire Export Forum  G. H. Snider  01355 230325

North of Scotland Export Club (Aberdeen)  R. Still  01224 212626

Scottish Borders Export Club (Galashiels)  M. Wilson
01896 755052

Tayside Export Club (Dundee)  Miss V. Lynch  01382 303810

---

## ENGLAND

### Midlands

Burton & District Export Club  M. Hunter  01283 545377

Gloucestershire Export Association  R.G. Marshall
01452 385151

North Oxfordshire Export Club  Miss Ann Jackson  01295 252221

West Midlands Export Club  T. Jones (S)  01905 640164

Worcester Export Club  T. Thomas  01432 268795

---

### Yorkshire & Humberside

East Coast Export Group, Filey  01723 514141

West Riding Branch (IOE) Leeds  G. D. Lloyd  01132 372269

Leeds & Bradford Export Exchange  Ms K. Ross  01132 363136

Rotherham International Association  K. Moss  01142 766667

Sheffield Export Club  R. Neale  01142 752394

Sheffield & District Branch (IOE)  D. Corbridge  01709 893423

South Humberside Export Association  Mrs C. Smith
01724 842109

Wakefield Export Group  A. Smith  01924 200646

York & North Yorkshire Export Club  Mrs S. Dunn  01904 629513

---

### North West

Bolton & Bury Export Club  N. Massey  01204 397350

Business Link Export Club, Cheshire  M. J. Collins  01606 734200

Cumbria Export Club  P. Fearn  01228 812255

Central & West Lancashire Export Club, Preston
Mrs N. Marsden  01772 653000

East Lancashire Export Club, Burnley  Mrs V. Miles
01254 388400

Halton Chamber of Commerce Export Club  D. Ogden
0151 4209420

Liverpool & North West Coast Branch IOE  R. Perkins
0151 236 4871

North Western Export Club, Manchester  E. Greenhalgh
01204 523367

Oldham Export Club  M. Hilton  0161 633 6133

Rochdale Chamber of Commerce Export Club  E. Lamb
01706 343810

Wigan Export Club  Ms L. Hardcastle  01942 324547

---

### East Midlands

North Derbyshire Export Association  Mrs J. Whiting
01246 211277

Southern Derbyshire Export Club  A. Monroe  01332 347031

East Midlands Branch (IOE) Leicester  Mrs M. Clarke
01162 871944

Leicestershire Export Club  Ms S. Bolton  01162 559944

Lincolnshire & East Nottinghamshire Export Association
Mrs J. McGeogham  01522 523333

Export Association of Nottingham  Miss N. Hardcastle
01159 415193

North Nottinghamshire Export Club  R. Clifford  01623 420366

---

## North-East

North East Export Club  B. Smith  01642 250888

---

South-West & South Coast

Avon International Business Club, Bristol  Miss J. Clarke
01179 737373

Cornwall Export Club, Redruth  M. Puzey  01209 314884

European Business Club, Bristol  R. Dennerey  01275 856700

International Business Club of the Southampton Chamber of
Commerce  Miss C. Farley  01703 223541

Isle of Wight Dev. Board Export Forum  01983 826222

North Devon Export Centre  Angela Brooks  01271 24808

Plymouth Chamber Export Services  B. Pickett  01752 221151

South Devon Export Group  G. A. Best  01803 296244

South East Hampshire Chamber of International Business Club
(Portsmouth)  M. Stead  01705 666622

South West Branch IOE, Bristol  Mrs P. Humphrey  01179 570699

Somerset Export Club  P. Lewis  01373 465151

Swindon Chamber of Commerce Export Club  C. Liew
01793 616544

Wessex Export Club  Mrs M. Wareham  01202 448804

---

## Outer London North & Anglia

Cambridge International Trade Group  G. Lee  01223 237414

Greater Peterborough Exporters Club  C. Street  01733 342658

Hemel Hempstead & District Export Club  Mrs A. Banks
01727 862568

Luton & District Export Association  Mrs C. Smart  01582 23456

Norfolk & Waveney International Trade Group  V. Honour
01603 782334

Suffolk International Trade Group  R. Baker  01473 210611

## WALES

Mid-Wales Export Association  Ms B. Richards  01938 555000

North Wales Exporters Club  G. E. Roberts  01492 544288

South Wales Exporters Association  Miss J. Rees  01633 251331

West Wales Exporters Association  Mrs S. Langdon
01792 473377

## London/Outer London & South East

Eastern Thames Valley Export Club  J. Rolstone  01753 577877

East Kent Exporters Club  S. D. S. Brown  01303 254197

Institute of Export, North Sussex & Surrey Export Club
R. K. Fendall  01892 536444

Kent Export Association  J. D. Day  01634 830001/2

Reading & District Export Association  J. N. Walters
01734 594424

South of England Exporters Association, Kent
S. V. Robbens  01732 452219

Southside Export Club, S. London  G. MacDonagh  0171 928 4722

Sussex Export Club, Brighton  P. Chester  01273 326282

Watford International Business Association  A. J. Bailey
01923 234469

West London Export Group  M. Voss  0181 965 7700

## NORTHERN IRELAND

International Trade Association (Belfast)  Mrs V. McWilliam
09603 52321

# EXPORT TRAINING – THE INSTITUTE OF EXPORT

An independent, registered educational charity providing professional training for those engaged in exporting activity

The Institute supports training courses at Colleges throughout the UK, leading to the Institute's professional examinations and export industry recognised qualifications

The Institute also has links with Universities whose degree courses at BA, MA and MBA level have been produced to conform with its professional qualification

There is a Home Study course for individuals

A Distance Learning Programme for companies wishing to become exporters

An Export Staff Recruitment Consultancy to assist members and exporting companies

Export training courses on a variety of subjects are run by Institute **Accredited Trainers and these courses are available to non-members of the Institute**, subject to course fees

A 'help-line' for export and trading queries is available

---

An Institute of Export qualification is evidenced by the addition of designated letters after a member's name in accordance with qualification and experience

The qualifications/designations are recognised Worldwide

Grades of membership   –  Student member

                            –  Associate member **(AMIEx)**

                            –  Member by experience **(MIEx)** – minimum of 10 years' exporting experience and holds a position of responsibility

                            –  Graduate member **(MIEx (Grad))** – member who has passed the

> Institute's professional examinations or their equivalents
> – Corporate membership for businesses

Benefits of membership:

- professional status: designated letters after member's name
- bi-monthly journal – EXPORT TODAY – to keep members up to date on all matters 'export', and a quarterly newsletter 'EXPORTER'
- Official Handbook issued to members annually
- local Branch membership (21 branches around the UK meeting regularly, each with an informative programme of speakers)
- free information and advisory service to members
- opportunity to purchase books on exporting (at members' special prices)
- Member Discounts on short course fees

---

IMPROVE YOUR EXPORT PERFORMANCE THROUGH TRAINING

Write now for more information:

> The Institute of Export,
> Export House,
> 64 Clifton Street,
> London, EC2A 4HB
>
> Tel:  0171 247 9812
> Fax: 0171 377 5343

# PROFESSIONAL EXPORT COURSES

The following institutions provide evening/day release courses in preparation for the professional examinations of The Institute

## LONDON & HOME COUNTIES

**City & Islington College,** Willen House, 8–26 Bath Street, London, EC1V 9PL  Mr T. Rawnsley  0171 638 4171 ext 321, or 0171 614 0321

**London College of Printing & Distributive Trades,** 65 Davies Street, London, W1Y 2DA  Mr M. Barnes  0171 514 6500 ext 6918

**ENAIP,** 134 Clerkenwell Road, London, EC1R 5DL (Italians only) Ms L. Bugitti  0171 278 0139/0

**Aylesbury College,** Oxford Road, Aylesbury, Bucks, HP21 8PD Mr R. Winks  01296 434111

**Croydon College,** Croydon Business School, Fairfield, Croydon, CR9 1DX  Mr A. Bravo  0181 686 5700 ext 3127

**Guildford College of Further & Higher Education,** Stoke Park, Guildford, Surrey, GU1 1EZ  Ms J. Morton  01485 31251 ext 4941

**Hammersmith and West London College,** Gliddon Road, Hammersmith, London, W14 9BL  Mr P. Modha  0181 741 1688

**Havering College of Further and Higher Education,** Ardleigh Green Road, Hornchurch, Essex, RM11 2LL  Mr G. Tofarides 01708 455011

**Reading College of Arts and Technology,** School of Advanced Business & Management, Crescent Road, Reading, RG1 5RQ Mr J. E. Bennett  01734 583501 ext 123

**South Kent College,** Maison Dieu Road, Dover, Kent, CT16 1DH Mr M. Markram  01304 204573

**West Herts College,** Watford Campus, Hempstead Road, Watford, Herts, WD1 3EZ  Miss F. N. Ekwulugo  01923 257594

**West Thames College,** PO Box 225, London Road, Isleworth, Middx, TW7 4HS (Also full-time course)  Mrs C. Kirkland 0181 568 0244 ext 385/335

**Westminster College,** Battersea Park Road, London, SW11 4JR
(also full-time course)  Mr R. Smith  0171 720 2121

---

**EAST ANGLIA**

**Suffolk College,** Rope Walk, Ipswich, Suffolk, IP4 1LT
Mr A. Matthews  01473 255885)

---

**NORTH WEST**

**Blackpool and Fylde College of Further & Higher Education,**
Department of Management Studies, Ashfield Road, Bispham,
Blackpool, FY2 0HB  Mr J. R. Sumner  01253 352352

**Manchester College of Arts & Technology,** Central Campus,
Lower Hardman Street, Manchester, M3 3ER
Mr J. G. Sherlock  0161 953 5995, ext 2210

**Stockport College of Further & Higher Education,** Davenport
Centre, Highfield Close, Davenport, Stockport, SK3 8UA
Mr J. H. Taylor  0161 958 3619

**Wirral Metropolitan College,** Carlett Park, Eastham, Wirral,
L62 0AY  Mr E. Brown  0151 327 4331

---

**SOUTH**

**Basingstoke College of Technology,** Worting Road, Basingstoke,
Hants, RG21 1TN  Mr A. E. Branch  01256 54141, ext 270

**Southampton Technical College,** St Mary Street, Southampton,
SO9 4WX  Mr J. Bridge  01703 635222 ext 390

**South Downs College,** College Road, Havant, Hants, PO7 8AA
Mr A. Fielder  01705 797979

---

**SOUTH WEST**

**Exeter College,** School of Business Administration, Episcopal
Centre, Dinham Road, Exeter, EX4 4EE  Course
Administrator  01392 384132

**Filton College,** Filton Avenue, Filton, Bristol, BS12 7AT (Also full-
time course)  Mr J. Beasley  0117 694217 ext 240

**Plymouth College of Further Education,** Dept of Business Studies,
Kings Road, Devonport, Plymouth, PL1 5QG
Mr F. Barker   01752 385858

## WALES

**Mid-Wales Export Association Ltd.,** 42 Broad Street, Welshpool,
Powys, SY21 7RR   Mrs J. Christie   01938 555000 (courses in
Wrexham)

**NCM Credit Insurance Ltd.,** Crown Buildings, Cathays Park,
Cardiff, CF1 3PX   Mrs A. Stafford   01222 824951

**Gwent Tertiary College,** Nash Road, Newport, Gwent,
NP9 0TS   Mrs Y. A. Davies   01633 274861

**The Language Export Centre,** The Innovations Centre, University
College, Singleton Park, Swansea, SA2 8PP
Ms Y. Van Kasteren   01792 295621

## EAST MIDLANDS

**Clarendon College,** Pelham Avenue, Mansfield Road,
Nottingham, NG5 1AL   Mr E. J. MacIntyre   0115 607201

**Wigston College of Further Education,** Station Road, Wigston
Magna, Leicester, LE8 2DW   Mr W. T. Parrish   0116 885051

## NORTH WEST MIDLANDS

**Newcastle-Under-Lyme College,** Liverpool Road, Newcastle-
Under-Lyme, Staffs, ST5 2DF   Mr D. Winter   01782 715111

## WEST MIDLANDS

**Sandwell College of Further & Higher Education,** Management
Centre, Wood Green Road, Wednesbury, West Midlands,
WS10 9QN   Mr A. Burns   0121 556 6000 ext 8307

**South Birmingham College,** Hall Green Centre, Cole Bank Road,
Birmingham, B28 8ES   Mr J. Cox   0121 778 2311

**Sutton College,** Lichfield Road, Sutton Coldfield, B74 2NW   Mr M.
McGuire   0121 355 5671 ext 271

## YORKSHIRE AND HUMBERSIDE

**Calderdale College,** Francis Street, Halifax, HX1 3UZ
Mrs L. Oliver  01422 357357

**Huddersfield Technical College,** New North Road, Huddersfield,
HD1 5NN  Mrs C. Cooper  01484 536521 ext 258

**Hull College of Further Education,** Queens Gardens, Hull,
HU1 3DG  Mr W. Paxton  01482 29943 ext 2574

**Park Lane College,** Hanover Way, Leeds, LS3 1AA
Mr M. Baker  0113 443011 ext 524

**Rockingham College of Further Education,** West Street,
Wath-upon-Dearne, Rotherham, South Yorks, S63 6PX
Mr V. Shafiee  01709 760310

**Rotherham College of Art & Technology,** Eastwood Lane,
Rotherham, South Yorks, S65 1EG  Mrs A. Goddard  01709 362111
ext 2755

**Sheffield Hallam University,** Sheffield Business School, Dyson
House, Suffolk Road, Sheffield, S1 1WB  Mrs C. A. White
0114 720911 ext 3626 or 3641

**Wakefield District College,** Whitwood Centre, Four Lane Ends,
Castleford, WF10 5NF  Mr B. Dalton  01924 370501

---

## NORTH EAST

**Durham University Business School,** Mill Hill Lane, Durham,
DH1 3LB (Training Programme for Graduates)
Ms Y. K. Gibb  0191 374 2267

**North Tyneside College,** Embleton Avenue, Wallsend,
NE28 9NJ  Mrs C. E. Carpenter  0191 262 4081

---

## NORTHERN IRELAND

**Lisburn College of Further Education,** Castle Street, Lisburn, Co.
Antrim, BT27 4SU  Mr E. Forester  01846 677225

---

## SCOTLAND

**Central College of Commerce,** Dept of Distributive and
Management Studies, 300 Cathedral Street, Glasgow, G1 2TA
Mr P. Provan  0141 552 3941, ext 2253

**Edinburgh Chamber of Commerce,** 3 Randolph Crescent,
Edinburgh, EH3 7UD  Mr M. Beaton  0131 225 5851

**Glenrothes College,** Stenton Road, Glenrothes, Fife, KY6 2RA
(Full-time course)  Ms B. Beedham  0592 772233

---

## PRIVATE COLLEGE (FULL-TIME COURSE)

**Central London College,** 213/5 Tottenham Court Road, London,
W1 4UA  Mr H. Deschampsneufs  0171 636 2212

---

### Correspondence Course

**The Institute of Export,** 64 Clifton Street, London, EC2A 4HB  Ms T.
Feury  0171 247 9812

---

### Graduate and Postgraduate Courses for which Exemption from the Professional Examinations is Granted

**Buckingham College of Higher Education,** Queen Alexandra
Road, High Wycombe, HP11 2JZ. One year full-time Diploma in
Export Marketing, MA in Export Marketing Management
Mr V. Edwards  01494 22141

**University of Central Lancashire,** Department of International
Business, Peston, PR1 2HE. MA in Export Marketing
Mr P. Ruddock  01772 201201

**The City University Business School,** Frobisher Crescent,
Barbican, London, EC2Y 8HB. One year, full-time or two year,
part-time, MBA in Export Management and International
Business  0171 477 8606

**Dunchurch: The GEC Management College,** Dunchurch, Rugby,
Warks, CU22 6QW. Postgraduate Certificate and Diploma in
Commercial Management  Mr B. Watt  01788 810656

**Napier University,** 219 Colinton Road, Edinburgh, EH14 1DJ.
Three year BA degree in Languages & Export Studies
Mr A. Todd   0131 444 2266

**University of Portsmouth,** School of Languages and Area Studies,
Wiltshire Building, Hampshire Terrace, Portsmouth, PO1 2EG.
Four year BA degree in International Trade & Languages
Mr H. Thiessen   01705 876543

**University of Surrey,** Surrey European Management School,
Guildford, Surrey, GU2 5XH. One-year full-time, two-year part-
time and two year distance learning MBA   Dr P. Kangis
01483 509347

Local Branches of The Institute of Export operate in the following
locations with a regular programme of meetings for students and
members, and they will welcome visitors interested in learning
more about how the Institute can assist exporters and those
interested in becoming exporters

---

Branches operate in the following areas:
ANGLIA (Gt. Yarmouth and Norwich)
CENTRAL SHIRES (Northampton and Milton Keynes)
COVENTRY & SOUTH MIDLANDS
EAST MIDLANDS (Leicester/Loughborough/Nottingham)
HERTS & BEDS (St Albans and Luton)
HUMBERSIDE (Hull)
LIVERPOOL & NORTH WEST COAST
LONDON & HOME COUNTIES
MANCHESTER & DISTRICT
MID-WESSEX & THAMES VALLEY
NORTH EAST
NORTHERN IRELAND
NORTH WEST MIDLANDS (Potteries)
SCOTLAND (Edinburgh and Glasgow)
SHEFFIELD & DISTRICT
SOUTHERN (Kent and Sussex)
SOUTH WEST
WALES (Cardiff)
WESSEX (Southampton)
WEST MIDLANDS
WEST RIDING (Bradford and Leeds)

---

The Institute of Export will gladly give you the contact name and
telephone number of the local Branch Secretary:
Telephone the Institute – 0171 247 9812

## CONTACT ADDRESSES FOR GOVERNMENT REGIONAL OFFICES

There is no shortage of specialist help for those wishing to export
– you can use it – let them assist you

This compendium of addresses is to help you access that help

The export services of the Department of Trade & Industry (DTI)
and the Foreign & Commonwealth Office (FCO) have been
brought together as OVERSEAS TRADE SERVICES at Kingsgate
House, 66–74 Victoria Street, London, SW1E 6SW Telephone:
0171 215 5000 or the appropriate Country Desk for your enquiry
(see Appendix C3) Telex: 8813148 DIHQ G DTHQ.G
Fax: 0171 222 2629

and there are Regional Offices in the following locations, there to
help you with information, access to the various services and
general advice and assistance:

### REGIONAL GOVERNMENT OFFICES, PROVIDING DTI SUPPORT FOR EXPORTERS:

### East Midlands

Government Office for the East Midlands, Severns House,
20 Middle Pavement, Nottingham, NG1 7DW Telephone:
(01159) 506181 Telex: 37143 Fax: (01159) 587074

Derby Office Telephone: (01332) 347031

Chesterfield Office Telephone: (01246) 239905

Leicester Office Telephone: (01162) 559944

Lincoln Office Telephone: (01522) 574046

Northampton Office Telephone: (01604) 791105

### West Midlands

Government Office for the West Midlands, 77 Paradise Circus,
Queensway, Birmingham, B1 2DT Telephone: 0121-212 5000
Telex: 337919 Fax: 0121-212 1010

Stoke-on-Trent Office Telephone: (01782) 285171
Worcester Office Telephone: (01905) 765339
Coventry Office Telephone: (01203) 632328
Telford Office Telephone: (01952) 290422

---

## South West

Government Office for the South West, The Pithay, Bristol,
BS1 2PB Telephone: (01179) 272666 Telex: 44214 Fax:
(01179) 299494
Plymouth Office Telephone: (01752) 221891
Penzance Office Telephone: (01736) 60440

---

## North East

Government Office for the North East, Stanegate House, 2 Groat
Market, Newcastle-upon-Tyne, NE1 1YN Telephone:
0191-235 4722 Telex: 53178 Fax: 0191-235 7798
Middlesbrough Office Telephone: (01642) 232220
Billingham Office Telephone: (01642) 553671

---

## North West

Government Office for the North West, Sunley Tower, Piccadilly
Plaza, Manchester, M1 4BE Telephone: 0161-952 4100 Telex:
667104 Fax: 0161 952 4199/0161 237 4040/0161 952 4193
Government Office for Merseyside, Liverpool Office, Graeme
House, Derby Square, Liverpool L2 7UP Telephone:
0151-224 6300 Telex: 627647 Fax: 0151-236 1140
Barrow-in-Furness Office Telephone: (01229) 830212
Cheshire Office Telephone: (01606) 737247
Cockermouth Office Telephone: (01900) 828328
Preston Office Telephone: (01772) 653000

---

## Yorkshire and Humberside

Government Office for Yorkshire and Humberside, 25 Queen Street, Leeds, LS1 2TW Telephone: (01132) 443171 Telex: 557925 Fax: (01132) 338301/2

Hull Office Telephone: (01482) 465741

Sheffield Office Telephone: (01742) 729849

## London & South East

Government Office for London, Bridge Place, 88/89 Eccleston Square, London, SW1V 1PT Telephone: 0171-215 0574 Telex: 297124 Fax: 0171-215 0875

Government Office for the South East, Reading Office, 40 Caversham Road, Reading, Berkshire, RG1 7EB Telephone: (01734) 395600 Telex: 847799 Fax: (01734) 502818

Reigate Office, Douglas House, London Road, Reigate, Surrey, RH2 9QP Telephone: (01737) 226900 Telex: 918364 Fax: (01737) 223491

Portsmouth Office Telephone: (01705) 818548

Margate Office Telephone: (01843) 290511

Chatham Office Telephone: (01634) 829299

## East

Government Office for the Eastern Region, Building A, Westbrook Centre, Milton Road, Cambridge CB4 1YG Telephone: (01223) 461939 Telex: 81582 Fax: (01223) 461941

Norwich Office Telephone: (01603) 761294

## SCOTLAND

### Scottish Trade International

Franborough House, 120 Bothwell Street, Glasgow, G2 7JP Telephone: (0141) 228 2869/2633 Telex: 0777883 Fax: (0141) 2213712

## WALES

### Welsh Office Industry Department

Crown Building, Cathays Park, Cardiff, CF1 3NQ Telephone:
(01222) 825111 Telex: 498228 Fax: (01222) 823088

---

## NORTHERN IRELAND

### Industrial Development Board

Export Development Branch, Marketing Development Division,
IDB House, 64 Chichester Street, Belfast, BT1 4JX Telephone:
(01232) 233233 Telex: 747025 Fax: (01232) 231328

## BOTB AREA ADVISORY GROUPS AVAILABLE TO ASSIST EXPORTERS

**AAG**

**Asia Pacific** Advisory Group (APAG)
Secretary, APAG,
Bay 565/70,
Kingsgate House,*
Tel: 0171-215 4889

APAG Subsidiary Committees
are:

i) **Anglo Taiwanese** Trade Comm (ATTC)
Deputy Director,
ATTC,
7th Floor,
Wettern House,
56 Dingwall Road,
Croydon, CR0 0XH
Tel: 0181-666 0440

ii) **Hong Kong** Action Committee (HKAC)
Secretary, HKAC
Bay 556,
Kingsgate House,*
Tel: 0171-215 5273

iii) **Korea** Trade Action Committee (KTAC)
Secretary, KTAC,
Bay 548,
Kingsgate House,
Tel: 0171-215 4807

iv) **South East Asia** Action Committee (SEAAC)
Secretary, SEACC,
Bay 567,
Kingsgate House*
Tel: 0171-215 5391

| | |
|---|---|
| **Australia and New Zealand** Trade Advisory Committee (ANZTAC) | Director, ANZTAC, Suite 10–16, Morley House, 314–322 Regent Street, London, W1R 5AJ Tel: 0171-636 4525 |
| British Overseas Trade Group for **Israel** (BOTGI) | Executive Secretary, BOTGI, 14–15 Rodmarton Street, London, W1H 3FW. Tel: 0171-935 4351 |
| **Caribbean** Trade Advisory Group (CARITAG) | Director, CARITAG, Nelson House, 8–9 Northumberland Street, London, WC2N 5RA Tel: 0171-976 1493 |
| **China** British Trade Group (CBTG) | Director, CBTG, 5th Floor, Abford House, 15 Wilton Road, London, SW1V 1LT Tel: 0171-828 5176/7 |
| Committee for **Middle East** Trade (COMET) | Executive Director, COMET, Bury House, 33 Bury Street, St James's, London, SW1Y 6AX Tel: 0171-839 1170/1191 |

**East European** Trade Council
(EETC)

Director, EETC,
Suite 10,
Westminster Palace
Gardens,
Artillery Row,
London, SW1P 1RL
Tel: 0171-222 7622

---

**European** Trade Committee
(ETC)

Secretary, ETC,
Room 953,
Kingsgate House,*
Tel: 0171-215 4787

---

**Indo–British** Partnership

Executive Secretary,
Bay 732,
Kingsgate House,*
Tel: 0171-215 4826

---

**Japan** Trade Advisors (JTA)
and **Japan** Trade Group

Secretary JTA,
Bay 532,
Kingsgate House,*
Tel: 0171-215 5426

---

**Latin America** Trade Advisory
Group (LATAG)

Chief Executive,
LATAG,
Canning House,
2 Belgrave Square,
London, SW1X 8PJ
Tel: 0171-235 2307

---

| | |
|---|---|
| **North America** Advisory Group (NAAG) | Secretary, NAAG, Bay 806/807 Kingsgate House,* Tel: 0171-215 5327 |
| **Southern Asia** Advisory Group (SAAG) | Executive Director, SAAG, Bay 723/32, Kingsgate House,* Tel: 0171-215 5280 |
| **Tropical Africa** Advisory Group (TAAG) | Executive Director, TAAG, Bay 728/730, Kingsgate House,* Tel: 0171-215 5032 |
| **South Africa** Committee on South African Trade (COSAT) | Chairman, COSAT c/o DTI South Africa Desk, Tel: 0171 215 5274 |

* An asterisk denotes a Kingsgate House address, the full details being:

    Kingsgate House,
    66–74 Victoria Street,
    London, SW1E 6SW

Switchboard Telephone: 0171-215 5000

# DTI COUNTRY DESKS

For specific information on export opportunities in individual countries DTI's overseas trade divisions in London ('country desks') are there to help; the address is Kingsgate House, 66–74 Victoria Street, London, SW1E 6SW. As well as being responsible for export promotion, the protection of UK commercial interests and general government-to-government relations, these country desks can also provide information on tariff regulations

To contact a country desk, **ring 0171-215** followed by the relevant extension given below

| Country | 0171-215 | Ext. | Country | 0171-215 | Ext. |
|---|---|---|---|---|---|
| Abu Dhabi (UAE) | | 5221/ 4246/ 8291 | Aruba | | 5040/ 5049* |
| Afghanistan | | 3787/ 4824* | Ascension Island | | 8471/ 4781* |
| Albania | | 4849/ 4812 | Australia | | 4760/ 5321/ 5319/ 2743* |
| Algeria | | 4948 | | | |
| Andorra | | 4357/ 4284*/ 5624/ 4768 | Austria | | 2663/ 4798 |
| | | | Azerbaijan | | 2671 |
| | | | Azores | | 2751/ 4776* |
| Angola | | 8471/ 4781* | Bahamas | | 5297/ 5049* |
| Anguilla | | 5297/ 5049* | Bahrain | | 8281 |
| Antigua | | 5297/ 5049* | Bangladesh | | 4824*/ 3787 |
| Argentina | | 5055/ 2646* | Barbados | | 5297/ 5049* |
| Armenia | | 2671 | Belarus | | 4257/ 5265 |

| Country | 0171-215 | Ext. | Country | 0171-215 | Ext. |
|---|---|---|---|---|---|
| Belgium | | 4227/ | Cameroon | | 4967/ |
| | | 4792/ | | | 4970* |
| | | 4794 | Canada Cons Gds | | 4593/ |
| Belize | | 5040/ | | | 4595* |
| | | 5049 | Cap Gds | | 4608/ |
| Benin | | 4967/ | | | 4563* |
| | | 8676*/ | Gen'l | | 5415 |
| | | 4970* | Canary Islands | | 4357/ |
| Bermuda | | 8286 | | | 5624*/ |
| Bhutan | | 3787/ | | | 5307* |
| | | 4824* | Cape Verde | | 4967/ |
| Bolivia | | 5289/ | | | 8676*/ |
| | | 5051* | | | 4970* |
| Bosnia-Herzegovina | | 4849 | Caribbean | | 5297/ |
| Botswana | | 4028/ | | | 5040/ |
| | | 5011/ | | | 5049* |
| | | 4781 | Cayman Islands | | 5297/ |
| Brazil | | 5347/ | | | 5049* |
| | | 8123 | Central African Rep | | 2860/ |
| British Indian Ocean | | 2860/ | | | 5608* |
| Territories (BIOT) | | 5608/ | Ceuta/Melilla | | 4772 |
| Brunei | | 8546/ | Chad | | 2860/ |
| | | 5465* | | | 5608* |
| Bulgaria | | 4812/ | Chile | | 5383* |
| | | 5152 | China | | 5357/ |
| Burkina Faso | | 4967/ | | | 4230* |
| | | 4970*/ | CIS | | 4257/ |
| | | 8676* | | | 5265 |
| Burma (Myanmar) | | 8546/ | Colombia | | 5289/ |
| | | 8479* | | | 5051* |
| Burundi | | 2860/ | Comoros | | 2860/ |
| | | 5608* | | | 5608* |
| Cambodia | | 8546/ | Congo | | 2860/ |
| | | 8479* | | | 5608* |

309

| Country | 0171-215 | Ext. | Country | 0171-215 | Ext. |
|---------|----------|------|---------|----------|------|
| Costa Rica | | 5288/ 5015* | Falkland Islands | | 5055/ 2646 |
| Cote d'Ivoire | | 4967/ 8676* | Faroes (see Denmark) | | 8657 |
| Croatia | | 4849/ 4812 | Fiji | | 5319/ 2743* |
| Cuba | | 5040/ 5049* | Finland | | 4783*/ 5134 |
| Cyprus | | 5358/ 8442* | France Cons Gds | | 4762 4765 |
| Czech Rep | | 4735/ 8194 | Cap Gds | | 5197 |
| Denmark | | 8657 | French Guiana | | 5297/ 5049* |
| Djibouti | | 4973/ 5608* | French Polynesia (Tahiti) | | 5319/ 2743* |
| Dominica | | 5297/ 5049* | French West Indies | | 5040/ 5049* |
| Dominican Republic | | 5040/ 5049* | Gabon | | 4967/ 4970* |
| Dubai (UAE) | | 5221/ 4246* | Gambia | | 4967/ 4970* |
| Ecuador | | 5289/ 5051* | Georgia | | 2671 |
| Egypt | | 4947/ 4948 | Germany, Fed Rep 1. Consumer goods and all general inquiries including regulations and tariffs | | 4795/ 5245 |
| El Salvador | | 5288/ 5015* | 2. Capital goods – market info only | | 4796 4285/ 5333 |
| Equatorial Guinea | | 4967/ 8676* | Ghana | | 4969/ 4970* 8676* |
| Eritrea | | 4973/ 5608* | | | |
| Estonia | | 5265 | | | |
| Ethiopia | | 4973/ 5608* | Gibraltar | | 4284 |

310

| Country | 0171-215 | Ext. | Country | 0171-215 | Ext. |
|---|---|---|---|---|---|
| Greece | | 5103/ 4774 | Iran | | 4367/ 4395/ 8323* |
| Greenland | | 8657 | | | |
| Grenada | | 5297/ 5049* | Iraq | | 4367/ 4395 |
| Guadeloupe | | 5040/ 5049* | Ireland | | 4782/ 8413 |
| Guatemala | | 5288/ 5015* | Israel | | 4949/ 4240/ 8442* |
| Guinea | | 4967/ 4970* | Italy | | 4385/ 5154 |
| Guinea Bissau | | 4967/ 4970* | Ivory Coast | | 4967/ 8676*/ 4970* |
| Guyana | | 5297/ 5049 | | | |
| Haiti | | 5040/ 5049 | Jamaica | | 5297/ 5049* |
| Honduras | | 5288/ 5015* | Japan Cons Gds | | 4804*/ 5667 |
| Hong Kong | | 4828/ 4829 | Ind Gds | | 4801/ 4805* |
| Hungary | | 8194/ 4735 | Priority Japan | | 4269 |
| | | | Jordan | | 5169/ 4394* |
| Iceland | | 4397 | Kazakhstan | | 2681 |
| India | | 4826/ 8477/ 5278/ 8290*/ 2745*/ 4825* | Kenya | | 5226/ 4964 |
| | | | Kiribati | | 5319 |
| Indo-China | | 5253 | Korea, South | | 4747/ 4809* |
| Indonesia | | 4738/ 5086* | Korea, North | | 4747/ 4809* |
| | | | Kuwait | | 8645 |
| | | | Kyrgyzstan | | 2681 |

| Country | 0171-215 Ext. | Country | 0171-215 Ext. |
|---|---|---|---|
| Laos | 8546/ 8479* | Malta | 8328/ 8442* |
| Latvia | 5265/ 8245 | Martinique | 5297/ 5049* |
| Lebanon | 5092/ 5376* | Mauritania | 4948 |
|  |  | Mauritius | 8188/ 5608* |
| Lesotho | 5011/ 4781* | Mayotte | 2860/ 5608* |
| Liberia | 4967/ 4970* | Mexico | 5290/ 4297* |
| Libya | 8216 |  |  |
| Liechtenstein | 4359/ 8353 | Moldova | 4257/ 5265 |
| Lithuania | 5265/ 4257 | Monaco | 4762/ 4765 |
| Luxembourg | 4792/ 4794 | Mongolia | 5357 |
|  |  | Montserrat | 5297/ 5049 |
| Macao | 4828/ 4829 | Morocco | 8326 |
| Macedonia | 4849/ 4812 | Mozambique | 8471/ 4028* |
| Madagascar | 2860/ 5608* | Myanmar (Burma) | 8546/ 8479* |
| Madeira | 2751/ 4776 | Namibia | 4308/ 4781*/ 4028* |
| Malawi | 8471/ 4028* | Nauru | 5319 |
| Malaysia | 5143/ 5465* | Nepal | 3787/ 4824* |
| Maldives | 3787/ 4824* | Netherlands | 4790/ 4791/ 4789 |
| Mali | 4967/ 4970* |  |  |

| Country | 0171-215 | Ext. | Country | 0171-215 | Ext. |
|---|---|---|---|---|---|
| Netherlands | | 5040/ | Portugal | | 4776/ |
| Antilles | | 5049* | | | 2751 |
| New Caledonia | | 4760 | Puerto Rico | | 5040/ |
| New Zealand | | | capital goods | | 4607* |
| Cap Gds | | 5321 | consumer goods | | 4597 |
| Cons Gds | | 4760 | Qatar | | 4811 |
| Serv Invisibles | | 5319 | Réunion | | 2860 |
| Tariffs | | 2743* | Cons Gds | | 4762* |
| Nicaragua | | 5288/ | Cap Gds | | 5197* |
| | | 5015* | Romania | | 5267/ |
| Niger | | 4967/ | | | 4812 |
| | | 4970* | Russia | | 4257/ |
| Nigeria | | 4968/ | | | 5265 |
| | | 4966/ | Rwanda | | 2860/ |
| | | 2844* | | | 5608* |
| Norway | | 8267 | San Marino | | 5103/ |
| Oman | | 4388 | | | 4776/ |
| Occupied Territories | | 5169/ | | | 4385 |
| (Palestinian Authority) | | 4394* | Sao Tomé & | | 4967/ |
| | | | Principe | | 4970* |
| Pakistan | | 4777/ | St Helena | | 8471/ |
| | | 4824* | | | 4781* |
| Palestinian Authority | | 5169/ | St Kitts/Nevis | | 5297/ |
| (Occupied Territories) | | 4394* | | | 5049* |
| Panama | | 5288/ | St Lucia | | 5297/ |
| | | 5015* | | | 5049* |
| Papua New Guinea | | 5319 | St Vincent | | 5297/ |
| Paraguay | | 8117/ | | | 5049* |
| | | 2646* | Saudi Arabia | | 5239/ |
| Peru | | 5289/ | | | 5052 |
| | | 5051* | Senegal | | 4967/ |
| Philippines | | 5614*/ | | | 4970* |
| | | 4742 | Serbia/Montenegro | | 4849 |
| Poland | | 8194/ | Seychelles | | 2860/ |
| | | 4735 | | | 5608* |

| Country | 0171-215 | Ext. | Country | 0171-215 | Ext. |
|---|---|---|---|---|---|
| Sierra Leone | | 4967/ | Tadjikistan | | 2681 |
| | | 4970* | Tahiti (French | | 5319/ |
| Singapore | | 8162/ | Polynesia) | | 2743* |
| | | 8479* | Taiwan | | 4729 |
| Slovak Republic | | 4735/ | Tanzania | | 5033/ |
| | | 8194 | | | 4964* |
| Slovenia | | 4849 | Thailand | | 3659/ |
| Solomon Islands | | 5319 | | | 5489/ |
| Somalia | | 2860/ | | | 4264* |
| | | 5608* | Togo | | 4967/ |
| South Africa | | 5011/ | | | 4970* |
| | | 5274*/ | Tonga | | 5319 |
| | | 4308 | Trinidad & Tobago | | 5297/ |
| South Pacific Islands | | 5319 | | | 5049* |
| Spain Gen Enq | | 4772 | Tristan da Cunha | | 8471/ |
| Cap Gds | | 4284 | | | 4781* |
| Cons Gds | | 5624 | Tunisia | | 8434 |
| (food & drink) | | | Turkey | | 5314/ |
| Cons Gds | | 5307 | | | 8332/ |
| (clothing, medical) | | | | | 4394* |
| Sri Lanka | | 5677/ | Turkmenistan | | 2671 |
| | | 4824* | Turks & Caicos Islands | | 5297/ |
| Sudan | | 8216/ | | | 5049* |
| | | 8442* | Tuvalu | | 5319 |
| Suriname | | 5297/ | Uganda | | 2860/ |
| | | 5049* | | | 4964* |
| Swaziland | | 5011/ | Ukraine | | 4257/ |
| | | 5274* | | | 5265 |
| Sweden | | 5341 | United Arab Emirates | | 4246/ |
| Switzerland | | 4359/ | | | 5221 |
| | | 8353 | | | |
| Syria | | 5376/ | | | |
| | | 5092/ | | | |
| | | 8246* | | | |

| Country | 0171-215 | Ext. | Country | 0171-215 | Ext. |
|---|---|---|---|---|---|
| United States of America | Cons Gds | 4595/<br>4593/<br>8286* | Virgin Islands (USA) | | 5297 |
| | Cap Gds | 4608/<br>4563 | | Cap Gds | 4607 |
| | Gen'l | 5632 | | Cons Gds | 4597 |
| Uruguay | | 5055/<br>2646* | Western Sahara | | 4948 |
| USSR (former) | | 5265/<br>4257 | Western Samoa | | 5319/<br>2743* |
| US Trust Territories of Pacific | | 5319 | Yemen, Republic of | | 8675 |
| Uzbekistan | | 2681 | Yugoslavia | | 4849/<br>4812 |
| Vanuatu | | 5319 | Zaïre | | 2860/<br>5608* |
| Venezuela | | 5288/<br>5015* | Zambia | | 3763/<br>4028* |
| Vietnam | | 5253/<br>5614* | Zimbabwe | | 5018/<br>4028* |
| Virgin Islands (British) | | 5297/<br>5049* | | | |

*Tariff and import
regulation inquiries

# CREDIT RISK INSURANCE PROVIDERS

**Credit Risk Insurance of debtors – see Section 3**
**NCM Offices Nederlandsche Credietverzekering Maatschappij**

**CARDIFF**
NCM Cardiff
Head Office Insurance
Services
Crown Building
Cathays Park
Cardiff CF1 3NH
01222 824000

**BELFAST**
NCM Belfast
12th Floor
Windsor House
9–12 Bedford Street
Belfast BT2 7EG
01232 231743

**BIRMINGHAM**
NCM Birmingham
Colmore Centre
115 Colmore Row
Birmingham B3 3SB
0121-233 1771

**BRISTOL**
NCM Bristol
3 Buckingham Court
Beaufort Office Park
Woodlands Lane
Almondsbury
Bristol BS12 4NF
01454 616999

**CAMBRIDGE**
NCM Cambridge
Three Crowns House
72–80 Hills Road
Cambridge CB2 1NJ
01223 68801

**CITY OF LONDON**
NCM City of London
Export House
50 Ludgate Hill
London EC4M 7AY
0171 382 7000

**CROYDON**
NCM Croydon
45 Friend's Road
Croydon
Surrey CR0 1ED
0181 680 5030

**GLASGOW**
NCM Glasgow
Berkeley House
285 Bath Street
Glasgow G2 4JL
0141 332 8707

**LEEDS**
NCM Leeds
West Riding House
67 Albion Street
Leeds LS1 5AA
01132 450631

**MANCHESTER**
NCM Manchester
Townbury House
Blackfriars Street
Manchester M3 5AL
0161 834 8181

## CREDIT RISK INSURANCE PROVIDERS Cont'd

**TRADE INDEMNITY PLC OFFICES**

**TRADE INDEMNITY PLC**

### HEAD OFFICE
12–34 Great Eastern Street
London EC2A 3AX
Telephone: 0171-739 4311
Telex: 21227
Fax: 0171-729 7682

### REGIONAL OFFICES

### BIRMINGHAM
Embassy House
60 Church Street
Birmingham B3 2DJ
Telephone: 0121-233 4535
Telex: 334204
Fax: 0121-233 3703

### BRISTOL
4 Buckingham Court
Beaufort Office Park
Woodlands
Almondsbury BS12 4NF
Telephone: 01454 617597
Telex: 44875
Fax: 01454 617456

### GLASGOW
5–6 Claremont Terrace
Glasgow G3 7XR
Telephone: 0141-331 1088
Telex: 779644
Fax: 0141-331 1627

### LEEDS
St James House
28 Park Place
Leeds LS1 2SP
Telephone: 01532 341808
Telex: 55268
Fax: 01532 342027

### LONDON
12–34 Great Eastern Street
London EC2A 3AX
Telephone: 0171-739 4311
Telex: 21227
Fax: 0171-739 8986

### MANCHESTER
Macintosh House
Market Place
Manchester M4 3AF
Telephone: 0161-832 3676
Telex: 667368
Fax: 0161-833 2645

## CREDIT RISK INSURANCE PROVIDERS Cont'd

---

### EXPORT CREDIT GUARANTEE DEPARTMENT
Britain's official export credit insurer, for medium-to-long term
credit periods and provision of finance guarantees

ECGD,
PO Box 2200,
2 Exchange Tower,
Harbour Exchange Square,
London, E14 9GS

ECGD
Crown Buildings,
Cathays Park,
Cardiff, CF1 3NH

Tel: 0171 512 7000
Fax: 0171 512 7649

Tel: 01222 784000
Fax: 01222 784448

---

HERMES Credit Services Ltd
(Short to medium term cover)

**HERMES CREDIT SERVICES LTD,**
1 Angel Court,
London, EC2R 7HJ
Tel: 0171 600 4406
Fax: 0171 600 4426
(w.o.s. of Hermes
Kreditversicherungs-AG,
Hamburg)

NAMUR
(Short to medium term cover)

**NAMUR – INSURANCES OF
CREDIT,**
8 Bedford Park,
Croydon, CR0 2AP
Tel: 0181 680 1565
Fax: 0181 688 4953
(w.o.s. of SA
Namur–Assurances du Credit,
registered in Belgium)

## CREDIT RISK INSURANCE PROVIDERS Cont'd

COFACE London Bridge
Finance Ltd
(Short to medium term cover)

**COFACE LONDON BRIDGE
FINANCE LTD,**
15 Appold Street,
London, EC2A 12DL
Tel: 0171-325 7500
Fax: 0171-325 7699
(w.o.s. of Coface France)

## Other useful addresses

### Export Market Information Centre

Ashdown House
123 Victoria Street
London SW1E 6RB
Tel: 0171 215 5444/5
Fax: 0171 215 4231

Section 1.3.1

### Export Marketing Research Scheme

The Association of British
Chambers of Commerce
4 Westwood House
Westwood Business Park
Coventry CV4 8HS
Tel: 01203 694484

Section 1.3.1 & 1.5.1

### Technical Requirements

Technical Help for Exporters
Linford Wood
Milton Keynes MK14 6LE
Tel: 01908 220022

Section 1.2.1

### Overseas Promotions Support

Dean Bradley House
Horseferry Road
London SW1P 2AG
Tel: 0171 276 2414
Fax: 0171 222 4707

Section 1.8

### Publications (incl OVERSEAS TRADE MAGAZINE)

DTI Export Publications
PO Box 55
Stratford upon Avon
Warwicks CV37 9NG
Tel: 01789 296212

### Export Documentation & EDI

SITPRO (the Simpler Trade
Procedures Board)
Venture House
29 Glasshouse Street
London W1R 5RG
Tel: 0171 287 3525
Fax: 0171 287 5751

Section 16.1

### Export Intelligence

Prelink Ltd
Export House
87A Wembley Hill Road
Wembley, Middx, HA9 8BU
Tel: 0181 900 1313
Fax: 0181 900 1268

Financial Times Profile
Information
Sunbury House
PO Box 12
Sunbury-on-Thames
TW16 7UD
Tel: 01932 761444
Fax: 01932 781425

Section 1.2

**VAT Recovery**
Cash Back Consulting (UK) Ltd
20 St. Dunstans Hill
London EC2R 8HL
Tel: 0171 626 3262
Fax: 0171 626 0384

Section 1.9

---

Quipsound Ltd
The Crown Building
London Road
Westerham
Kent, TN16 1DP
Tel: 01959 563228
Fax: 01959 564740

---

**British Consultants Bureau**
1 Westminster Palace Gardens
1–7 Artillery Row
London, SW1P 1RJ
Tel: 0171 222 3651
Fax: 0171 222 3664

---

**Export Licences**
The Enquiry Unit
Export Control Organisation
6th Floor
Kingsgate House
66–74 Victoria Street
London SW1E 6SW
Tel: 0171 215 8070

---

**International Chamber of Commerce**
(ICC United Kingdom)
14–15 Belgrave Square
London SW1X 8PS
Tel: 0171 823 2811

Sections 6 & 14.1

---

**THE PATENT OFFICE AND REGISTRIES – see Section 1.2**

THE PATENT OFFICE and TRADE MARKS REGISTRY
  The Patent Office
  Cardiff Road
  Newport
  Gwent
  NP9 1RH
  Tel: 01633 814000

THE DESIGNS REGISTRY

The Designs Registry
The Patent Office
Chartist Tower
Upper Dock Street
Newport
Gwent
NP9 1DW
Tel: 01633 814000 General Enquiries ext 5162

Queries and matters relating to COPYRIGHT should be addressed to:

Industrial Property and Copyright Department
Copyright Enquiries
Hazlitt House
45 Southampton Buildings
Chancery Lane
London
WC2A 1AR
Tel: 0171 438 4778

The SEARCH AND ADVISORY SERVICE operates from:

Search and Advisory Service
The Patent Office
Hazlitt House
45 Southampton Buildings
Chancery Lane
London
WC2A 1AR
Tel: 0171 438 4747/8

Requests for literature, and general enquiries relating to the services of the Patent Office, should be made to: 0171 829 6512

The DTI has a Large Project Support section, split into a number of industry sections, available to assist UK exporters involved or likely to become involved in large projects:

**Large Project Support**
Projects and Export Policy Division
Ashdown House
123 Victoria Street
London SW1E 6RB

**Branch 1**
Airports, civil aviation equipment, roads, bridges and tunnels:
0171 215 6632

Railways, urban transport systems (other than European or Eastern Bloc), ports and shipyards, road and rail vehicles:
0171 215 6052

European and Eastern Bloc rail and urban transit projects:
0171 215 6608

**Branch 2**
Hydroelectric projects worldwide except India; cement: 0171 215 6552

Nuclear, renewable and alternative energy power projects worldwide and all non-hydro power projects in China, Taiwan, Hong Kong, Malaysia, Thailand, Turkey: 0171 215 6731

All mining projects (underground and open cast), all power projects in India:
0171 215 6602

Major overseas thermal power generation, transmission and distribution projects and gas turbines worldwide except for Pakistan: 0171 215 6842

Major thermal power generation, transmission and distribution and gas turbine projects in Pakistan:
0171 215 6124

**Branch 3**
Telecommunications, postal services, electronics and educational equipment:
0171 215 6721/6105

Water and sewerage, hospitals, housing, urban development, public buildings, educational establishments: 0171 215 6523

Agricultural and agro-industrial projects, fisheries, forestry (including pulp and paper); sports and leisure projects, including hotels:
0171 215 6762

Industrial projects not
elsewhere specified:
0171 215 6568

**Branch 4**
Major overseas oil and gas
projects, refineries and
pipelines: 0171 215 6742

Ferrous metallurgical projects:
0171 215 6683

Non-ferrous metallurgical
projects, petrochemical
(except primary processing
and refining), chemical,
biotechnology and
pharmaceutical:
0171 215 6688/6683

---

**WORLD AID SECTION DATABASE OF ALL AID-FUNDED,
AND WORLD BANK FINANCED PROJECTS THROUGHOUT THE
WORLD:**

**World Aid Section**
Room 290
Ashdown House
123 Victoria Street
London SW1E 6RB

Information on the multilateral development agencies and
projects financed by them: World Bank Group: 0171 215 6735/6330

European Development Funds, European Structural Funds,
Eastern Europe, European Bank for Reconstruction and
Development (EBRD): 0171 215 6157/6765/6089

Asian Development Bank, Inter-American Development Bank,
Caribbean Development Bank, African Development Bank, Arab
Aid Agencies and United Nations Agencies: 0171 215 6586/6587

---

**Sector**
The sectors are the areas in which the Banks fund projects as
follows:

**WORLD AID SYSTEM**
01    Agricultural and Rural Development
02    Development Finance Companies
04    Energy

| | |
|---|---|
| 05 | Industry |
| 06 | Non-Project |
| 07 | Health, Population and Nutrition |
| 08 | Small Scale Enterprises |
| 09 | Technical Assistance |
| 10 | Telecommunications |
| 11 | Transportation |
| 12 | Urbanisation |
| 13 | Water Supply and Sewerage |
| 14 | Structural Adjustment Loans |
| 15 | Multi-sector |
| 16 | Economic Reports |
| 17 | Tourism |
| 18 | Education |
| 19 | Environmental Protection |

---

European Structural Funds are categorised as follows:

| | |
|---|---|
| AG | Agriculture |
| CS | Culture, Sport and Leisure |
| EC | Economic Reports and Development Plans |
| ED | Education and Training |
| EN | Energy |
| ENV | Environmental Protection |
| FI | Fisheries and Aquaculture |
| HE | Health, Population and Nutrition |
| HO | Housing |
| IN | Industry |
| MS | Multi-Sector |
| NP | Non-Project |
| PO | Ports and Harbours |
| SM | Small Scale Enterprises |
| TA | Technical Assistance |
| TC | Telecoms & Information Technology |
| TO | Tourism |
| TR | Transportation |
| UR | Urbanisation |
| WS | Water Supply and Sewerage |

---

## EIS Status

The current stage of development of a project as follows:

1  Project Identification
2  The project is at an early stage and only limited information is available at present
3  Negotiation
4  Appraisal/Approval – Full Project Documents now available in WAS or local regional office for inspection

## Remarks

MOS means Monthly Operational Summary. Followed by date, this refers to the first official listing given by a Bank to a project.

BOS means Bi-Monthly Operational Summary

QOS means Quarterly Operational Summary

Prepipe means projects under consideration but not officially identified on an Operational Summary yet.

## COMPANY INFORMATION REPORT PROVIDERS

CCN Systems Ltd
Customer Service Department
Abbey House
Abbeyfield Road
Lenton
Nottingham NG7 2SW
Tel: 01159 863864

Section 8.2

Dun & Bradstreet Ltd
Holmers Farm Way
High Wycombe
Bucks HP12 4UL
Tel: 01494 422000

Section 8.2

Infocheck Ltd
28 Scrutton Street
London EC2A 4RQ
Tel: 0171 377 8872
Fax: 0171 247 4194

Section 8.2

## CRONERS REFERENCE BOOK FOR EXPORTERS published by

Croner Publications Ltd
Croner House
173 Kingston Road
New Malden
Surrey KT3 3SS
Tel: 0181 942 8966

Section 16.1

## FOR INFORMATION ON FREIGHT FORWARDERS

British International Freight
Association
Redfern House
Browells Lane
Feltham
Middx TW13 7EP
Tel: 0181 844 2266

Section 20.2

---

Freight Transport Association
Hermes House
157 St. John's Road
Tunbridge Wells
Kent, TN4 9UZ
Tel: 01892 526171
Fax: 01892 534989

Section 20.2

---

Association of International
Courier and Express Services
Unit 1B, Galleymead Road
Colnbrook
Berks SL3 0EN
Tel: 01753 680550
Fax: 01753 681710

Section 20.2

---

## PRE-SHIPMENT INSPECTION AGENCIES

Cotecna International Ltd
Hounslow House
730 London Road
Hounslow
Middx TW3 1PD
Tel: 0181 577 6000

Section 25

---

SGS
SGS House
217/221 London Road
Camberley
Surrey GU15 3EY
Tel: 01276 691133

Section 25

---

Bureau Veritas
British Central Office
Capital House
42 Western Street
London SE1 3QL
Tel: 0171 403 6266

Section 25

---

**OFFICIAL GOVERNMENT PUBLICATIONS ARE AVAILABLE FROM**

HM Stationery Office
Publications Centre
PO Box 276
London SW8 5DT

Section 26

---

**CUSTOMS & EXCISE HEAD OFFICE**

HM Customs & Excise Dept
Kings Beam House
Mark Lane
London EC3R 7HE (for general enquiries)
Tel: 0171 626 1515

Section 26

---

**FOR ASSISTANCE IN PREPARING OVERSEAS PUBLICITY MATERIAL, NEW STORIES AND PRESS RELEASES, AND USE OF THE 'NEW PRODUCTS FROM BRITAIN' SERVICE, contact:**

Central Office of Information (accessed through the Regional Government Offices)

Section 1.12.1

---

## OTHER USEFUL ORGANISATIONS:

### The Defence Export Services Organisation

Helps British firms market and sell their defence products and services overseas. Part of the Ministry of Defence, DESO can assist companies with advice on defence market prospects on a worldwide, regional or country basis, by providing military assistance in support of sales, and in other guidance

For information, contact the Director of Marketing Services, Defence Export Services Organisation, Room 707, Stuart House, 23–25 Soho Square, London W1V 5JF Telephone: 0171 632 4826

### Trade Associations

Provide advice and services for their members on export matters relevant to their industry. Some organise trade missions and participation in trade fairs abroad.

328

### Training and Enterprise Councils (TECs) (Department of Employment)

The Business Enterprise Training scheme operated by TECs provides business advice and counselling, consultancy support and business training in subjects such as marketing, accounting and resource management. Further information can be obtained from your local TEC, (**LEC** – Local Enterprise Council in Scotland) or the Department of Employment Telephone: 0171 273 6969

### The Banks

Provide a whole range of services and assistance to exporters, particularly through their international banking centres

### Association of Language-Export (LX) Centres

A network of LX Centres bringing together universities, colleges and polytechnics has been set up with Government help to provide language courses and cultural briefings which are tailor made to the specific business needs of individual firms. Further information can be obtained from the Secretary, P.O. Box 15, London NW1 4NJ Fax: 0171 224 3518 Telephone: 0171 224 3748

### Centre for Information on Language Teaching and Research (CILT)

Is an independent organisation sponsored by Government. It plays an important role in improving language competence in the UK. The CILT library collects and disseminates information on foreign language training. CILT does not run language courses, but it can help analyse a company's needs and help identify a potential provider. For further information contact CILT, Regent's College, Inner Circle, Regent's Park, London NW1 4NS Telephone: 0171 486 8221 Fax: 0171 224 3518

### Assistance with Language Translations and Interpreters

Institute of Linguists
24A Highbury Grove
London N5 2EA
Tel: 0171 359 7445

### Resource

An independent organisation, jointly sponsored by the British Government and BSI. It aims to promote technical co-operation in key overseas markets in the fields of standards, quality assurance, metrology, testing and the way these practices are applied to industrial and agricultural development and technology areas

Further information can be obtained from the Director, Resource, 1–3 Birdcage Walk, London SW1H 9JH Telephone: 0171 222 5373.

### Shipping Companies

Are responsible for the movement of a large proportion of UK exports. For further information contact the General Council of British Shipping, 30–32 St Mary Axe, London EC3A 8ET Telephone: 0171 283 2922

## SELLING FOOD FROM BRITAIN

See Section 1.17

### 'FOOD FROM BRITAIN' offices

### UNITED KINGDOM

Food from Britain
301–344 Market Towers
New Covent Garden Market
London, SW8 5NQ
Tel:  0171 720 2144
Fax: 0171 627 0616

### BELGIUM

Food from Britain (Belgium) BV BA
Rue du Biplan 187
B1140 Evere-Brussels
Belgium
Tel:  00 322 245 6420
Fax: 00 322 245 8210

## FRANCE

Food from Britain (France)
SARL
112–114 rue de la Boetie
75008 Paris
France
Tel: 00 33 1 42 25 01 86
Fax: 00 33 1 42 25 01 85

## GERMANY

Food from Britain (Germany)
GmbH
Lindenstrasse 1
60325, Frankfurt/Main
Germany
Tel: 00 49 69 74 02 77
Fax: 00 49 69 75 14 79

## ITALY

Food from Britain (Italy) Srl
Via Mauro Macchi 50, 20124
Milan
Italy
Tel: 00 39 2 6671 0814/0870
Fax: 00 39 2 6671 1303

## THE NETHERLANDS

Food from Britain (The
Netherlands) BV
Saffierborch 16
5241 LN Rosmalen
(postal address is:
PO Box 280,
5240 AG Rosmalen)
Tel: 00 31 4192 21222
Fax: 00 31 4192 10043

## NORTH AMERICA

Food from Britain (North
America) Inc
4700 Magnolia Circle
Marietta
Georgia 30067
USA
Tel: 00 1 404 955 4074
Fax: 00 1 404 952 9792

## SPAIN (now privatised)

Food from Britain (Spain) SL
Edificio Espana
Gran Via 86
Grupo 1
Planta 5$^a$B 28013 Madrid
Spain
Tel: 00 34 1 559 2612/2661
Fax: 00 34 1 559 4062

# BRITISH CHAMBERS OF COMMERCE

Local Chambers are, with very few exceptions, affiliated to the ASSOCIATION OF BRITISH CHAMBERS OF COMMERCE, and they provide a range of business services in their respective localities, including training courses related to exporting. Membership is by local application and approval

**Membership is strongly recommended: Chambers help exporters**

---

Contact addresses:     Association of British Chambers of
                       Commerce
London Office:         9 Tufton Street,
                       London SW1P 3QB
                       0171 222 1555   Fax: 0171 799 2202
Coventry Office:       4 Westwood House,
                       Westwood Business Park,
                       Coventry CV4 8HS
                       (01203) 694484   Fax: 01203 694690

(Export Marketing Research Scheme is operated from the Coventry Office – see Section 1.5.1)

---

Chambers of Commerce issue CERTIFICATES OF ORIGIN (See Section 16.5.1)

---

Chambers marked Ø are authorised to issue Arab Certificates and authenticate other documents.@ = sub agent

---

The following Chambers are authorised to issue Customs CARNETS:

| | |
|---|---|
| BIRMINGHAM | LEEDS, BRADFORD, YORK |
| BRISTOL | LEICESTER |
| DORSET | LIVERPOOL |
| EDINBURGH | LONDON |
| GLASGOW | MANCHESTER |

| NORFOLK & WAVENEY | SOUTH-EAST HAMPSHIRE |
|---|---|
| NORTHAMPTONSHIRE | (PORTSMOUTH) |
| NORTHERN IRELAND | THAMES VALLEY |
| NOTTINGHAMSHIRE | TYNE & WEAR |
| SOUTHAMPTON | |

A good number of Chambers organise TRADE MISSIONS to Overseas markets

– contact your local Chamber for details of their Mission programme or details of Missions organised by other Chambers

– contact BCC (Coventry) for a full BCC Mission brochure

Chambers organise training courses for Exporters

– ask your local Chamber for details of its Training Course Programme – contact ABCC (Coventry) (Tel: 01203 694484 Fax: 01203 694690) for details of NVQs for International Trade

Some Chambers offer a Language Training and Translation Service

---

**British Chambers Overseas** – There are British Chambers in many overseas countries, and you can obtain the address and contact details from your local Chamber of Commerce – contact list follows:

**SCOTLAND**

| | | |
|---|---|---|
| Ø | ABERDEEN Chamber of Commerce | 01224 212626 |
| | CENTRAL SCOTLAND C of C (Polmont) | 01324 716868 |
| Ø | DUNDEE & TAYSIDE | 01382 201122 |
| Ø | EDINBURGH C of C & Manufacturers | 0131 225 5851 |
| | FIFE C of C & Industry (Kirkcaldy) | 01592 201932 |
| Ø | GLASGOW C of C & M | 0141 204 2121 |
| | LEITH C of C | 0131 225 5851 |
| | PAISLEY C of C & I | 0141 848 5588 |
| | PERTHSHIRE C of C (Perth) | 01738 37626 |

---

## ENGLAND
## MIDLANDS

| | |
|---|---|
| Ø BIRMINGHAM C of I & C (Birmingham) | 0121 454 6171 |
| Solihull C of I & C | 0121 704 6406 |
| Ø BURTON UPON TRENT & DIS. C of C & I | 01283 563761 |
| Ø COVENTRY & WARWICKSHIRE C of C & I | 01203 633000 |
| ◎ DUDLEY C of I & C | 01384 484466 |
| KIDDERMINSTER & DIS. C of C | 01562 515515 |
| Ø NORTH STAFFORDSHIRE C of C & I | |
| (Stoke on Trent) | 01782 202222 |
| REDDITCH & DIS. C of I & C | 01527 67692 |
| RUGBY & DIS. C of C | 01788 544951 |
| SANDWELL C of C & I | 0121 553 2821 |
| Ø EAST MERCIA C of C & I | 01922 721777 |
| Ø WOLVERHAMPTON C of C & I | 01902 26726 |

## YORKSHIRE & HUMBERSIDE

| | |
|---|---|
| BARNSLEY C of C & I | 01226 201166 |
| Ø BRADFORD C of C | 01274 728166 |
| CALDERDALE C OF C & I (Halifax) | 01422 365356 |
| DONCASTER C of C | 01302 341000 |
| GOOLE & DIS. C of C & Shipping Inc. | 01405 769164 |
| ◎ GRIMSBY & IMMINGHAM C of C & Shipping | 01472 342 981 |
| Ø HULL Incorp. C of C & Shipping | 01482 24976 |
| HUMBER C of C & I | 01652 68838 |
| (Humberside Int'l Airport) – (Ass. Member) | |
| Ø LEEDS C of C & I | 01132 363136 |
| Ø MID YORKSHIRE C of C | 01484 426591 |
| ROTHERHAM C of C & I | 01709 828425 |
| SCUNTHORPE, GLANFORD & | |
| GAINSBOROUGH (Scunthorpe) | 01724 842109 |
| Ø SHEFFIELD C of C & Manu. Inc. | 01142 766667 |
| YORK C of C, Trade & I | 01904 629513 |

## NORTH-WEST

| | | |
|---|---|---|
| ⊘ | BOLTON AND BURY C of C | 01204 526526 |
| | BURY & DIS.C of C | 0161 764 8640 |
| | CARLISLE C of C | 01228 21884 |
| Ø | CENTRAL & WEST LANCASHIRE C of C | |
| | (Preston) | 01772 653000 |
| | CHESTER & NORTH WALES C of C | |
| | (Chester) | 01244 674111 |
| | (Colwyn Bay) | 01492 532106 |
| | EAST LANCS C of C & I | 01254 388400 |
| | HALTON C of C (Widnes) | 0151 420 9420 |
| | KENDAL & DIS. C of C, T & I | 01539 729959 |
| | LANCASTER & DIS. C of C, T & I | 01524 39467 |
| Ø | LIVERPOOL C of C & I | 0151 227 1234 |
| Ø | MANCHESTER C of C & I | 0161 236 3210 |
| | SALFORD C of C & I | 0161 236 3210 |
| | TAMESIDE C of C & I | 0161 236 3210 |
| | MANCHESTER INTERNATIONAL | |
| | AIRPORT (Altrincham) (Export | |
| | Documentation Centre) | 0161 489 3170 |
| ⊘ | OLDHAM & DIS. C of C | 0161 633 6133 |
| ⊘ | ROCHDALE C of C, T & I | 01706 343810 |
| ⊘ | ST. HELENS C of C, T & I | 01744 613068 |
| ⊘ | STOCKPORT C of C | 0161 480 0321 |
| | WARRINGTON C of C & I | 01925 635054 |
| ⊘ | WIGAN & DIS. Inc. C of C | 01942 324547 |

---

## EAST MIDLANDS

| | | |
|---|---|---|
| | BOSTON C of C | 01205 351144 |
| | DERBY & DERBYSHIRE C of C & I (Derby) | 01332 347383 |
| | GRANTHAM C of C | 01476 68970 |
| Ø | LEICESTERSHIRE C of C & I | 01162 512300 |
| ⊘ | LINCOLN Inc. C of C | 01522 523333 |
| | NEWARK C of C | 01636 640555 |

Ø NORTH DERBYSHIRE C of C & I
    (Chesterfield)                      01246 211277
    High Peak (Buxton & Glossop)   01298 73070
Ø NORTHAMPTONSHIRE C of C & I
    (Northampton)                 01604 790792
Ø NOTTINGHAMSHIRE C of C & I
    (Nottingham)                  01159 624624
    Mansfield (Mansfield)         01623 420366
    PETERBOROUGH C of C & I     01733 342658/
    (Euro Info Bureau)            891993

---

## LONDON

Ø CROYDON & SOUTH LONDON C of C    0181 680 2165
Ø LONDON C of C & I (38 Queen St)    0171 248 4444
    * Southern Area & Gatwick Airport
      Office (Crawley)           01293 530017
     * South-East Region (Ashford)   01233 639562
     * Barking & Dagenham Office (Barking)  0181 594 3195
     * Greenford Office          0181 575 3542
Ø WESTMINSTER C of C (177 Regent St)  0171 734 2851
    NORTH LONDON C of C        0181 882 0180
    Palmers Green N13 (Ass. Member)

---

## OUTER LONDON & SOUTH EAST

Ø BEDFORDSHIRE & DISTRICT C of C & I
    (Luton)                     01582 23456
    Bedford Area Office         01234 269555
Ø HERTFORDSHIRE              01727 813680
Ø MEDWAY & GILLINGHAM C of C (Chatham)  01634 830001
Ø MILTON KEYNES C of C        01908 662123
Ø OXFORD & DIS. Inc. C of C      01865 792020
Ø READING & CENTRAL BERKSHIRE C of C,
    T & I (Reading)           01734 595049
Ø THAMES VALLEY C of C & I (Slough)    01753 577877

| | |
|---|---|
| Area Offices: | |
| London Airport Heathrow | 0181 759 9321 |
| High Wycombe | 01494 445909 |
| Aylesbury | 01296 434392 |
| Bracknell | 01344 860343 |
| Thames-Chiltern Training Ltd (Slough) | 01753 824541 |
| WEALD & WEST KENT C of C & I (Tunbridge Wells) | 01892 546888 |

## SHROPSHIRE & SOUTH WEST MIDLANDS AREA

| | | |
|---|---|---|
| ⊘ | SHROPSHIRE C of I & C (Telford) | 01952 208228 |
| ⊘ | THREE COUNTIES C of C & I (Worcester) | 01905 611611 |
| | Hereford Area Office (Hereford) | 01432 268795 |

## NORTH EAST

| | | |
|---|---|---|
| | TEESSIDE & DIS. C of C & I (Middlesbrough) | 01642 230023 |
| | Darlington Office | 01325 384045 |
| | TYNEDALE C of C (Hexham) | 01434 601380 |
| Ø | TYNE & WEAR C of C (Newcastle on Tyne) | 0191 261 1142 |
| | Chamber's Centres: | |
| | Sunderland | 0191 510 9090 |
| | South Shields | 0191 427 0663 |
| | North Shields | 0191 258 1795 |

## EAST ANGLIA

| | | |
|---|---|---|
| Ø | CAMBRIDGE & DIS. C of C & I | 01223 237414 |
| Ø | IPSWICH & SUFFOLK C of C, I & Shipping | 01473 210611 |
| | LOWESTOFT Inc. C of C | 01502 569383 |
| Ø | NORFOLK & WAVENEY C of C & I | 01603 625977 |
| Ø | NORTH & MID ESSEX | 01206 765277 |
| | GREAT YARMOUTH C of C & I | 01493 842184 |
| | Documentation Office (Kings Lynn) | 01553 768505 |
| | PETERBOROUGH C of C & I | 01733 342658 |

| | |
|---|---|
| SOUTH ESSEX C of C, T & I | 01702 77090/ |
| (Westcliff-on-Sea) | 78380 |

## SOUTH WEST

| | |
|---|---|
| Ø BRISTOL C of C & I | 01179 737373 |
| ⓪ PLYMOUTH C of C & I | 01752 221151 |
| ⓪ SWINDON C of C & I | 01793 616544 |
| Ø CORNWALL | 01209 314884 |

## SOUTH COAST/HOME COUNTIES

| | |
|---|---|
| Ø DORSET C of C & I | 01202 448800 |
| FAREHAM C of C | 01329 822250 |
| GUILDFORD C of C | 01483 37449 |
| Ø SOUTH-EAST HAMPSHIRE C of C & I | |
| (Portsmouth) | 01705 294111 |
| Ø SOUTHAMPTON C of C | 01703 223541 |
| HOVE – Sussex C of C & I | 01273 326282 |

## WALES

| | |
|---|---|
| Ø CARDIFF C of C & I | 01222 481648 |
| Ø NEWPORT & GWENT C of C & I (Newport) | 01633 257871 |
| CHESTER & NORTH WALES C of C | 01244 674111 |
| Colwyn Bay Office | 01492 532106 |
| WEST WALES C of C (Swansea) | 01792 653297/8 |

## NORTHERN IRELAND

| | |
|---|---|
| Ø NORTHERN IRELAND C of C & I (Belfast) | 01232 244113 |

## OFF-SHORE

| | |
|---|---|
| GUERNSEY C of C (St. Peter Port) | 01481 727483 |

| | |
|---|---|
| JERSEY C of C & I Inc. (St. Helier) | 01534 24536/ 71031 |
| ISLE OF MAN C of C, T & I (Douglas) | 01624 674941 |
| ISLE OF WIGHT C of C (Newport, I O W) | 01983 524390 |

# OVERSEAS CHAMBERS OF COMMERCE IN LONDON

See Section 1.3.2

| | |
|---|---|
| AMERICAN C of C | 0171 493 0381 |
| | Fax: 0171 493 2394 |
| ARAB–BRITISH C of C (A/M BCC) | 0171 235 4363 |
| | Fax: 0171 245 6688 |
| BRITISH–AMERICAN C of C | 0171 404 6400 |
| | Fax: 0171 404 6828 |
| AUSTRALIAN–BRITISH C of C (UK) | 0171 636 4525 |
| | Fax: 0171 636 4511 |
| BELGIAN–LUXEMBOURG C of C | 0171 831 3508 |
| | Fax: 0171 831 9151 |
| BRAZILIAN C of C in GB | 0171 499 0186 |
| | Fax: 0171 493 5105 |
| BRITISH BULGARIAN C of C | 0171 584 8333 |
| | Fax: 0171 589 4875 |
| BRITISH–ISRAEL C of C | 0171 486 2371 |
| | Fax: 0171 224 1783 |
| BRITISH LATVIAN C of C | 0171 680 0627 |
| BSCC | 0171 403 1706 |
| *(Note: Covers all former Soviet republics)* | Fax: 0171 403 1245 |
| CANADA-UNITED KINGDOM C of C | 0171 930 7711 |
| | Fax: 0171 930 9703 |
| CROATIAN C of C | 0181 896 1230 |
| | Fax: 0181 896 2577 |
| CYPRUS–BRITISH C of C & I | 0171 734 4791 |
| | Tx:          22540 |
| | CYTOUR G |
| CYPRUS TURKISH C of C | 0171 582 1007 |
| | Fax: 0171 494 0491 |
| EGYPTIAN BRITISH C of C | 0171 323 2856 |
| | Fax: 0171 323 5739 |
| FRENCH C of C | 0171 304 4040 |
| | Fax: 0171 304 7034 |

| | |
|---|---|
| GERMAN C of I & C in UK | 0171 233 5656 |
| | Fax: 0171 233 7835 |
| ITALIAN C of C for GB | 0171 637 3153 |
| | Fax: 0171 436 6037 |
| JAPANESE C of C & I (UK) | 0171 628 0069 |
| | Fax: 0171 628 0248 |
| NETHERLANDS–BRITISH C of C | 0171 405 1358 |
| | Fax: 0171 405 1689 |
| NEW ZEALAND–UNITED KINGDOM C of C | 0171 636 4525 |
| | Fax: 0171 636 4511 |
| NIGERIAN C of C | 01435 872 731 |
| | Fax: 01635 200 799 |
| NORWEGIAN C of C | 0171 930 0181 |
| | Fax: 0171 930 7946 |
| PAPUA NEW GUINEA–UNITED KINGDOM C of C | 0171 636 4525 |
| | Fax: 0171 636 4511 |
| PORTUGUESE (UK) C of C | 0171 494 1844 |
| | Fax: 0171 494 1822 |
| SPANISH C of C | 0171 637 9061 |
| | Fax: 0171 436 7188 |
| SWEDISH C of C | 0171 486 4545 |
| | Fax: 0171 935 5487 |
| TURKISH–BRITISH C of C & I | 0171 499 4265 |
| | Fax: 0171 493 5548 |

# BRITISH–OVERSEAS CHAMBERS OF COMMERCE

The Chambers listed below will provide information and advise on local matters for UK exporters. (BCC) indicates Associate Members of British Chambers of Commerce

UNITED STATES OF AMERICA
British–American Chamber of Commerce
Room 1714                                   00 (1) 415 296 8645
275 Madison Avenue                  Fax: 00 (1) 415 296 9649
New York
NY 10016

British–American Chamber of Commerce
41 Sutter Street                            00 (1) 415 296 8645
Suite 303                                Fax: 00 (1) 415 296 9649
San Francisco
California 94104

ARGENTINA
Anglo–Argentine Chamber of Commerce
Av. Corrientes 457                        00 (54) 1 394 2318
Piso 10$^0$                                 Tx: 23645 CAMAB AR
1043 Buenos Aires                  Fax: 00 (54) 1 394 2282

AUSTRALIA
Australian– British Chamber of Commerce
Level 12                                     00 (61) 2 299 5474
83 Clarence Street                Fax: 00 (61) 2 299 5483
Sydney
New South Wales 2000

Australian–British Chamber of Commerce
Level 5                                       00 (61) 3 614 7173
520 Collins Street                  Tx: 00 (61) 3 629 8298
Melbourne, Victoria 3000

AUSTRIA
British Trade Council
Mollwaldplatz 1                           00 (43) 1 505 4363
A–1040 Vienna                      Fax: 00 (43) 1 505 4914

British Chamber of Commerce in BELGIUM (BCC)
Avenue Du Col Vert 1                    00 (32) 2 678 4790
Groenkraaglan                  Fax: 00 (32) 2 678 4791
B–1170 Brussels

BRAZIL
The British Chamber of Commerce in Brazil
Avenida Rio Branco 181,                 00 (55) 21 262 5926
Room 2007                      Fax: 00 (55) 21 533 1486
CEP 20040–007 Rio de Janeiro–RJ

The British Chamber of Commerce in Brazil
PO Box 1621                             00 (55) 11 255 4286
Rua Barao de Itapetininga 275  Fax: 00 (55) 11 231 3742
7th Floor
CEP 01059–970 Sao Paulo–SP

CHILE
The British–Chilean Chamber of
Commerce in the Republic of Chile       00 (56) 2 231 4366
Avenida Suecia 155–C           Fax: 00 (56) 2 231 8211
Casilla 536
Santiago

COLOMBIA
The Colombo–British Chamber of Commerce
Calle 106, No. 25–41                    00 (57) 1 215 8949
Apartado Aereo 054728          Fax: 00 (57) 1 215 1190
Bogota D.E.

DENMARK
British Import Union
Borsbygningen                           00 (4533) 136349
DK–1217                        Fax: 00 (4533) 142404
Copenhagen K

FRANCE
French–British Chamber of Commerce
& Industry                              00 (33) 1 44 59 25 20
41 Rue de Turenne              Tx: 614806 BRCOMFPAF
F–75003 Paris                  Fax: 00 (33) 1 44 59 25 45

British Chamber of Commerce in GERMANY (BCC)
Severinstrasse 60                               00 (49) 221 314458
D–50678 Köln                         Fax: 00 (49) 221 315335
Germany

BRITISH–HELLENIC Chamber of Commerce (BCC)
25 Vas Sofias Avenue                           00 (01) 7210361
GR–106 74 Athens                       Fax: 00 (01) 7218751
Greece

British Chamber of Commerce in HONG KONG (BCC)
Room 1712, Shui On Centre                    00 (852) 824 2211
8 Harbour Road                       Fax: 00 (852) 824 1333
Wanchai
Hong Kong

British Chamber of Commerce in HUNGARY (BCC)
Iskola u. 37.1/4                 Tel/Fax: 00 (36) 1 201 9142
H1011 Budapest
Hungary

ISRAEL
Israel–British Chamber of Commerce           00 (972) 3 6959732
76 Ibn Gvirol Street                       Tx: 34315 PCENT IL
642 Tel Aviv                          Fax: 00 (972) 3 221873
Mail Address: PO Box 16065, Tel Aviv 61160

British Chamber of Commerce for ITALY (BCC)
Via Camperio 9                                 00 (39) 2 876 981
20123 Milan                           Fax: 00 (39) 864 61885
Italy

British Chamber of Commerce in JAPAN (BCC)
3rd Floor Kenkyusha Eigo Centre Building
1–2 Kagurazaka                               00 (81) 3 3267 1901
Shinjuku-ku, Tokyo 162              Fax: 00 (81) 3 3267 1903
Japan

British Chamber of Commerce for LUXEMBOURG (BCC)
c/o The Secretariat                           00 (35) 2 346 351
BP 2740                               Fax: 00 (35) 2 349 145
L.1027 Luxembourg

British Chamber of Commerce in MEXICO (BCC)
Rio de la Plata No. 30                    00 (525) 256 0901
Col Cuauhtemoc                    Tx: 76 1274 BCCME
06500 Mexico, DF                    Fax: 00 (525) 211 5451
Mexico

British Chamber of Commerce for MOROCCO (BCC)
Holiday Inn Crowne Plaza                    00 (212) 2 271519
Suite 201, Rond Point Hassan II                    Fax: 00 (212) 2 269744
Casablanca
Morocco

NETHERLANDS–BRITISH Chamber of Commerce (BCC)
Holland Trade House                    00 (31) 70 347 8881
Bezuidenhoutseweg 181                    Fax: 00 (31) 70 347 8769
NL–2594 AH The Hague
The Netherlands
and in London
0171 405 1358
Fax: 0171 405 1689

NEW ZEALAND
British–New Zealand Trade Council
PO Box 37162                    Tel/Fax: 00 (64) 9 522 0526
Auckland

British Chamber of Commerce in POLAND (BCC)
Ul. Krolewska 27a                    00 (48) 22 273582
Warsaw 00–060                    Fax: 00 (48) 22 276915
Poland

BRITISH–PORTUGUESE Chamber of Commerce (BCC)
Rua da Estrela, 8                    00 (351) 1 396 1586
P–1200 Lisbon                    Fax: 00 (351) 1 601513
Portugal

RUSSIA
BSCC                    00 (7) 095 230 6120
Suite 102, Ground Floor                    Tx: 413523 BRIS SU
Bolshoi Stochenovsky per. 22/25                    Fax: 00 (7) 095 230 6124
Moscow 113054

SPAIN
British Chambers of Commerce in Spain
Paseo de Gracia, 11A                          00 (34) 3 317 3220
E 08007 Barcelona                     Fax: 00 (34) 3 302 4896

BRITISH–SWEDISH Chamber of Commerce (BCC)
Nybrogatan 75                                 00 (08) 665 3425
114 40 Stockholm                      Fax: 00 (08) 665 0935
Sweden

The British Chamber of Commerce of TURKEY (BCC)
Mesrutiyet Caddesi                            00 (90) 1 249 0658
No 34 Tepebasi                        Fax: 00 (90) 1 252 5551
Istanbul
(PO Box 190, Karakoy, Istanbul)

# EUROPEAN COMMISSION OFFICES

European Commission
200 rue de la Loi
1049 Brussels
Tel: (00 322) 235 1111

---

European Commission
Batiment Jean Monnet
rue Alcide de Gasperi
L-2920 Luxembourg
Tel: (00 352) 43011

---

In UK:  LONDON OFFICE        – 8 Storey's Gate
                                London SW1P 3AT
                                0171 973 1992
                                Fax: 0171 973 1900

        BELFAST OFFICE        – Windsor House
                                9–15 Bedford Street
                                Belfast
                                01232 240708

        CARDIFF OFFICE        – 4 Cathedral Road
                                Cardiff CF1 9SG
                                01222 371631

        EDINBURGH OFFICE      – 9 Alva Street
                                Edinburgh EH2 4PH
                                0131 225 2058

---

## EURO INFORMATION CENTRES IN UK

### Northern Ireland
### Local Enterprise Development Unit
LEDU House
Upper Galwally
Belfast BT8 4TB
Tel: 01232 491031

### North-West
### North West Euro Services Ltd
Liverpool Central Libraries
William Brown Street
Liverpool L3 8EW
Tel: 0151 298 1928

### Manchester Chamber of Commerce and Industry
Euro Info Centre
56 Oxford Street
Manchester M60 7HJ
Tel: 0161 236 3210

### Shropshire
### Shropshire Chamber of Commerce and Industry
Euro Info Centre
Industry House
16 Halesford
Telford
Shropshire TF7 4TA
Tel: 01952 588766

### Cheshire
Mold – Tel: 01352 704748

### Wales
### Wales Euro Info Centre
University College Cardiff
PO Box 430
Cardiff CF1 3XT
Tel: 01222 229525

### South-West
### Bristol Chamber of Commerce and Industry
16 Clifton Park
Bristol BS8 3BY
Tel: 01179 737373 x311

### Exeter Enterprises Ltd
University of Exeter
Hailey Wing
Reed Hall
Exeter EX4 4QR
Tel: 01392 214085

### South Coast area
### Southern Area Euro Info Centre
Central Library
Civic Centre
Southampton SO9 4XP
Tel: 01703 832866

## Scotland
### Highland Opportunity Ltd
Development Department
Highland Regional Council
Regional Buildings
Glenurquhart Road
Inverness IV3 5NX
Tel: 01463 702560

### Scottish Development Agency
Euro Info Centre
21 Bothwell Street
Glasgow G2 6NR
Tel: 0141 221 0999

## East Midlands
### Nottinghamshire Chamber of Commerce and Industry
Euro Info Centre
Faraday Building
Highfield Science Park
Nottingham NG7 2QP
Tel: 01159 624624

### Euro Info Centre
30 New Walk
Leicester LE1 6TF
Tel: 01162 559944

## Midlands
### Birmingham Chamber of Industry and Commerce
75 Harborne Road
PO Box 360
Birmingham B15 3DH
Tel: 0121 454 6171

**Stafford** – Tel: 01785 59528

**Worcester** – Tel: 01905 765335

## Berkshire, Oxon
### Thames Chiltern Chamber of Commerce
Commerce House
2–6 Bath Road
Slough
Berks SL1 3SB
Tel: 01753 577877

## London area
### London Chamber of Commerce and Industry
69 Cannon Street
London EC4N 5AB
Tel: 0171 261 1163 &
0171 248 4444

## South-East
### Kent County Council
Euro Info Centre
Springfield
Maidstone ME1 2LL
Tel: 01622 694109

### Sussex Chamber of Commerce and Industry
Seven Dials
Brighton BN1 3JS
Tel: 01273 326282

**North-East**
**Northern Development Company**
Euro Info Centre
Great North House
Sandyford Road
Newcastle-upon-Tyne
NE1 8ND
Tel: 0191 261 0026

**Yorkshire & Humberside**
**Yorkshire and Humberside Euro Info Centre**
Westgate House
Wellington Street
Leeds LS1 4LT
Tel: 01132 833126

**Bradford** – Tel: 01274 754262

**Sheffield** – Tel: 01142 5321236

**East Anglia**
**Norwich and Norfolk Chamber of Commerce and Industry**
Euro Info Centre
112 Barrack Street
Norwich NR3 1UB
Tel: 01603 625977

# EUROPEAN DOCUMENTATION CENTRES

(Located mainly in Universities)
*EUROPEAN REFERENCE CENTRES\**

---

**Contact numbers:**
**Northern Ireland**
Belfast            01232 245133 x 3605
Coleraine          01265 44141 x 4257

---

**North-West**
Lancaster          01524 592539
Manchester         0161 275 3727 x 3770/3751
*\*Preston*          *01772 892267*
Salford            0161 745 5846

---

**Staffordshire**
Keele              01782 621111 x 7738

---

**Wales**
*\*Aberystwyth*      *01970 6233 111 x 2401*
Cardiff            01222 874262
*\*Swansea*          *01792 205678 x 4037*
*\*Wrexham*          *01978 291 355*

---

**South-West**
Bath               01225 826826 x 5594
Bristol            01179 303370
Exeter             01392 263263 x 2072
*\*Exmouth*          *01395 255 352*

---

## South Coast area

| | |
|---|---|
| Guildford | 01483 300800 x 3323 |
| Portsmouth | 01705 843242 |
| Southampton | 01703 593451 |

## Scotland

| | |
|---|---|
| Aberdeen | 01224 272588 |
| Dundee | 01382 23181 x 4102 |
| Edinburgh | 0131 650 2041 and * |
| Glasgow | 0141 339 8855 x 6747 |
| *Stirling | 0131 226 4531 |

## East Midlands

| | |
|---|---|
| Leicester | 01162 522044 |
| Loughborough | 01509 222344 |
| *Northampton | 01604 735500 |
| Nottingham | 01159 514560 |

## Midlands

| | |
|---|---|
| Birmingham | 0121 331 5298 |
| | 0121 414 5833 |
| Coventry | 01203 838295 |
| | 01203 523523 x 2041 |
| Wolverhampton | 01902 322727 |

## Thames Valley/Oxfordshire

| | |
|---|---|
| *Chalfont St. Giles | 01494 873906 |
| Oxford | 01865 271463 |
| Reading | 01734 318782 |
| *Reading | 01734 318651 |

## East Anglia

| | |
|---|---|
| Cambridge | 01223 333138 |
| *Chelmsford* | *01245 493131 x 3200* |
| Colchester | 01206 873181 |
| *Hatfield* | *01707 284678* |
| *Ipswich* | *01473 233411 x 125* |
| Norwich | 01603 56161 x 2412 |

## South East & London

| | |
|---|---|
| Ashford | 01233 812401 x 497 |
| Brighton | 01273 678159 |
| *Brighton* | *01273 691297* |
| Canterbury | 01227 764000 x 3108 |
| London SW1 | 0171 957 5700 x 221 |
| London E1 | 0171 775 3321 |
| London NW5 | 0171 607 2789 x 4110 |
| London WC2 | 0171 955 7273 |
| *London W5* | *0181 231 2246* |

## North East

| | |
|---|---|
| Durham | 0191 374 3041 |
| *Middlesbrough* | *01642 218121 x 2100* |
| Newcastle | 0191 227 4136 |

## Yorkshire & Humberside

| | |
|---|---|
| Bradford | 01274 383402 |
| *Halifax* | *01422 358221 x 2117* |
| Hull | 01482 465966 |
| Leeds | 01132 335041 |
| | 01132 833126 |
| Sheffield | 01142 532126 |
| *Sheffield* | *01142 768555 x 6779* |

## EUROPEAN DEPOSIT LIBRARIES

A comprehensive collection of EU official documentation can be consulted at the following locations:

| | |
|---|---|
| LIVERPOOL | 0151 225 5430 |
| LONDON | 0171 798 2034 |
| WETHERBY | 01937 546044 |

Many local libraries provide EU information and stock EU publications for reference purposes

# UNIVERSITIES WORK FOR EXPORTS – CONTACTS FOR INDUSTRY

ABERDEEN    External Funding & Industrial Services, University of Aberdeen. Tel: 01224 272124 Fax: 01224 272319

ABERDEEN    Industrial Unit, The Robert Gordon University. Tel: 01224 262000 Fax: 01224 639559

ABERYSTWYTH    Industrial Liaison, University College of Wales. Tel: 01970 622385 Fax: 01970 617172

BANGOR    Manager of Commercial Services, University College of North Wales, 9th Floor Chemistry Block, Bangor, Gwynedd LL57 2DG. Tel: 01248 382500/1 Fax: 01248 370528

BATH    Director Technical & Commercial Marketing, University of Bath, Claverton Down, Bath, Avon BA2 7AY. Tel: 01225 826822 Fax: 01225 826675

BELFAST    Director of Industrial Liaison, The Queens University of Belfast, 10 Malone Road, Belfast BT9 5BN Tel: 01232 245133 Extn: 4143/4004 Fax: 01232 663015

BEDFORD    Economic Development Officer, Bedfordshire Economic Development Unit, County Hall, Bedford MK42 9AP

BIRMINGHAM    Pro-Vice-Chancellor, Aston University, Aston Triangle, Birmingham B4 7ET. Tel: 0121 359 3611 Fax: 0121 359 2792

BIRMINGHAM    Director of Research Support, The University of Birmingham, Edgbaston, Birmingham B15 2TT. Tel: 0121 414 3884/1/0 Fax: 0121 414 3850

BIRMINGHAM    Head of Enterprise Unit, University of Central England in Birmingham, Perry Barr, Birmingham B42 2SU. Tel: 0121 331 5253 Fax: 0121 331 5256

BOLTON    Head of Marketing, Bolton Institute of Higher Education, Dean Road, Bolton BL3 5AB. Tel: 01204 28851 Fax: 01204 399074

BOURNEMOUTH    Head of External Affairs & Marketing, Bournemouth University, Poole House, Talbot Campus, Fern Barrow, Poole, Dorset BH12 5BB. Tel: 01202 595531 Fax: 01202 595034

BRADFORD    Director of Business Development Services, University of Bradford, 14 Claremont, Bradford, West Yorkshire BD7 1DP. Tel: 01274 383170/1 Fax: 01274 720910

BRIDGWATER    Head of Marketing, Industrial Liaison, Bridgwater College, Bath Road, Bridgwater, Somerset TA6 4PZ. Tel: 01278 455464 Fax: 01278 444363

BRIGHTON    Senior Finance Officer, University of Sussex, Sussex House, Falmer, Brighton BN1 9RH. Tel: 01273 606755 Fax: 01273 678335

BRIGHTON    Head of Marketing and Business Development, University of Brighton, Moulsecoomb Place, Lewes Road, Brighton BN2 4GA. Tel: 01273 681941 Fax: 01273 681895

BRISTOL    Head of Research Support and Industrial Liaison Office, University of Bristol, 3rd Floor, Senate House, Tyndall Avenue, Bristol BS8 1TH. Tel: 01179 303120 or 303030 Extn 8036/8120/8039 Fax: 01179 298383

BRISTOL    Project Development Manager, Centre for Innovation and Industry, University of the West of England, Bristol, Coldharbour Lane, Bristol BS16 1QY. Tel: 01179 656261 Fax: 01179 763839

BUXTON    Training Consultant, High Peak College, Harpur Hill, Buxton, Derbyshire. Tel: 01298 71100 Fax: 01298 27261

CAMBRIDGE    Director in Industrial Co-operation, The University of Cambridge, Industrial Liaison & Technology Transfer Office, 20 Trumpington Street, Cambridge CB2 1QA. Tel: 01223 334755 Fax: 01223 332797

CAMBRIDGE    Industrial Liaison Officer, Anglia Polytechnic University, East Road, Cambridge CB1 1PT. Tel: 01223 352962 Fax: 01223 352935

CANTERBURY    Research Grants & Contracts Officer, University of Kent, The Registry, Canterbury, Kent CT2 7NZ. Tel: 01227 764000 Extn 3523 Fax: 01227 452196

CARDIFF    Head – Research & Commercial Development, University of Wales College of Cardiff, PO Box 78, Cardiff CF1 1XL. Tel: 01222 874837 Fax: 01222 874189

CARDIFF    Deputy Registrar, University of Wales College of Medicine, Heath Park, Cardiff CF4 4XN. Tel: 01222 742028 Fax: 01222 742914

CHATHAM    Midken Ltd, Mid-Kent College of HE & FE, Maidstone Road, Chatham, Kent ME5 0UQ. Tel: 01634 844265 Fax: 01634 830224

CHELMSFORD    Marketing Officer, Chelmsford Colleges of FE, Dovedale, Moulsham Street, Chelmsford, Essex CM2 0JQ. Tel: 01245 265611

CHELMSFORD    ILO, Anglia Polytechnic University, Victoria Road South, Chelmsford CM1 1LL. Tel: 01245 493131 Fax: 01245 495419

CHELTENHAM    Employer Link Co-ordinator, Cheltenham & Gloucester College of HE, Fullwood Lodge, Park Campus, PO Box 220, The Park, Cheltenham, Gloucestershire GL50 2QF. Tel 01242 543304 Fax: 01242 532810

CHESTER    Enterprise Officer, Cheshire County Council, Shipgate House, Shipgate Street, Chester CH1 1RT. Tel: 01244 602619/603152 Fax: 01244 314349

COLCHESTER    Director – Industrial Liaison, University of Essex, Wivenhoe Park, Colchester, Essex CO4 3SQ. Tel: 01206 872411 Fax: 01206 873375

COLERAINE    Head – Research & Consultancy Services, University of Ulster, Coleraine, Co Londonderry, Northern Ireland BT52 1SA. Tel: 01265 44141 Extn 4378/9 Fax: 01265 40905

CORK    Industrial Liaison Officer, University College Cork, Cork, Ireland. Tel: 00 353 21 276871 Fax: 00 353 21 273365

COVENTRY    Director, Commercial Affairs, Coventry University, Priory Street, Coventry CV1 5FB. Tel: 01203 838727 Fax: 01203 221396

COVENTRY    Director of Industrial Development, University of Warwick, Senate House, Coventry CV4 7AL. Tel: 01203 523716 Fax: 01203 524573

CUDDESDON    AILO/UDIL Secretariat, Hamlet, Denton Green, Cuddesdon, Oxon OX44 9JD. Tel: 01865 872228 Fax: 01865 874671

DAGENHAM    University of East London, Longbridge Road, Dagenham, Essex RM8 2AS. Tel: 0181 590 7722

DERBY    Assistant Marketing Officer, University of Derby, Kedleston Road, Derby DE22 1GB. Tel: 01332 47181 x 1043 Fax: 01332 294861

DONCASTER    Marketing Administrator, Doncaster College, Waterdale, Doncaster DN1 3EX. Tel: 01302 322122 Fax: 01302 738065

DUBLIN    Director – University Industry Programme, University College Dublin, Belfield, Dubin 4, Ireland. Tel: 00 353 1 693244

DUBLIN    Director of Innovation Services, The University of Dublin, O'Reilly Institute, Trinity College, Dublin 2. Tel: 00 353 1 702 1427/1155 Fax: 00 353 1 679 8039

DUBLIN    Director – Industrial & International Affairs, Dublin City University, Glasnevin, Dublin 9. Tel: 00 353 1 7055175 Fax: 00 353 1 7045505

DUNDEE    Director of Industrial Liaison, University of Dundee, Dundee DD1 4HN. Tel: 01382 25468 Fax: 01382 202178

DUNDEE    Industrial Liaison Officer, Duncan of Jordanstone College of Art, Perth Road, Dundee DD1 4HT. Tel: 01382 23261 Fax: 01382 27304

DUNDEE    Director, Technology Transfer Centre, Dundee Institute of Technology, Bell Street, Dundee DD1 1HG. Tel: 01382 27225 Fax: 01382 200782

DURHAM    Industrial Liaison Officer, University of Durham, Mountjoy Research Centre, South Road, Durham DH1 3LE. Tel: 0191 374 2599 Fax: 0191 374 2591

EDINBURGH    Managing Director – UNIVED, University of Edinburgh, 16 Buccleuch Place, Edinburgh EH8 9LN. Tel: 0131 650 3479 Fax: 0131 650 6532

EDINBURGH    Director – Industrial Liaison, Heriot-Watt University, Riccarton, Edinburgh EH14 4AS. Tel: 0131 449 5111 Fax: 0131 451 3070

EDINBURGH    Managing Director, Napier University Ventures Ltd, Napier University, Room C1, Sighthill Court, Sighthill Campus, Edinburgh EH11 4BN. Tel: 0131 455 2250 Fax: 0131 452 8532

EDINBURGH    Director of Business Development, Queen
   Margaret College, 38b Drumsheugh Gardens, Edinburgh EH3
   7SW. Tel: 0131 539 7095 Fax: 0131 539 7096

EDINBURGH    Assistant Principal, Telford College, Crewe Toll,
   Edinburgh EH4 2NZ. Tel: 0131 332 2491 Fax: 0131 343 1218

EDINBURGH    Commercial Services Manager, The Scottish
   Agricultural College, Central Office, West Mains Road,
   Edinburgh EH9 3JG. Tel: 0131 662 1303 Fax: 0131 662 1323

EGHAM    Royal Holloway Enterprise Account Executive, Royal
   Holloway, University of London, Egham Hill, Egham, Surrey
   TW20 0EX. Tel: 01784 434455 Fax: 01784 437520

EXETER    Assistant Registrar Finance Division, University of
   Exeter, Northcote House, The Queens Drive, Exeter EX4 4QJ.
   Tel: 01392 263057 Fax: 01392 263108

GALWAY    Director – Industrial Liaison Office, University of
   Galway, Galway, Ireland. Tel: 00 353 91 24411 Fax: 00 353 91
   26388

GLASGOW    Chief Executive, Glasgow Poly Enterprises Ltd,
   Glasgow Caledonian University, Cowcaddens Road, Glasgow
   G4 0BA. Tel: 0141 331 3725 Fax: 0141 331 3005

GLASGOW    Director – ICD, University of Glasgow, 2 The Square,
   Glasgow G12 8QQ. Tel: 0141 330 5199 Fax: 0141 330 5643

GLASGOW    Director of R&D Services, University of Strathclyde,
   Marland House, 50 George Street, Glasgow G1 1BA. Tel: 0141
   552 4400 Extn 2476 Fax: 0141 552 4409

GUILDFORD    Intellectual Property Manager – Office for
   Research & Commercial Services, University of Surrey,
   Guildford, Surrey GU2 5XH. Tel: 01483 259361 Fax: 01483
   505629

GUILDFORD    Pro-Vice-Chancellor, Commercial Affairs, Office
   of Research and Commercial Services, University of Surrey,
   Guildford, Surrey GU2 5XH. Tel: 01483 259361 Fax: 01483
   505629

GUILDFORD    Industrial Liaison Officer, Guildford College of
   Technology, Stoke Park, Guildford GU1 1EZ. Tel: 01483 31251
   Fax: 01483 63409

HATFIELD   Commercial Development Manager, UH Ventures Ltd, University of Hertfordshire, PO Box 109, Hatfield AL10 9AB. Tel: 01707279339 Fax: 01707279670

HEREFORD   Lecture/Tourism Marketing, Herefordshire College of Technology, Folly Lane, Hereford HR1 1LS. Tel: 01432 352235 Fax: 01432 353449

HIGH WYCOMBE   Buckinghamshire College of HE, Queen Alexandra Road, High Wycombe HP11 2JZ. Tel: 01494 522141 Fax: 01494 524392

HUDDERSFIELD   Assistant Rector, University of Huddersfield, Queensgate, Huddersfield HD1 3DH. Tel: 01484 422288 Fax: 01484 516151

HULL   Director of DIRECT, University of Hull, Cottingham Road, Hull HU6 7RX. Tel: 01482 465510 Fax: 01482 466477

HULL   Polygon (Humber) Ltd, University of Humberside, 246 Cottingham Road, Hull HU6 7RT. Tel: 01482 492776 Fax: 01482 440279

INVERNESS   Assistant Principal, Inverness College of F & HE, 3 Longman Road, Longman South, Inverness IV1 1SA. Tel: 01463 236681 Fax: 01463 711977

KEELE   Assistant Director – Research Development, Keele University, Keele, Staffordshire ST5 5BG. Tel: 01782 583369 Fax: 01782 713127

KINGSTON UPON THAMES   General Manager, Kingston University Enterprises Ltd, Kingston University, Penrhyn Road, Kingston upon Thames, Surrey KT1 2EE. Tel: 0181 547 7273 Fax: 0181 974 8035

LANCASTER   Research Support Officer, Lancaster University, University House, Bailrigg, Lancaster LA1 4YW. Tel: 01524 65201 Extn 4526 Fax: 01524 594069

LANCASTER   Manager, Enterprise Unit, St Martins College, Lancaster, Lancashire LA1 3JD. Tel: 01524 63446 Fax: 01524 68943

LEEDS   Director – Research Support Unit, The University of Leeds, Leeds LS2 9JT. Tel: 01132 336028 Fax: 01132 334123

LEEDS   Short Course Manager, Leeds Metropolitan University, Calverly Street, Leeds LS1 3HE. Tel: 01132 832600 Fax: 01132 833115

LEICESTER   Development Officer, University of Leicester, University Road, Leicester LE1 7RH. Tel: 01162 523334 Fax: 01162 522028

LEICESTER   Marketing Manager, Leicester Expertise Ltd, De Montfort University, 1 Gateway House, Gateway Street, Leicester LE2 7DP. Tel: 01162 577377 Fax: 01162 577250

LEICESTER   Charles Keen College of FE, Painter St, Leicester LE1 3WA. Tel: 01162 516037 Fax: 01162 620592

LIMERICK   Director – Co-op Education & External Affairs Division, University of Limerick, Limerick, Ireland. Tel: 00 353 61 333644

LIVERPOOL   Director – Research Support & Industrial Liaison, The University of Liverpool, Senate House, PO Box 147, Liverpool L69 3BX. Tel: 0151 794 2079/2080 Fax: 0151 708 6502

LIVERPOOL   Industrial Liaison Officer, Commercial Development Unit, Liverpool John Moores University, 2 Rodney St, Liverpool L3 5UX. Tel: 0151 231 3471 Fax: 0151 707 0199

LONDON   University of London, Birkbeck College, Malet Street, London WC1E 7HX. Tel: 0171 631 6257 Fax: 0171 631 6270

LONDON   Director – Industrial Liaison Unit, The British Postgraduate Medical Federation, 33 Millman Street, London WC1N 3EJ. Tel: 0171 831 6222 Fax: 0171 831 1387

LONDON   The Secretary, City University, Northampton Square, London EC1V 0HB. Tel: 0171 477 8100 Fax: 0171 250 0837

LONDON   General Manager CoPEL, University of East London, 1 Water Lane, Romford Road, London E15 4LZ. Tel: 0181 519 3188 Fax: 0181 534 8457

LONDON   University of Greenwich, Riverside House, Beresford St, Woolwich, London SE18 6BU. Tel: 0181 316 9000 Fax: 0181 316 9005

LONDON   Pro Rector (Research Contracts), Imperial College, Room 539 Sherfield Building, South Kensington, London SW7 2AZ. Tel: 0171 225 8619/8620 Fax: 0171 589 3553

LONDON   Director of Industrial Liaison, Kings College London, Campden Hill Road, London W8 7AH. Tel: 0171 333 4650 Fax: 0171 333 4650

LONDON   Head of EPS Dept, Lewisham College, Wickham Building, Lewisham Way, London SE4 2PU. Tel: 0181 692 0353 Fax: 0181 694 9163

LONDON   Director – Research Support, London Business School, Sussex Place, Regents Park, London NW1 4SA. Tel: 0171 262 5050 Fax: 0171 724 7875

LONDON   Assistant College Secretary, London Hospital Medical College, Turner Street, London E1 2AD. Tel: 0171 377 7607 Fax: 0171 377 7677

LONDON   Head of Research Services, London School of Economics, Houghton Street, London WC2A 2AS. Tel: 0171 831 4262 Fax: 0171 955 7427

LONDON   Commercial Manager, Middlesex University, Bounds Green Road, London N11 2NQ. Tel: 0181 362 5687 Fax: 0181 362 5736

LONDON   Head of Economic Development, University of North London, Holloway Road, London N7 8DB. Tel: 0171 753 5151 Fax: 0171 753 7064

LONDON   Assistant Accountant (External Grants), Queen Mary & Westfield College, Mile End Road, London E1 4NS. Tel: 0171 975 5021 Fax: 0171 975 5500

LONDON   Commercial Director, Royal Postgraduate Medical School, Commonwealth Building, Du Cane Road, London W12 0NN. Tel: 0181 740 3111 Fax: 0181 749 5284

LONDON   Director External Affairs Division, The School of Oriental and African Studies, Thornhaugh Street, Russell Square, London WC1H 0XG. Tel: 0171 637 2388 Fax: 0171 436 3844

LONDON   Head of Industrial Liaison Unit, South Bank University, London SE1 0AA. Tel: 0171 928 8989 Fax: 0171 261 9115

LONDON   Corporate Relations Manager, Thames Valley University, St Mary's Road, Ealing, London W5 5RF. Tel: 0181 231 2387 Fax: 0181 231 2644

LONDON   Director of Finance, United Medical and Dental Schools, Medical School Building, Guy's Hospital, London SE1 9RT. Tel: 0171 955 4109

LONDON   Managing Director UCLi Ltd, University College, London, 5 Gower Street, London WC1E 6HA. Tel: 0171 636 7668 Fax: 0171 637 7921

LONDON   University Director for Industrial Liaison, University of Westminster, 115 New Cavendish Street, London W1M 8JS. Tel: 0171 911 5080 Fax: 0171 911 5026

LONDON   Manager of Industrial Research Support Unit, University of Westminster, 115 New Cavendish Street, London W1M 8JS. Tel: 0171 911 5811 Fax: 0171 580 6732

LOUGHBOROUGH   General Manager – Loughborough Consultants Ltd, Loughborough University of Technology, Ashby Road, Loughborough, Leicestershire LE11 3TF. Tel: 01509 222597 Fax: 01509 231983

LUTON   Marketing Officer, Industrial Unit, University of Luton, The Research Centre, 24 Crawley Green Road, Luton, Beds LU1 3LF. Tel: 01582 456843 Ext 18 Fax: 01582 459787

MANCHESTER   Industrial Liaison Manager, University of Manchester, Oxford Road, Manchester M13 9PL. Tel: 0161 275 2194 Fax: 0161 275 3000

MANCHESTER   Managing Director – UMIST Ventures Ltd, UMIST, PO Box 88, Manchester M60 1QD. Tel: 0161 200 3054 Fax: 0161 200 3052

MANCHESTER   Head of Research Development, Manchester Metropolitan University, All Saints, Manchester M15 6BH. Tel: 0161 247 2000 Fax: 0161 236 7383

MIDDLESBROUGH   Chief Executive, Teesside Polytechnic Enterprises, University of Teesside, Borough Road, Middlesbrough TS1 3BA. Tel: 01642 218121 Fax: 01642 226822

MILTON KEYNES   Director of Development Fund, Open University, 17 Beeward Close, Green Leys, Milton Keynes MK12 6LY. Tel: 01908 655191 Fax: 01908 655159

NEWCASTLE UPON TYNE    Director of Research Studies, University of Newcastle Upon Tyne, 6 Kensington Terrace, Newcastle Upon Tyne NE1 7RU. Tel: 0191 222 6091 Fax: 0191 222 6229

NEWCASTLE UPON TYNE    Managing Director, Unique Business Services Ltd, University of Northumbria at Newcastle, Library Building, Ellison Place, Newcastle Upon Tyne NE1 8ST. Tel: 0191 227 4148 Fax: 0191 227 4563

NORTHAMPTON    ILO, Timken Business & Innovation Centre, Nene College, Boughton Green Road, Northampton NN2 7AH. Tel: 01604 791179 Fax: 01604 971114

NORWICH    Senior Assistant Registrar, University of East Anglia, The Registry, Norwich NR4 7TJ. Tel: 01603 592221 Fax: 01603 58553

NORWICH    Manager, City College Enterprises, Norwich City College of F & HE, Elmhurst, 5 Ipswich Road, Norwich NR2 2LJ. Tel: 01603 767922 Fax: 01603 760910

NOTTINGHAM    Director of Industrial & Business Liaison Services, University of Nottingham, University Park, Nottingham NG7 2RD. Tel: 01159 513634/5 Fax: 01159 513633

NOTTINGHAM    Industrial Liaison Manager, The Nottingham Trent University, Unit 17, Heathcoat Building, Highfields Science Park, Nottingham NG7 2QJ. Tel: 01159 224256 Fax: 01159 225820

NOTTINGHAM    Manager, Clarendon Business Services, Hanwell House, Vivian Avenue, Nottingham NG5 1AF. Tel: 01159 692480 Fax: 01159 693382

OXFORD    Director – Research Support & ILO, University of Oxford, University Offices, Wellington Square, Oxford OX1 2JD. Tel: 01865 270142/270043 Fax: 01865 270708

OXFORD    Head of Contracts and Commercial Services, Marketing and Communications Dept, Oxford Brookes University, Gipsy Lane Campus, Headington, Oxford OX3 0BP. Tel: 01865 484854 Fax: 01865 484883

PAISLEY    Manager, Technology & Business Centre, University of Paisley, High Street, Paisley PA1 2BE. Tel: 0141 848 3734 Fax: 0141 887 0812

PAISLEY   Director of Development & Enterprise, University of Paisley, High Street, Paisley PA1 2BE. Tel: 0141 848 3731 Fax: 0141 848 3814

PLYMOUTH   PEP Research & Consultancy Ltd, University of Plymouth, Charles Cross Centre, Plymouth PL4 8BD. Tel: 01752 225999 Fax: 01752 222943

PONTYPRIDD   Pro-Vice-Chancellor, University of Glamorgan, Pontypridd, Mid Glam. CF37 1DL. Tel: 01443 480480 Fax: 01443 480558

PORTSMOUTH   Resource Development Manager, UPEL, University of Portsmouth, Town Mount, Hampshire Terrace, Portsmouth PO1 2QG. Tel: 01705 843901 Fax: 01705 843384

PRESTON   Head of Commercial and Trading, University of Central Lancashire, Preston, Lancs PR1 2HE. Tel: 01772 892250 Fax: 01772 892938

READING   Director – Industrial Liaison Bureau, University of Reading, Palmer Building, Whiteknights, Reading RG6 2AH. Tel: 01734 318978 Fax: 01734 318979

ROCHESTER   Training Adviser, Short Course & Conference Unit, Kent Institute of Art & Design, Fort Pitt, Rochester, Kent ME1 1DZ. Tel: 01634 830022 Fax: 01634 829461

SALFORD   Director of Development, University of Salford, Maxwell Building, 43 The Crescent, Salford M5 4WT. Tel: 0161 745 5000 Fax: 0161 745 5885

SALFORD   Salford College of Technology, Salford M6 6PU. Tel: 0161 736 6541 Fax: 0161 745 8386

SHEFFIELD   Director – Commercial & Industrial Development Bureau, University of Sheffield, Western Bank, Sheffield S10 2TN. Tel: 01142 824040 Fax: 01142 725004

SHEFFIELD   Commercial Development Project Officer, Business Development Office, Sheffield Hallam University, Collegiate Crescent Campus, Sheffield S10 2BP. Tel: 01142 720911

SHEFFIELD   Head of Commercial Activities, School of Engineering, Sheffield Hallam University, City Campus, Sheffield S1 1WB. Tel: 01142 720911

SOUTHAMPTON    Office of Industrial Affairs, University of Southampton, Highfield, Southampton SO9 5NH. Tel: 01703 593095 Fax: 01703 593585

SOUTHAMPTON    Company Secretary, SRTC Ltd, Southampton Institute of HE, East Park Terrace, Southampton SO9 4WW. Tel: 01703 319307 Fax: 01703 222259

ST ANDREWS    Director of Continuing Education, University of St Andrews, 66 North Street, St Andrews KY16 9AH. Tel: 01334 76161 Extn 564 Fax: 01334 75892

ST AUSTELL    Consultancy & Training for Business Co-ordinator, Mid-Cornwall College, Sedgemoor, Priory Road, St Austell PL25 5AB. Tel: 01726 67714 Fax: 01726 68499

STIRLING    University Secretary, University of Stirling, Stirling FK9 4LA. Tel: 01786 67017 Fax: 01786 62087

STOCKPORT    Head of Industrial Liaison Centre, Stockport College of Technology, Wellington Road South, Stockport SK1 3UQ. Tel: 0161 480 3897 Fax: 0161 480 6636

STOKE ON TRENT    Director, Staffordshire University Enterprises, Staffordshire University, College Road, Stoke on Trent ST4 2DE. Tel: 01782 573629 Fax: 01782 745447

SWANSEA    Director of University Innovation Centre, University College of Wales – Swansea, Singleton Park, Swansea SA2 8PP. Tel: 01792 295556 Fax: 01792 295613

SWINDON    Head of Business Link Office, ESRC, Polaris House, North Star Avenue, Swindon SN2 1UJ. Tel: 01793 413000 Fax: 01793 413001

SWINDON    Head of Industrial Affairs Unit, EPSRC, Polaris House, North Star Avenue, Swindon, Wilts SN2 1ET. Tel: 01793 444000 Fax: 01793 444010

TRURO    Business Liaison Manager, Cornwall Economic Development Office, Trevint House, Strangways Villas, Truro, Cornwall TR1 2PA. Tel: 01872 77322/71324 Fax: 01872 77373

TWICKENHAM    Marketing Officer, St Mary's College, Strawberry Hill, Waldegrave Road, Twickenham, Middlesex. Tel: 0181 892 0051 Fax: 0181 744 2080

TWICKENHAM   Schools Liaison Officer, West London Institute of HE, 300 St Margaret's Road, Twickenham, Middlesex TW1 1PT. Tel: 0181 891 0121 Fax: 0181 744 1441

UXBRIDGE   Head – Research Services Bureau, Brunel – The University of West London, Kingston Lane, Uxbridge, Middlesex UB8 3PH. Tel: 01895 239234/274000 Fax: 01895 230883

WALSALL   Manager, Business Development, Walsall College of Technology, St Paul's, Walsall WS1 1XN. Tel: 01922 720824 Fax: 01922 29967

WINCHESTER   Business Services Manager, King Alfred's College, Sparkford Road, Winchester, Hants SO22 4NR. Tel: 01962 841515 Fax: 01962 842280

WOLVERHAMPTON   Director, Corporate Enterprise Centre, University of Wolverhampton, Wulfruna Street, Wolverhampton WV1 1SB. Tel: 01902 321000/322478 Fax: 01902 25015

WYE   Secretary, Wye College, Wye, Kent TN25 5AH. Tel: 01233 812401 Fax: 01233 813320

YORK   Director of Industrial Development, University of York, Heslington, York YO1 5DD. Tel: 01904 433245 Fax: 01904 432917

---

**AIESEC UK** – See Section 1.15.2

The following are AIESEC UK addresses:

ABERDEEN            AIESEC Aberdeen
                            Department of Economics
                            Edward Wright Buildings
                            Dunbar Street
                            Old Aberdeen
                            AB0 2TY
                            Tel: 01224 484811
                            Fax: 01224 487084

ASTON

AIESEC Aston
Societies Room
Guild of Students
University of Aston
Birmingham
B4 7EG
Tel: 0121 359 6531 x 4065
Fax: 0121 333 4218

BIRMINGHAM

AIESEC Birmingham
Strathcona Building
Faculty Commerce & Social Sciences
University of Birmingham
Birmingham
B15 2TN
Tel: 0121 472 2726
Fax: 0121 414 3971

BOURNEMOUTH

AIESEC Bournemouth
F Floor
Bournemouth Polytechnic
Fern Barrow
Poole
BH12 5BB
Tel: 01202 595362
Fax: 01202 513293

BRISTOL

AIESEC Bristol
c/o Manor Hall
Lower Clifton Hill
Bristol
BS8 1BU
Tel: 01179 745204

CAMBRIDGE

AIESEC Cambridge
4A All Saints Passage
Cambridge
CB2 3LS
Tel: 01223 60034

CARDIFF

AIESEC Cardiff
Aberconway Building
Cardiff Business School

|          | Colum Road<br>Cardiff<br>CF1 3EU<br>Tel: 01222 874000 x5185<br>Fax: 01222 874419 |
|----------|---|
| CITY | AIESEC City<br>c/o Careers Service<br>City University<br>Myddletton Building<br>Northampton Square<br>London<br>EC1V 0HP<br>Tel: 0171 477 8790 |
| EDINBURGH | AIESEC Edinburgh<br>Societies Centre<br>60 The Pleasance<br>Edinburgh<br>EH8 9TJ<br>Tel: 0131 557 0984<br>Fax: 0131 667 7938 |
| EXETER | AIESEC Exeter<br>Societies Rack A<br>Devonshire House<br>University of Exeter<br>Exeter<br>EX4 4PZ<br>Tel: 01392 436431<br>Fax: 01392 263108 |
| HULL | AIESEC Hull<br>Regional Electronics Centre<br>University of Hull<br>Cottingham Road<br>Hull<br>HU6 7RX<br>Tel: 01482 466405<br>Fax: 01482 466666 |
| KENT | AIESEC Kent<br>c/o Enterprise Kent |

|  | The University<br>Canterbury<br>Kent<br>CT2 7LT<br>Tel: 01227 761288<br>Fax: 01227 761288 |
|---|---|
| LEEDS | AIESEC Leeds<br>Leeds Business School<br>5 Queens Square<br>Leeds<br>LS2 8AF |
| LIVERPOOL | AIESEC Liverpool<br>PO Box 197<br>2 Bedforth North Street<br>Liverpool<br>L69 7BR<br>Tel: 0151 794 4164<br>Fax: 0151 794 4174 |
| LOUGHBOROUGH | AIESEC Loughborough<br>Students Union Building<br>Ashby Road<br>Loughborough<br>Leics<br>LE11 3TT<br>Tel: 01509 263171 x 4014<br>Fax: 01509 235593 |
| LSE | AIESEC LSE<br>Dept of Economics<br>LSE<br>Houghton Street<br>London<br>WC2A 2AE<br>Tel: 0171 955 6785 |
| MANCHESTER | AIESEC Manchester<br>MSS Building<br>UMIST<br>PO Box 88<br>Sackville Street |

|  | Manchester |
|--|--|
|  | M60 1QD |
|  | Tel: 0161 200 3399 |
|  | Fax: 0161 200 3505 |
| NEWCASTLE | AIESEC Newcastle |
|  | c/o Porters Lodge |
|  | Claremont Tower |
|  | University of Newcastle upon Tyne |
|  | Tyne and Wear |
|  | NE1 7RU |
|  | Tel: 0191 232 7054 |
|  | Fax: 0191 232 3467 |
| NOTTINGHAM | AIESEC Nottingham |
|  | Cripps Hall |
|  | University of Nottingham |
|  | Nottingham |
|  | NG7 2QW |
|  | Tel: 01159 514322 |
|  | Fax: 01159 513666 |
| OXFORD | AIESEC Oxford |
|  | 13 Bevington Road |
|  | Oxford |
|  | OX2 6NB |
|  | Tel: 01865 311004 |
|  | Fax: 01865 240409 |
| PORTSMOUTH | AIESEC Portsmouth |
|  | 2 Kings Terrace |
|  | Southsea |
|  | Portsmouth |
|  | Hants |
|  | PO5 3AR |
|  | Tel: 01705 876543 |
|  | Fax: 01705 876804 |
| QUEENS | AIESEC Queens |
|  | Students Union |
|  | University Road |
|  | Belfast |
|  | BT7 1PE |

|  |  |
|---|---|
|  | Tel: 01232 313993 |
|  | Tel: 01232 324803 x147 |
|  | Fax: 01232 247895 |
| READING | AIESEC Reading |
|  | Students Union |
|  | White Knights |
|  | Reading |
|  | Berkshire |
|  | RG6 2AW |
|  | Tel: 01734 860222 x 246 |
|  | Fax: 01734 314404 |
| SHEFFIELD | AIESEC Sheffield |
|  | 85 Wilkinson Street |
|  | Sheffield |
|  | S10 3GJ |
|  | Tel: 01142 768555 x 4983 |
|  | Fax: 01142 725103 |
| SOUTHAMPTON | AIESEC Southampton |
|  | Students Union |
|  | University of Southampton |
|  | Highfield |
|  | Southampton |
|  | SO9 5NH |
|  | Tel: 01703 593363 |
|  | Fax: 01703 593939 |
| ST ANDREWS | AIESEC St Andrews |
|  | St Andrews University |
|  | Students Association Building |
|  | St Mary's Place |
|  | St Andrews |
|  | Fife |
|  | KY16 9UZ |
|  | Tel: 01334 74653 |
|  | Fax: 01334 77761 |
| STIRLING | AIESEC Stirling |
|  | Aithrey Castle |
|  | University of Stirling |
|  | Stirling |

|  |  |
|---|---|
|  | FK9 4LA |
|  | Tel: 01786 466066 |
|  | Fax: 01786 67190 |
| STRATHCLYDE | AIESEC Strathclyde |
|  | Graham Hills Building |
|  | 50 Richmond Street |
|  | University of Strathclyde |
|  | Glasgow |
|  | G1 1XH |
|  | Tel: 0141 522 4400 x 3528 |
|  | Fax: 0141 552 0775 |
| ULSTER | AIESEC Ulster |
|  | University of Ulster & Jordanstown |
|  | Room 12G15 |
|  | Shore Road |
|  | Newton Abbey |
|  | Northern Ireland |
|  | BT37 0GB |
|  | Tel: 01232 365131 x 3112 |
| WARWICK | AIESEC Warwick |
|  | c/o SIBS |
|  | University of Warwick |
|  | Coventry |
|  | Warwickshire |
|  | CV4 7AL |
|  | Tel: 01203 524374 |
|  | Fax: 01203 461606 |

Sheffield Business School
**China Services Centre**
Unit 4, Sheffield Science Park
60 Howard Street
Sheffield S1 2NS
01142 533365

### The OPEN UNIVERSITY BUSINESS SCHOOL

> The Open University
> PO Box 71
> Milton Keynes
> MK7 6AG

The Open Business School is a training organisation within the OU and provides a range of business training courses leading to professional qualifications in Management and Business Administration

- suitable for business managers at any stage of their career
- distance learning course based tuition
- practical use in day to day work
- Certificate, Diploma and Degree levels of qualification

---

> The Open Business School,
> Open University,
> PO Box 71
> Milton Keynes,
> MK7 6AG
>
> Tel: 01908 653231

Contact and information can be obtained through the OU Regional Offices:

| | |
|---|---|
| London Region 01 (London) | 0171 794 0575 |
| South Region 02 (Oxford) | 01865 327000 |
|   Sub-Centre (Winchester) | 01962 867969 |
| South West Region 03 (Bristol) | 01179 299641 |
|   Sub-Centre (Plymouth) | 01752 228321 |
| West Midlands 04 (Birmingham) | 0121 426 1661 |
| East Midlands 05 (Nottingham) | 01159 473072 |
| East Anglian 06 (Cambridge) | 01223 61650 |
| Yorkshire 07 (Leeds) | 01132 444431 |
| North West 08 (Manchester) | 0161 861 9823 |
| North Region 09 (Newcastle upon Tyne) | 0191 284 1611 |
|   Resource Centre | |

| | |
|---|---|
| – (Cumbria – Penrith) | 01768 64720 |
| – (Middlesbrough) | 01642 816227 |
| Wales 10 (Cardiff) | 01222 397911 |
| Scotland 11 (Edinburgh) | 0131 226 3851 |
| Sub-Centre (Glasgow) | 0141 332 4364 |
| Northern Ireland 12 (Belfast) | 01232 245025 |

# FOREIGN EMBASSIES AND HIGH COMMISSIONS IN LONDON

Key:

E – Embassy. HC – High Commission. CS – Commercial Section

| Country | | Telephone | Fax |
|---|---|---|---|
| **Afghanistan** | E | 0171 589 8891 | 0171 581 3452 |
| **Albania** | E | 0171 976 5925 | 0171 834 2508 |
| **Algeria** | E | 0171 221 7800 | |
| **Angola** | E | 0171 495 1752 | 0171 495 1635 |
| **Antigua & Barbuda** | HC | 0171 486 7073 | 0171 486 9970 |
| **Argentina** | E | 0171 584 6494 | 0171 589 3106 |
| | CS | 0171 730 9334 | |
| **Armenia** | E | 0171 938 5435 | 0171 938 2595 |
| **Australia** | HC | 0171 379 4334 | 0171 240 5333 |
| **Austria** | E | 0171 235 3731 | 0171 235 8025 |
| | CS | 0171 584 4411 | |
| **Bahamas** | HC | 0171 408 4488 | 0171 499 9937 |
| **Bahrain** | E | 0171 370 5132/3 | 0171 370 7773 |
| **Bangladesh** | HC | 0171 584 0081 | 0171 589 4842–4 |
| **Barbados** | HC | 0171 631 4975 | 0171 323 6872 |
| **Belarus** | E | 0171 225 4568 | |
| **Belgium** | E | 0171 235 5422 | 0171 259 6213 |
| **Belize** | HC | 0171 499 9728 | 0171 491 4139 |
| **Benin** | E | 0181 954 8800 | 0181 954 8844 |
| **Bolivia** | E | 0171 235 4248/ 2257 | 0171 235 1286 |
| **Bosnia & Herzegovina** | E | 0171 734 3758 | 0171 734 3765 |
| **Botswana** | HC | 0171 499 0031 | |
| **Brazil** | E & CS | 0171 499 0877 | |
| **Brunei** | HC & CS | 0171 581 0521 | 0171 235 9717 |
| **Bulgaria** | E | 0171 584 9000 | 0171 584 4948 |
| | CS | 0171 581 3144 | |
| **Burkina** | E | 0171 738 1800 | 0171 738 2820 |

| Country | | Telephone | Fax |
|---|---|---|---|
| **Burma (Myanmar)** | E | 0171 629 6966 | 0171 629 4169 |
| **Burundi** | | – see list of Embassies in Europe | |
| **Cameroon** | E | 0171 727 0771/ 0713 | 0171 792 9353 |
| **Canada** | HC | 0171 258 6600 | 0171 258 6333 |
| **Cape Verde** | E | 0171 493 4840 | |
| **Central African Republic** | | – see list of Embassies in Europe | |
| **Chad** | | – see list of Embassies in Europe | |
| **Chile** | E | 0171 580 6392 | 0171 436 5204 |
| **China** | E | 0171 636 9375/5726 | |
| | CS | 0171 262 3911 | |
| **Colombia** | E | 0171 589 5037/ 9177 | 0171 581 1829 |
| **Congo** | E | 0171 222 7575 | 0171 233 2087 |
| **Costa Rica** | E | 0171 495 3985 | 0171 495 3992 |
| **Cote d'Ivoire** | E | 0171 235 6991 | |
| **Croatia** | E | 0171 434 2946 | |
| **Cuba** | E | 0171 240 2488 | 0171 836 2602 |
| **Cyprus** | E | 0171 499 8272 | 0171 491 0691 |
| **Czech Rep** | E | 0171 243 1115 | 0171 727 9654 |
| **Denmark** | E | 0171 333 0200 | 0171 333 0270 |
| **Djibouti** | | – see list of Embassies in Europe | |
| **Dominica** | H | 0171 370 5194/5 | 0171 373 8743 |
| **Dominican Rep** | E | 0171 602 1885 | |
| **E. Caribbean States** | HC | 0171 937 9522 | 0171 937 5514 |
| **Ecuador** | E | 0171 584 1267/ 8084 | 0171 823 9701 |
| **Egypt** | E | 0171 499 2401/ 3002 | 0171 355 3568 |
| **El Salvador** | E | 0171 430 2141 | 0171 430 0484 |
| **Equa. Guinea** | | – see list of Embassies in Europe | |
| **Eritrea** | E | 0171 713 0096 | 0171 713 0161 |

| Country | | Telephone | Fax |
|---|---|---|---|
| **Estonia** | E | 0171 589 3428 | 0171 589 3430 |
| **Ethiopia** | E | 0171 589 7212–5 | |
| | CS | 0171 580 0174 | |
| **Fiji** | E | 0171 584 3661 | 0171 584 2838 |
| | CS | 0171 584 2838 | |
| **Finland** | E | 0171 839 7262 | 0171 235 3680 |
| **France** | E | 0171 201 1000 | 0171 259 6498 |
| **Gabon** | E | 0171 823 9986 | 0171 584 0047 |
| **The Gambia** | HC | 0171 937 6316–8 | 0171 937 9095 |
| **Germany** | E | 0171 235 5033 | 0171 235 0609 |
| **Ghana** | HC | 0181 342 8686 | 0181 342 8566 |
| **Greece** | E | 0171 727 8860 | 0171 727 8960 |
| **Grenada** | HC | 0171 737 7809 | 0171 370 7040 |
| **Guatemala** | E | 0171 351 3042 | 0171 376 5708 |
| **Guinea** | E | 0171 333 0044 | |
| **Guinea-Bissau** | E | 0171 589 5253 | |
| **Guyana** | HC | 0171 229 7684–8 | 0171 727 9809 |
| **Holy See** | | 0171 946 1410/ 7971 | 0181 947 2494 |
| **Honduras** | E | 0171 486 4880 | 0181 486 4880 |
| **Hungary** | E | 0171 235 4048/ 7191 | 0171 823 1348 |
| **Iceland** | E | 0171 730 5131/2 | 0171 730 1683 |
| **India** | HC | 0171 836 8484 | 0171 836 4331 |
| **Indonesia** | E | 0171 499 7661 | 0171 491 4993 |
| **Iran** | E | 0171 584 8101 | 0171 589 4440 |
| **Rep. Ireland** | E | 0171 235 2171 | 0171 245 6961 |
| **Israel** | E | 0171 957 9500 | 0171 957 9555 |
| **Italy** | E | 0171 312 2200 | 0171 312 2230 |
| **Jamaica** | HC | 0171 823 9911 | 0171 589 5154 |
| **Japan** | E | 0171 465 6500 | 0171 491 9348 |
| **Jordan** | E | 0171 937 3685 | 0171 937 8795 |
| **Kenya** | HC | 0171 636 2371/5 | 0171 323 6717 |
| **Kiribati** | | 0171 222 6952 | |

| Country | | Telephone | Fax |
|---|---|---|---|
| **Korea** | E | 0171 581 0247 | 0171 589 9134 |
| **Kuwait** | E | 0171 589 4533 | 0171 589 2978 |
| **Laos** | | – see list of Embassies in Europe | |
| **Latvia** | E | 0171 727 1698 | 0171 221 9740 |
| **Lebanon** | E | 0171 229 7265 | 0171 243 1699 |
| **Lesotho** | HC | 0171 235 5686 | 0171 235 5023 |
| **Liberia** | E | 0171 221 1036 | |
| **Libya** | | – see Saudi Arabia | |
| **Lithuania** | E | 0171 938 2481 | 0171 938 3329 |
| **Luxembourg** | E | 0171 236 6961 | 0171 235 9734 |
| **Macedonia** | E | 0171 404 6558 | |
| **Madagascar** | E | 0171 746 0133 | |
| **Malawi** | HC | 0171 491 4172/7 | |
| **Malaysia** | HC | 0171 235 8033 | 0171 235 5161 |
| **Mali** | | – see list of Embassies in Europe | |
| **Malta** | HC | 0171 938 1712/6 | 0171 937 8664 |
| **Mauritania** | E | 0181 980 4382 | 0171 556 6032 |
| **Mauritius** | HC | 0171 581 0294/5 | 0171 823 8437 |
| **Mexico** | E | 0171 499 8586 | 0171 495 4035 |
| **Mongolia** | E | 0171 937 0150 | |
| **Morocco** | E | 0171 581 5001/4 | 0171 225 3862 |
| **Mozambique** | E | 0171 383 3800 | 0171 383 3801 |
| **Myanmar** | | – see Burma | |
| **Namibia** | HC | 0171 636 6244 | 0171 792 9861 |
| **Nepal** | E | 0171 229 1594/<br>6231 | 0171 637 5694 |
| **Netherlands** | E | 0171 584 5040 | 0171 581 3450 |
| **New Zealand** | HC | 0171 930 8422 | 0171 839 4580 |
| **Nicaragua** | E | 0171 584 4365 | 0171 823 8790 |
| **Niger** | | – see list of Embassies in Europe | |
| **Nigeria** | HC | 0171 839 1244 | 0171 839 8746 |
| **Norway** | E | 0171 235 7151 | 0171 245 6993 |
| **Oman** | E | 0171 225 0011 | 0171 589 2505 |
| **Pakistan** | HC | 0171 235 2044 | |

| Country | | Telephone | Fax |
|---|---|---|---|
| **Panama** | E | 0171 487 5633 | |
| **Papua New Guinea** | HC | 0171 930 0922/7 | 0171 930 0828 |
| **Paraguay** | E | 0171 937 1253 | |
| **Peru** | E | 0171 235 1917 | 0171 235 4463 |
| **Philippines** | E | 0171 937 1600/ 1898 | 0171 937 2925 |
| **Poland** | E | 0171 580 4324/9 | 0171 323 4018 |
| **Portugal** | E | 0171 235 5331 | 0171 245 1287 |
| **Qatar** | E | 0171 493 2200 | 0171 493 2661 |
| **Romania** | E | 0171 937 9666/9 | 0171 927 8069 |
| **Russian Fed.** | E | 0171 229 2666/ 3628/6412 | 0171 727 8625 |
| **Rwanda** | | – see list of Embassies in Europe | |
| **St. Christopher & Nevis** | | – see Eastern Caribbean States | |
| **St. Lucia** | | – see Eastern Caribbean States | |
| **St. Vincent & Grenadines** | | – see Eastern Caribbean States | |
| **Sao Tomé & Principe** | E | 0171 499 1995 | |
| **Saudi Arabia** | E | 0171 917 3000 | |
| **Senegal** | E | 0171 937 0925/6 | |
| **Seychelles** | HC | 0171 224 1660 | |
| **Sierra Leone** | HC | 0171 636 6483–6 | 0171 927 8130 |
| **Singapore** | HC | 0171 235 8315 | 0171 245 6583 |
| | CS | 0171 222 0770 | |
| **Slovak Rep.** | E | 0171 243 0803 | 0171 727 5824 |
| **Slovenia** | E | 0171 495 7775 | 0171 495 7776 |
| **Solomon Is.** | E | 0181 946 5552 | 0181 946 1744 |
| **South Africa** | HC | 0171 930 4483 | 0171 321 0835 |
| **Spain** | E | 0171 235 5555–7 | 0171 235 9905 |
| | CS | 0171 486 0101 | |
| **Sri Lanka** | HC | 0171 262 1841–7 | 0171 262 7970 |
| **Sudan** | E | 0171 839 8080 | |
| **Suriname** | | – see list of Embassies in Europe | |
| **Swaziland** | HC | 0171 581 4976–8 | 0171 589 5332 |

| Country | | Telephone | Fax |
|---|---|---|---|
| **Sweden** | E | 0171 917 6400 | 0171 724 4174 |
| **Switzerland** | E | 0171 723 0701 | 0171 724 7001 |
| **Syria** | E | 0171 245 9012 | 0171 235 4621 |
| **Tanzania** | HC | 0171 499 8951–4 | 0171 491 9321 |
| **Thailand** | E | 0171 589 2944 | 0171 823 9695 |
| **Tonga** | HC | 0171 724 5828 | |
| **Trinidad & Tobago** | HC | 0171 245 9351 | 0171 823 1065 |
| **Tunisia** | E | 0171 584 8117 | 0171 823 1065 |
| **Turkey** | E | 0171 235 5252–4 | |
| | CS | 0171 235 4233/ | |
| | | 4991/2743 | |
| **Uganda** | HC | 0171 839 5783 | 0171 839 8925 |
| **Ukraine** | E | 0171 727 6312 | 0171 792 1708 |
| **United Arab Emirates** | E | 0171 581 1281 | 0171 581 9616 |
| | CS | 0171 589 3434 | |
| **United States** | E | 0171 499 9000 | |
| **Uruguay** | E | 0171 584 8192 | 0171 581 9585 |
| **Venezuela** | E | 0171 584 4206/7 | 0171 589 8887 |
| **Vietnam** | E | 0171 937 1912/ | 0171 937 6108 |
| | | 8564 | |
| **Western Samoa** | E | 0171 229 4067 | |
| **Yemen** | E | 0171 584 6607 | 0171 589 3350 |
| **Yugoslavia** | E | 0171 370 6105/9 | 0171 370 3838 |
| **Zaïre** | E | 0171 235 6137 | 0171 235 9048 |
| **Zambia** | E | 0171 589 6655 | 0171 581 1353 |
| **Zimbabwe** | HC | 0171 836 7755 | |

## FOREIGN EMBASSIES IN EUROPE

The following countries do not have Embassies in the United Kingdom, but matters can be referred to the Embassies in Europe Contact numbers are:

**Burundi**                          00 32 2 230 45 35
Brussels

**Central African Republic**         00 32 2 42 24 42 56
Brussels

**Chad**                             00 32 2 215 19 75
Brussels

**Djibouti**                         00 33 47 27 49 22
Paris

**Laos**                             00 33 45 53 02 98
Paris

**Mali**                             00 32 2 345 74 32
Brussels

**Niger**                            00 33 4505 80 60
Paris

**Rwanda**                           00 32 2 763 07 02
Brussels

**Suriname**                         00 31 70 3 650844
The Hague, Netherlands

# BUSINESS LINK CONTACT ADDRESSES

**OUTLETS OPEN AS AT 1 MAY 1995**

Business Link contacts: (those wanting to offer services should write to HUB in first instance)

BARNSLEY

Business Link Barnsley
Tel: 01226 771000
Fax: 01226 770066

BIRMINGHAM

Business Link Birmingham
Tel: 0121 6070 8090
Fax: 0121 6079 8999

CALDERDALE AND KIRKLEES

**Halifax (HUB)**
Business Link Calderdale &
    Kirklees
Halifax
Tel: 0345 697866
Fax: 01422 343899

**Brighouse**
Business Link Calderdale &
    Kirklees
Tel: 0345 697866
Fax: 01484 710110

**Batley**
Business Link Calderdale &
    Kirklees
Tel: 0345 697866
Fax: 01924 424883

**Huddersfield**
Business Link Calderdale &
    Kirklees
Tel: 0345 697866
Fax: 01484 427340

CHESTER AND ELLESMERE
PORT

**Chester (HUB)**
Business Link Chester &
    Ellesmere Port
Tel: 01244 674111
Fax: 01244 674333

**Hoole Bridge**
Business Link Chester &
    Ellesmere Port
Chester
Tel: 01224 311474
Fax: 01244 310690

**South Wirral**
Business Link Chester &
    Ellesmere Port
Great Sutton
Tel: 0151 348 0744
Fax: 0151 348 0750

COUNTY DURHAM

**Aykley Heads (HUB)**
Business Link County Durham
Tel: 0191 3744000
Fax: 0191 3744010

**Chester-le-Street**
Business Link Chester-le-
Street
Tel: 0191 3892648

**Durham City**
Chester-le-Street and City of
Durham Enterprise Agency
Tel: 0191 3845407
Fax: 0191 3868673

**Derwentside**
The Derwentside Industrial
Development Agency
Consett
Tel: 01207 509124
Fax: 01207 591477

**Easington**
The East Durham Development
Agency
Tel: 0191 5863366
Fax: 0191 5180332

**Sedgefield**
Development Agency of
Sedgefield
Tel: 01325 307270
Fax: 01325 307226

**Barnard Castle**
The Teesdale Enterprise
Agency

Tel: 01833 631851
Fax: 01833 637269

**Wear Valley**
The Wear Valley Development
Agency
Bishop Auckland
Tel: 01388 776688
Fax: 01388 777116

**Wear Valley**
Durham Dales Centre
Stanhope
Tel: 01388 527650
Fax: 01388 527461

COVENTRY & WARWICKSHIRE
(all outlets available on
Tel: 0345 125600)

**Coventry (HUB)**
Business Link Coventry &
Warwickshire
Tel: 01203 837800
Fax: 01203 837837

**Nuneaton**
Business Link Coventry &
Warwickshire
Tel: 01203 375469
Fax: 01203 641339

**Leamington Spa**
Business Link Coventry &
Warwickshire
Tel: 01926 433344
Fax: 01926 431711

**Stratford-upon-Avon**
Business Link Coventry &
   Warwickshire
Tel: 01789 414311
Fax: 01789 414265

DEVON AND CORNWALL

**Redruth**
Business Link West Cornwall
Tel: 01209 314555
Fax: 01209 314442

**Exeter**
Business Link Central Devon
Tel: 01392 490700
Fax: 01392 490499

DONCASTER

Business Link Doncaster
Tel: 01302 761000
Fax: 01302 739999

DORSET

**Poole (HUB)**
Business Link Dorset
Tel: 0345 448844
Fax: 01202 448838

**Weymouth**
Business Link Dorset

**Gillingham**
Business Link North Dorset
Tel/Fax: 01747 824065

DUDLEY

Business Link Dudley
Brierley Hill

Tel: 01384 868000
Fax: 01384 868400

GLOUCESTERSHIRE

Business Link Gloucestershire
Cheltenham
Tel: 0800 135235
Fax: 01452 509500

HEREFORD AND WORCESTER

**Hereford (HUB)**
Business Link Hereford
Tel: 01432 356699
Fax: 01432 274499

**Leominster**
Business Link Hereford and
   Worcester
Tel: 01568 616344
Fax: 01568 616355

**Malvern**
Business Link Hereford and
   Worcester
Tel: 01684 567070
Fax: 01684 567080

**Ross on Wye**
Business Link Hereford and
   Worcester
Tel: 01989 769744
Fax: 01432 274499

**Worcester**
Business Link Hereford and
   Worcester
Tel: 01905 22877
Fax: 01905 22878

**Pershore**
Business Link Hereford and
  Worcester
Tel: 01386 555577
Fax: 01386 555588

HERTFORDSHIRE

**St Albans (HUB)**
Business Link Hertfordshire
Tel: 01727 813400
Fax: 01727 813443

**Letchworth**
Business Link Hertfordshire
Tel: 01462 484222
Fax: 01462 686868

ISLE OF WIGHT

Business Link Isle of Wight
Newport
Tel: 01983 535353
Fax: 01983 535354

LEICESTERSHIRE

**Leicester (HUB)**
Business Link Leicestershire
Tel: 0116 255 9944
Fax: 0116 255 3470

**Coalville**
Business Link North West
Tel: 01530 810470
Fax: 01530 510452

**Hinckley**
Business Link Hinckley
Tel: 01455 891848
Fax: 01455 891923

**Market Harborough**
Business Link Market
  Harborough
Tel: 01858 461914
Fax: 01858 464181

**Melton Mowbray**
Business Link Melton
  Mowbray
Tel: 01664 410 401
Fax: 01664 500 730

**Oakham**
Business Link Rutland
Tel: 0157 272 4321
Fax: 0157 272 4628

**Loughborough**
Business Link Loughborough
Tel: 01509 215415
Fax: 01509 269723

LINCOLNSHIRE

**Lincoln (HUB)**
Business Link Lincolnshire
Tel: 01522 574000
Fax: 01522 574005

**Louth**
Business Link Louth
Tel: 01507 608811
Fax: 01507 601811

**Spalding**
Business Link Spalding
Tel: 01775 712833
Fax: 01775 712834

**Sleaford**
Business Link Sleaford
Tel: 01529 414155

**Skegness**
Business Link Skegness
Tel: 01754 610381
Fax: 01754 761987

**Grantham**
Business Link Grantham
Tel: 01476 72375
Fax: 01476 77781

**Boston**
Business Link Boston
Tel: 01205 351144
Fax: 01204 352182

**Gainsborough**
Business Link Gainsborough
Tel: 01427 617052
Fax: 01427 617057

MANCHESTER

**Manchester (HUB)**
Business Link Manchester
Tel: 0161 237 4000
Fax: 0161 237 4040

**Salford**
Business Link Salford
Tel: 0161 742 4400
Fax: 0161 742 4401

**Trafford Park**
Business Link Trafford Park
Manchester

Tel: 0161 848 4500
Fax: 0161 848 4313

**Tameside**
Business Link Tameside
Denton
Tel: 0161 337 4200
Fax: 0161 343 7367

**Openshaw**
Business Link East
    Manchester
Tel: 0161 237 4050
Fax: 0161 231 0695

MERSEYSIDE

**Liverpool (HUB)**
Business Link Merseyside
Liverpool
Tel: 0151 224 2400
Fax: 0151 224 2401

**Knowsley**
Business Link Merseyside
Tel: 0151 224 2410
Fax: 0151 548 4007

**Bootle**
Business Link Merseyside
Tel: 0151 224 2420
Fax: 0151 944 1464

**Brunswick Dock**
Business Link Merseyside
Liverpool
Tel: 0151 709 2375
Fax: 0151 709 9867

**Southport**
Business Link Merseyside
Tel: 01704 544 173
Fax: 01704 539 396

**Mount Pleasant**
Business Link Merseyside
Liverpool
Tel: 0151 224 2445
Fax: 0151 708 9957

NORTH AND MID CHESHIRE

**Widnes (HUB)**
Business Link Halton
Tel: 0151 420 9420
Fax: 0151 423 2749

**Runcorn**
Business Link Runcorn
Tel: 0151 420 9420
Fax: 0151 423 2749

ROTHERHAM

Business Link Rotherham
Tel: 01709 371611
Fax: 01709 539004

SANDWELL

**Oldbury**
Business Link Sandwell
Tel: 0121 543 2222
Fax: 0121 543 2233

SHROPSHIRE

**Telford (HUB)**
Business Link Shropshire
Tel: 0345 543210
Fax: 01952 208208

**Oswestry**
Business Link Oswestry
Tel: 01691 679915
Fax: 01691 670865

SOUTHERN DERBYSHIRE

**Derby (HUB)**
Business Link Southern
　Derbyshire
Tel: 01332 371071
Fax: 01332 299736

**Derby Inner City**
Business Link Derby Inner City
Tel: 01332 298123
Fax: 01332 298345

**Swadlincote**
Business Link Swadlincote
Tel: 01283 551324
Fax: 01283 552566

SOUTH AND EAST CHESHIRE

**Congleton**
Business Link Congleton
Tel: 01260 294500
Fax: 01260 294501

**Macclesfield**
Business Link Macclesfield
Tel: 01625 664400
Fax: 01625 664401

**Crewe**
Business Link Crewe and
　Nantwich
Crewe
Tel: 01270 504700
Fax: 01270 504701

TEESSIDE

**Middlesbrough**
Business Link Teesside
Tel: 0345 556575
Fax: 0345 697728

THAMES VALLEY

**Reading (HUB)**
Business Link Thames Valley
Tel: 01734 512288
Fax: 01734 569024

**Aylesbury**
Business Link Aylesbury
Tel: 01296 392288
Fax: 01296 434142

**Slough**
Business Link Slough
Tel: 01753 512288
Fax: 01753 533523

TYNESIDE

**Gateshead (HUB)**
Business Link Tyneside
Tel: 0191 491 6161
Fax: 0191 491 6199

**Gateshead**
Business Link Gateshead
Tel: 0191 477 5544
Fax: 0191 477 4650

**Newcastle Upon Tyne**
Business Link Newcastle

Tel: 0191 2305989
Fax: 0191 2305517

**North Shields**
Business Link North Tyneside
Tel: 0191 296 4477
Fax: 0191 296 4499

**South Shields**
Business Link South Tyneside
Jarrow
Tel: 0191 4283400
Fax: 0191 4283399

WALSALL

Business Link Walsall
Tel: 01922 433333
Fax: 01922 433343

SUNDERLAND (WEARSIDE)

Business Link Sunderland
Tel: 0191 5168088
Fax: 0191 5484044

WIGAN

Business Link Met Wigan
Tel: 01942 324547
Fax: 01942 821410

WIRRAL

Business Link Wirral
Birkenhead
Tel: 0151 650 6900
Fax: 0151 650 0101

BUSINESS LINKS have been approved for the following locations, and are expected to open later in 1995/early 1996. Contact numbers may be used to ascertain when the services will be operating

## AVON

Business Link Avon
Clifton
Bristol
Tel: 01179 737373
Fax: 01179 745365

## BEDFORDSHIRE

Business Link Bedfordshire
Kempston
Tel: 01234 855222
Fax: 01234 843211

## BOLTON AND BURY

Bolton and Bury TEC
Tel: 01204 397350
Fax: 01204 363212

## BRADFORD

Bradford & District TEC
Tel: 01274 723711
Fax: 01274 370980

## CENTRAL ENGLAND

Central England TEC
Redditch
Tel: 01527 545415
Fax: 01527 543032

## CUMBRIA

Business Link Cumbria
Cockermouth

Tel: 01900 828228
Fax: 01900 828979

## GREATER NOTTINGHAM

Nottingham
Tel: 0115 941 3313
Fax: 0115 948 4589

## GREATER PETERBOROUGH

Greater Peterborough TEC
Peterborough
Tel: 01733 890808
Fax: 01733 890809

## HAMPSHIRE

Fareham Enterprise Centre
Tel: 01329 317602
Fax: 01329 317333

## HUMBERSIDE

Humberside TEC
Hull
Tel: 01482 226491
Fax: 01482 213206

## KENT

Business Link Kent
West Malling
Tel: 01732 874 819
Fax: 01732 874 818

LEEDS
Leeds TEC
Tel: 0113 2347666
Fax: 0113 2438126

PAN-LONDON
**City & Inner London North**
80 Great Eastern Street
London
Tel: 0171 324 2424
Fax: 0171 324 2400

**South West London**
c/o AZTEC
Kingston Upon Thames
Tel: 0181 5473934
Fax: 0181 5473884

**West London**
c/o West London TEC
Hounslow
Tel: 0181 5771010
Fax: 0181 5709969

**North London**
c/o North London TEC
Palmers Green
Tel: 0181 447 9422
Fax: 0181 882 5931

MID ANGLIA
Business Link Mid Anglia
c/o Cambstec
Histon
Cambridge
Tel: 01223 235633
Fax: 01223 235631

MILTON KEYNES AND NORTH
BUCKINGHAMSHIRE
Milton Keynes and North Bucks
  TEC
Wolverton
Tel: 01908 661881
Fax: 01908 222839

NORFOLK AND WAVENEY
Business Link Norfolk and
  Waveney
Norwich
Tel: 01603 626642
Fax: 01603 617949

NORTH DERBYSHIRE
North Derbyshire TEC
Chesterfield
Tel: 01246 551158
Fax: 01246 238489

NORTH NOTTINGHAMSHIRE
North Nottinghamshire TEC
Mansfield
Tel: 01623 842624
Fax: 01623 842070

NORTHUMBERLAND
Business Link
  Northumberland
Blyth
Tel: 01670363239
Fax: 01670363655

ROCHDALE

Business Link Partnership
Rochdale
Tel: 01706 44664
Fax: 01706 713211

SHEFFIELD

Business Link Sheffield
Tel: 0114 2700612
Fax: 0114 2734159

SOLIHULL

Business Link Solihull
Tel: 0121 7048159
Fax: 0121 7048180

SOMERSET

Business Link Somerset
Bridgwater
Tel: 01278 452978
Fax: 01278 453058

SUFFOLK

Suffolk Enterprise Centre
Ipswich
Tel: 01473 259832
Fax: 01473 211903

STAFFORDSHIRE

Business Link Staffordshire
Beaconside
Staffordshire

Tel: 01785 222300
Fax: 01785 53207

ST HELENS

Business Link St Helens
St Helens
Tel: 01744 24433
Fax: 01744 453030

STOCKPORT

c/o Stockport and High Peak
  TEC
Stockport
Tel: 0161 477 8830
Fax: 0161 480 7243

WAKEFIELD

Wakefield TEC
Tel: 01924 299907
Fax: 01924 201837

WILTSHIRE

Business Link Wiltshire
Swindon
Tel: 01793 513644
Fax: 01793 542006

WOLVERHAMPTON

Wolverhampton TEC
Tel: 01902 397787
Fax: 01902 397786

The number of BUSINESS LINKS will increase during 1996:
details of new locations and approximate dates of opening can be
obtained from:

> DTI Small Firms Section,
> Business Links Division,
> Sheffield
> Tel: 0114 259 7549
> Fax: 0114 259 7540

# INDEX